# POTTERY
## techniques of decoration

# POTTERY
## techniques of
## decoration

# JOHN COLBECK

## PHOTOGRAPHS BY
## BONNIE VAN DE WETERING

 VAN NOSTRAND REINHOLD COMPANY
NEW YORK    CINCINNATI    TORONTO    LONDON    MELBOURNE

Copyright © 1983 by B.T. Batsford Limited

Library of Congress Catalog Card Number 83-10444

ISBN 0-442 - 21692-0

Printed in Great Britain

Published by Van Nostrand Reinhold Company Inc.
135 West 50th Street
New York, New York 10020

16 15 14 13 12 11 10 9 8 7 6 5 4 3 2 1

**Library of Congress Cataloging in Publication Data**
Colbeck, John.
 Pottery : techniques of decoration.

 Bibliography: p.
 Includes indexes.
 1. Pottery craft.  I.  Title.
TT920.C63 1983    738.1'5    83-10444
ISBN 0-442-21692-0

# Contents

# Acknowledgment

I acknowledge the careful and prompt work of Mrs Alice Gingold, Mrs Pat Hills, Karin Hiscock and Hayley Morriss who, at different stages, typed the manuscript.

I am grateful to Andrew Crouch, Gilbert Harding-Green, Mark Henderson and Peter Turnbull for permission to use photographs of work owned by them and to Felicity Aylieff, Andrew Crouch, Wayne Hathaway, Mark Henderson, Jill Radford and Judy Trim to use photographs of their work.

I acknowledge permission to use illustrations of work in the collections of the British Museum, London; the Crafts Study Centre, Bath; the Horniman Museum, London; Verulamium Museum, St Albans; the Victoria and Albert Museum, London; the Agora Museum, Athens; the Alhambra Museum, (Generalife), Granada, Spain; Archaelogical Museum, Granada, Spain; the National Archaelogical Museum, Athens; and Topkapi Sarayi Museum, Istanbul. Particularly I thank Barley Roscoe at the Crafts Study Centre, Bath and Mrs Wood at the Horniman Museum, London for their kind help. Likewise I thank Mrs Ann Hartree for permission to photograph Judy Trim's work during an exhibition at the Prescote Gallery, Banbury.

Most particularly I acknowledge the encouragement, advice and patient care of Thelma M Nye and the tireless work in taking and printing all the photographs and the encouragement and advice of Bonnie van de Wetering.

John Colbeck
Bath 1983

# Introduction

The intention of this book is to describe practical aspects of the processes of pottery decoration which require no machinery. This reflects an acceptance of the need to impose limits on what is an extraordinarily broad subject.

With some slight variation each section combines a short outline of each process with series of demonstration photographs with their accompanying text, and a number of photographs of examples of each process.

Every demonstration produces, or begins to produce, an image or an artefact, so to show a process in isolation, whether live or through a series of photographs, is not practical. The danger is that in showing aspects of processes, demonstration may inhibit individual intentions and development. It is important therefore to stress that a second aim of this book is to assist in educating, not to instruct. The distinction is both complex and fundamental: *education* offers information for an individual to pursue and to extend; *instruction* offers models to be copied. Only when the need is accepted to vary, develop and, on occasion, reject the content of demonstration, is the danger avoided. To this end the photographic sequences aim to communicate common principles and practices of processes rather than to emphasise particular means or end results, except in so far as these contain information about the potential of processes, and show a norm which may be varied. Similarly it should be understood that the photographs of examples which follow the practical sequences are shown not simply for their quality as objects but because they exemplify aspects of processes which extend those shown in the demonstration sequences.

The decision to include a preponderance of historical examples is based on the fact that a greater diversity of processes and use of processes is more evident in these than in contemporary work. The relative sparcity of contemporary

examples in this book shows neither a disregard for the present nor for its protagonists. The present and recent past have produced new uses and non-traditional combinations of processes but there has been little if any change in the nature and principles of non-mechanised processes. History is rich in examples which can be given new and particular uses. The development of museums, and the modern ease of travel have made people more aware of ancient and foreign traditions and the objects which exemplify these provide not only sources of inspiration but also show the variation and diversity of technique which is of considerable potential relevance to the practitioner.

What exactly is the nature of decoration is a question, unrelated to history, which clearly requires some answer. The connotations of the word and the diversity of the topic do not make it easy to evolve a precise answer. However, decoration may be defined as *those aspects of a form which begin where the essentials of form and function end.*

Within this definition the idea of an undecorated pot is a near impossibility. Such definition creates an overlap between the concerns of decorating and the concerns of form making. While it would be wrong to suggest that the concerns of form making are limited to the essentials of function, it is entirely right that the concerns of decoration begin long before any form is complete.

Aspects of the making of form include both elements conventionally thought of as decoration, and those not normally considered as such. The diverse textured surfaces which arise when coils are joined are one obvious example of the simultaneous making of form and elements normally thought of as decoration. The detailing of thrown edges, their fullness or sharpness, their roundness or underlying angularity and the smoothing of surfaces are examples which are not conventionally thought of as decoration, yet these integral elements profoundly affect the nature of subsequent decoration, if any occurs, or, if it does not occur, they profoundly affect the qualitative nature of the object. Some aspects of final quality are determined before any work begins simply by the selection of a particular clay body.

While this definition is one which widens the conventional concerns of decoration (and indeed widens them beyond the scope of this book to include virtually the whole process of ceramics) the intention is not to emphasise disproportionately the importance or the diversity of decoration but simply to stress that it is one of various elements which interrelate to comprise the quality of a pot. This interrelationship is an essential fact in understanding the whole process of ceramics. Both the diversity and the interrelationship of decoration destroy the not uncommon ideas that decoration is solely a graphic concern and that it is a concern which becomes relevant only subsequent to making.

What is ultimately worthwhile in a pot, beyond its function, are those aspects which are in some way awareness provoking. The history of pottery eloquently proclaims the human need for a pot to be endowed with more than its obvious function. Thus the function of a pot fulfils a physical need and its other qualities fulfil an intellectual or sensual, even a spiritual, need and the fulfilment of this latter need becomes another, much more diverse, function. Decoration, however it may be defined, is one aspect of this more diverse function.

The processes described in this book, though exemplified almost exclusively in the context of pots, may be applied in other contexts of ceramics. With tiles, for example, some of the processes are technically easier and the visual possibilities of these may be altered by this fact alone. With forms which are completely enclosed, the absense of the need to consider both the inside and outside of a form may also alter and simplify technical considerations.

The belief that knowledge of technique and material is important is an obvious foundation of a technical book. Ignorance of the nature and potential of technique and material may lead to the danger of contrivance, or, through too exclusive a concern for visual aims, insensitively forcing techniques and materials to comply with rigidly predetermined intentions. This danger though is not the only one and it is a necessary caution to state here that too exclusive a concern for technique and material is also a danger. Through the prejudice of incomplete knowledge, technique or material may be thought to impose constraints which in fact are unnecessary. Through a misunderstanding of the conventions of some traditional practice, technique or material may be seen to impose limitations which in fact are invalid outside the traditional context. These dangers may be avoided in the same way as those of contrivance by commitment to acquiring knowledge and experience of the breadth of available materials and techniques, through thoughtful and unprejudiced experiment. Certainly, if material failure is to be avoided, materials and techniques impose their limits but these limits should be discovered, not presumed. Certainly a knowledge of precedents suggests possibilities but a material or process will do what it will do, not just what it may have done before.

Notable protagonists of the present and notable cultures of the past have frequently used only a narrow range of materials and techniques. The reasons for this may differ but it is important that a harmonious balance exists between means and end. In such a context that balance allows particular intentions to be clarified, modified and refined by particular means, through a sensitive response to material and technique. It is arguable that there can be no such thing as good technique, that technique can only be appropriate or inappropriate to particular intentions. Evolving appropriate technique is central to achieving a quality of end result and this underlines the importance of knowledge of the breadth of possibilities from which to select the appropriate. It is the possibility of acquiring a breadth of knowledge from which to select whatever is appropriate to particular and diverse visual ends that places the late twentieth century potter in a unique position in history.

# TECHNIQUES OF DECORATION
# Impressed relief

That clay can be impressed is a fundamental aspect of its nature as a plastic material and is one which enables a wide range of qualities to be achieved.

It is easy to become excited by the range of impressed marks which can be made into sheets of soft clay. While such work has rich possibilities its relevance is limited to relief tiles, slabs and dishes formed in hollow moulds. The possibilities of this aspect of impressing are quite distinct from those of impressing marks into the walls of coiled or thrown pots. The distinction is simply that the unsupported walls of a soft pot are as readily indented as they are impressed. Impressed work on formed pots which have been allowed to stiffen somewhat is limited in two ways. Firstly, the area of any stamp should not be too large as enormous pressure is needed to press large stamps into anything but very soft clay. Secondly, stamp relief needs to be simple and bold as firm clay will not readily accept finely detailed impressions. The use of convex stamps and roulettes does overcome some aspects of the first of these limitations because, as these are rolled onto the clay, little of the stamp surface is in contact with the clay at any time so less pressure is needed to leave a clear impression. The second limitation is less easy to overcome as firm clay does simply lack the mobility to be finely impressed. Soft clay can however be added to the walls of a pot and then be finely impressed, and sprigging is also a possible option. Both of these alternatives enable fine relief to be made but both place that relief above, rather than in, the wall surface.

As carving, modelling, sprigging, incising and impressing all deal with relief it will help to consider them as complementary processes offering different but related possibilities. All are concerned with relief which may be revealed by light and shade alone or may be treated with oxide, glaze or some other material to alter or emphasise the work in some way.

Two main types of stamp exist: firstly, stamps which are pressed straight into the clay and, secondly, stamps which are convex or round which are rolled on to the clay. Stamps may be specifically carved and made but an immense variety of found objects, man-made or natural, may also be used. Stamps made of porous material, such as plaster of paris or fired clay, usually release quickly and cleanly from clay in a variety of conditions but if they tend to stick or clog they should be cleaned and dusted with talc as often as necessary to keep them working freely. Stamps of non porous material, such as metal, will usually produce a few clear impressions in stiff clay but then they begin to stick and clog. Metal is usually hopeless with soft clay. Several measures can be taken to prevent non porous stamps sticking and clogging and these depend to some extent on the state of the clay and the complexity of the stamp. The two major alternatives are to dust the clay surface with talc wherever impressions are to be made, or to oil the surface of the stamp frequently with an oily cloth.

The qualitative possibilities of impressed relief are complex, partly because of the contrast of opportunity between making and applying stamps. While the making of stamps allows and invites precise and controlled work, the application of stamps permits free, speedy repetition of the stamped unit. It is worth remembering that the possibility of the speedy application of stamped impressions does not preclude the possibility of thoughtful planning of their overall distribution on a form, and also that the spacing and relationships of the stamped units are usually as visually important as the nature of each individual stamp.

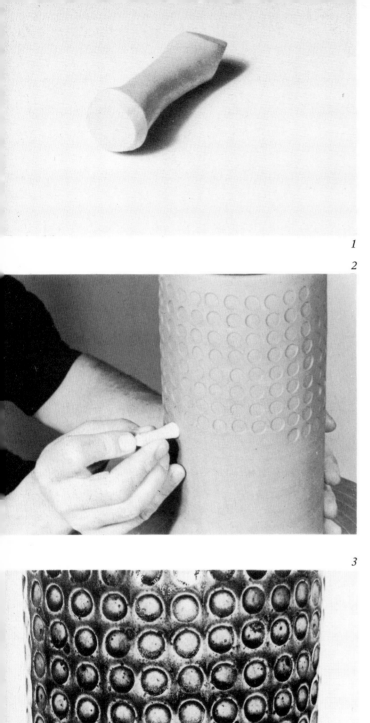

1 The simplest form of stamp is one which solely impresses a shaped flat area into the clay. Such stamps are made from plaster, clay or wood. Short lived ones can be made from sticks of blackboard chalk. If made of clay, as here, they are pinched to shape when plastic and are made as precise as necessary when leatherhard. They are easiest to use if they are only low biscuit fired to retain a fairly strong porosity — the actual temperature will of course depend on the clay

2 Such stamps are simply pushed into the clay surface. They are much easier to control if they have, as here, sufficient length to provide an easy grip. Producing an area of impressed marks of even depth requires a little more control than might be imagined, and catching the clay at just the right state makes work much easier. Obviously the clay has to be left until the wall itself will not be deformed by the impressing but the best time is as soon after this as possible, before the clay has developed the stiffness associated with true leatherhardness

3 With a glaze that is sensitive to relief even a simple stamp can produce a rich surface

4 A development of a basic stamp is to carve lines into the simple outline shape

5 Such carved lines are left as raised lines within the stamped impression. As here, impressed relief is frequently combined with incised lines

6 Glazed with a coloured translucent glaze, incised lines in the clay and the impressed outline show as tonally darker than the overall glaze, and the carved line in the stamp, being raised, projects into the glaze layer and shows as a lighter tone

7 This rolled slab of clay shows different impressions all made by a single stamp. By placing, spacing, tilting and overstamping, immense variety is possible. With simple stamps these aspects are at least as important as the shape of the stamp itself

8 This shows the working surface of a convex stamp. Impressed relief need not be thought of as consisting solely of recessed and unrecessed lines and areas, but can, as here, be carved more three dimensionally. The possible and appropriate quality is simpler than with sprigging but the possibility does exist, and the fact that it has been little used in traditional impressed work does not mean it should be ignored

5

6

8

7

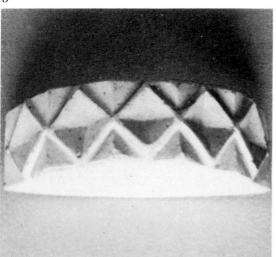

9, 10 and 11 In use, a convex stamp is simply rolled onto the clay. As so little of the mould surface touches the clay, especially with stamps as fully convex as this, the pressure needed to make a good impression is slight. The fact that, being supported in a dish mould, the clay in this example is soft, should not be misleading. Certainly the soft clay facilitates the making of a crisp impression but it is by no means essential to the good register of carved relief nor to the use of rolled convex stamps

12 In use, roulettes are simply rolled on to the clay

11

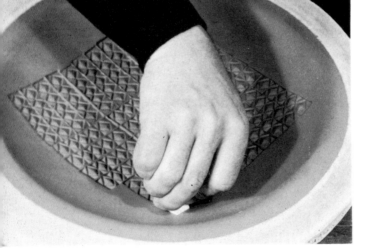

12

*13 and 14* To facilitate rolling they are sometimes made with handles but with narrow roulettes unless the axle is a good fit, they can make it inclined to tilt from side to side giving uneven impressions. Roulettes with handles, usually narrow ones, were occasionally used after turning, or even immediately after throwing, to impress the walls of wheel made pots

*15, 16 and 17* Of more limited relevance is the possibility of applying pieces of soft clay to the surface of a pot and stamping into these. Stamps can be relatively simple and more deeply impressed than would normally be possible by pressing directly into a pot or, as the clay is soft, more finely detailed stamps can be used. The shape of the piece of applied clay is usually as important an element in such work as the stamp itself

13

14

15

16

17

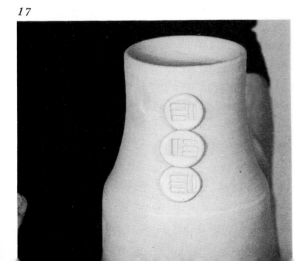

*18*

*19*

As well as for their decorative use impressed stamps have for long been widely used to certify the origins of pottery or its contents.

*18 and 19* These two fragments are handles of amphorae. Ancient Greek and Roman amphorae are a fascinating subject. For a thousand years they were the bulk liquid containers for the trade which flourished in the Mediterranean and deep into the hinterlands of its many ports. Their original use was for the distribution and export mainly of wine but also of oil and some preserved foodstuffs. Just as today distinctive bottle shapes, such as Burgundy or Bordeaux, denote the general origin of wines, so in the ancient world the shape of an amphora was evidence of the general origin of its contents. More expensive, better quality wines needed further certification and this was stamped onto the handles by the local potters who made the amphorae. Such stamps detailed the specific location of origin, sometimes including the vineyard and maker. Potters' stamps sometimes accompany the wine stamp. The information of both stamps is carved into the flat face of the stamp producing raised detail in the impression. *Museum of the Agora, Athens, Greece*

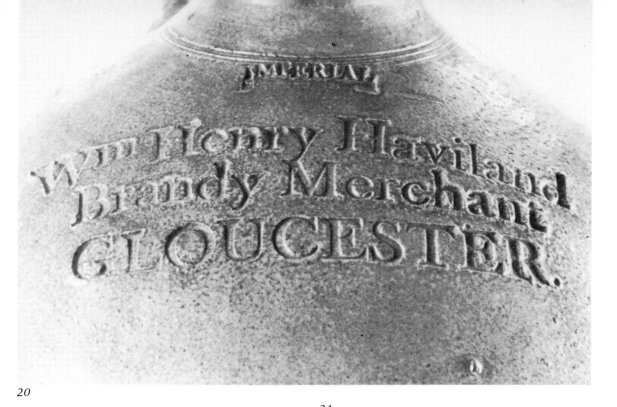

20

20 The 'Imperial' stamp here is also a type of certification but of amount not quality in this case. The stamping of the merchant's name is partly a guarantee of the quality of the contents, partly advertising and possibly partly for the identification and return of the container. The stamp letters in this case were raised giving a crisp sunken impression. In all probability they were printers' type, set as usual in a strip, and simply rolled onto the curved form of the bottle shoulder. Late nineteenth or early twentieth century. English

Impressed potters marks exist from most cultures in vast variety.

21 and 22 These two are Roman marks, *Urbinus* and *Castellus*, both rolled onto the convex edges of large kitchen bowls. *Verulamium Museum, St Albans, England*

21

22

*23*

*24*

*23* This mark is on the base of a Tzu-chou, Sung Dynasty tomb pillow. Chinese

*24* This mark is from the base of the plate illustrated in figure 293 *Winchcombe Pottery, England. 1930s*

In all of the four preceding examples the marks were cut into the flat faces of stamps. In pre- and non-industrial contexts this was and is the almost universal practise. In industrial contexts the standard practice is to use stamps with raised metal type to give a recessed impress.

25 This detail shows a combination of incised and impressed marks. The impressions have been made freely and quickly with the clear intention of forming a background texture to emphasise the incised shape of the flower and leaves. As bamboo, of both large and small diameter, is the common oriental tool-making wood, it seems likely that the end of a length of narrow bamboo was used to make these impressions; but any hollow tube will impress this type of mark. Both the incised and the impressed marks have been treated with pigment probably freely brushed over the whole surface and, when dry, rubbed or scraped clean. The glaze, being very thin, has no depth to distract attention from the crispness of the surface. Tzu-chou. Sung Dynasty, China. *Victoria and Albert Museum, London, England*

26 The impressions at the base of the neck of this posset-pot were clearly rouletted while the pot was on the wheel probably at the turning stage. English. Late seventeenth century. *Victoria and Albert Museum, London*

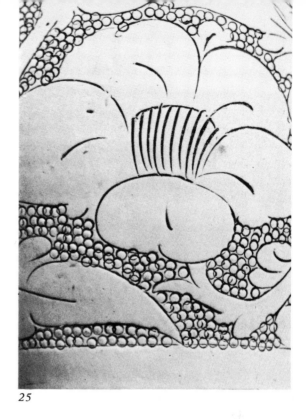

25

26

27

27 This detail is of two of a number of bands of relief ornament on a very large Greek pot. All the bands are formed by continuous roulettes. The majority of the work is very well defined but a few small patches show little relief even though parts which would have been simultaneously impressed as the roulette was rolled round the pot are clear. Nowhere is there the side to side unevenness often associated with roulette work, especially wide roulette work. The quality of the work — the evenness of the surface and the sharpness of the relief with its strangely bald patches — suggest the interesting possibility that rather than being rolled into the body clay of the pot the roulettes were rolled into a thickish slurry of clay basted on to the pot surface. This would explain the existence of bald patches side by side with crisp impressions on a basically even surface. Whether or not this is how it was done is of no great importance in this context but the idea of the process is an interesting one in that the firm surface of the pot would allow the roulette to work very evenly over the surface leaving crisp impressions from a minimum of pressure, provided the slurry layer was an appropriate and even thickness. In practice, the slurry could not be very wet and the routlette would need a ready porosity. Greek. Eighth century BC. *British Museum, London*

# Plastic and leatherhard modifications to pots

There is no single term to express the many ways in which the form of pots may be altered by indenting, stroking, stroking outwards from within, tapping, beating and other similar actions.

A clear distinction exists between the possibilities of modifying a form when it is soft and when leatherhard. With hand building some of the modification processes described could be argued to be inseparable from the forming. All the processes however may be applied to thrown pots and in this context the separateness of forming and modification is quite clear. The description and illustrations which follow are of the various processes in the context of thrown pots so it is important to stress that this is not their sole possible context.

## PLASTIC MODIFICATION

It would be understandable if it was thought that to attempt to modify a freshly thrown form would be to court disaster. In fact it is surprising just how much a newly thrown pot can be altered before it collapses. While modifications can be made to pots formed by processes other than throwing, it is true that thrown pots offer uniquely plastic qualities.

Plastic modifications fall into two main categories: those which solely affect the edge and those which affect the body of the pot.

Historically, modification to the edge of a pot is more common. The pulling of jug spouts is an obvious example of this though here the prime intention is functional. But even excluding the immense diversity of jug spouts, edges can be treated in many ways by pinching, pushing or stroking to profoundly alter the nature of a pot.

The character of the main body of a form, no less than that of an edge, obviously affects the type of alterations which may be made to it. Broadly there are two possibilities: firstly, the whole form, by stroking or pushing may be simply altered and, secondly, indentations or bumps, potentially numerous, may, in a number of separate actions, be pushed into or out from the wall changing a round form into a broadly fluted or lobed one.

Many cultures have used plastic modification and a rich selection of very diverse content and quality exists.

28 The simplest modifications can be made by pushing the sides of open forms. The surface of the form will be least marked if it is cleanly thrown, and therefore free of slip, and if the hands are wet with clean water

*28*

19

29 To square a form the sides are firmly pressed with the flat of the hands

30 The rounded ends are then pressed in. With some clays and with some forms a cleaner surface and profile will be achieved if the inward pressure is combined with a slow upwards or downwards stroking action. Some clays will tend to spring back towards a round shape and these will need working over more than once

31 and 32 A triangular shape can be formed in a single action with the thumbs used to form the third side

*29*

*30*

*31*

*32*

33 Any slurry left on the surface at the plastic stage is best left to be cleaned off with a fine sponge or chamois leather at an early leather-hard stage

Clearly this simple controlled distortion from the thrown circle is open to very varied exploitation. Bowl forms can be shaped in this way more readily and freely than more spherical forms as with these the upper enclosing part tends to hold the wall steady.

34 Indentations can be formed fairly precisely using just fingers or spreading the pressure with a sponge or folded piece of chamois

35 The action is rarely if ever one of simply pressing. In this case the movement is a gentle but firm circular one, each movement deepening and enlarging the indentation

36 How much the clay around the indentation is affected depends on the clay body, the wall thickness and the actual form. Here, mainly because of the placing of the indentation on the particular form the walls above and below the area of pressure are little affected but those to left and right are tending to give way and are therefore being supported from the inside. Where inside support is possible this can extend the depth and definition of indentation possible

33

34

36

35

37

38

39 *By stroking, quite deep marks can be made*

37 Where access to the inside is easy, a form can be altered from within. Here a vertical stroking action produces a soft angularity in the outer form

38 The action of extending the wall from within, whether with ridges formed by stroking or bumps formed by pushing, has a much softer effect than work done on the outside of a pot. This is mainly because the seen outside surface is not touched and the thickness of the wall reduces the sharp definition of the inside marks. The thicker the wall the more the sharpness of the inside marks are softened. See figure 53 for an example of this

39 By stroking, quite deep marks can be made into the walls of a pot with no damage to the thrown wall. When doing this sort of work the finger should be kept wet and wiped clean of any build up of slip

40 Marks can be further deepened or defined by a second or subsequent action. Here the initial upward stroking is being both deepened and defined at its top by a downward action. It is much better to work round a form a number of times, reworking each mark once only each time as this has a much less distorting effect on the whole form

39

40

41 The various modifications possible with thrown edges and ridges, are numerous. Many of the possibilities are created by the initial form of the edge or ridge. Complex edges can be pinched together, thin edges can be folded over and thick edges can be pinched thinner

42 *and* 43 Wooden or other tools, as well as fingers, can be used to indent the walls of pots. Such tools clearly enable a different, sharper quality of indentation to be made

44 Even quite thin tools have a pushing, indenting rather than a cutting effect on soft clay. In fact it takes sudden, brutal movements to cut through a soft thrown wall. Ironically the firmer the clay becomes the easier it is to cut as it resists rather than distorts when pressure is applied

41

42

44

43

45 The most plastic indenting can be done when the clay is softest straight after throwing. At this stage and especially with open forms where the top edge, as well as the sides, has been indented some degree of tilt or lean can easily occur. This can be readily corrected by appropriate pressure at the base either immediately or when the pot has stiffened a little. When indented forms require turning they should be thrown with a clear idea of the extent of the indenting, and indented with a clear idea of the extent of the turning. Where the edge itself has been indented they need to be supported on or in a clay chuck

45

Historical examples of plastic modifications exist in great diversity.

46 The outward flaring edge on this Chinese, Sung Dynasty, bowl has been stroked regularly in and up with a fairly narrow tool. The strong plastic folds of the edge are the initial and strongest impact of the form. *Victoria and Albert Museum, London*

46

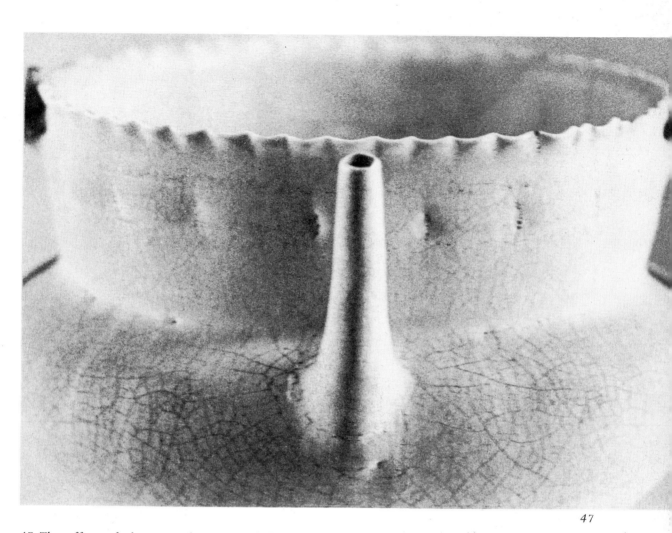

47 The effect of the more frequent and finer
indenting on the edge of this pot is quite
different from the previous example. The
delicate frillyness of the whole edge forms a
stronger impression than the form of the
individual folds. Persian. Twelfth century AD.
*Victoria and Albert Museum, London*

48 This detail is of the top of a softly detailed, nearly spherical form. The goblet-like form of the top was possibly thrown onto the bottle after the body and neck had stiffened. Certainly the indenting was done while that part of the form was very plastic. Though strongly decorative the folds would clearly have served efficiently as pouring spouts when the bottle was used. Persian. Thirteenth century AD. *Victoria and Albert Museum, London*

48

49 The thrown ridge on this jar is folded up and down alternately and the fairly fluid glaze has gathered on the relief of the folds. It is possible the ridge was made partly to hold the glaze. While the angular shoulder and the lugs are the primary feature of the pot, the folded ridge and the varying tonalities of the glaze on this are a strong and complementary feature. Chinese. Late Tang or early Sung Dynasty. *Victoria and Albert Museum, London*

50 This detail is of a small Roman beaker 4 in. (10 cm) in diameter. The unglazed surface is covered with a fine, slightly shiny slip giving the indentations a crispness often lost in glazed work. This crisp surface and the soft fullness of the forms between the indentation marks give this small pot a most distinct quality. *Verulamium Museum, St Albans, England*

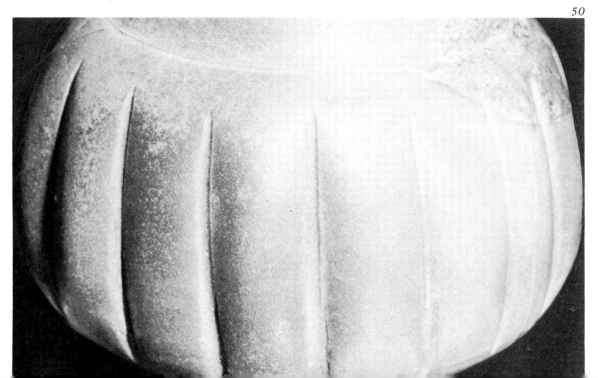

51

51 and 52 A common type of Roman beaker has indented sides like these two examples. The indentations, which may have been intended as finger holds, range in quality from the deep rather irregular ones shown in figure 51 to the shallower more controlled ones in figure 52. Both beakers are just under 5½ in. (14 cm) high. *British Museum, London*

52

*53* The bumps on this Roman jar have been pressed out from the inside. The relative sharpness of the indentations inside compared with the bumps outside can be clearly seen. This is the least common process of plastic modification. Roman 10 in. (25 cm) high. *British Museum, London*

## LEATHERHARD MODIFICATION

Modifications done at a leatherhard stage usually involve tapping or beating a pot with broad faced wooden tools. This work is necessarily slower than work with soft clay and, because of the economics implicit in that fact, traditional examples are rarer. The main possibilities of work at the leatherhard stage are with simple rather than complex form quite simply because the clay is so much less readily formable. With edges particularly, attempts to alter the form even at an early leatherhard stage run the risk of cracking the clay.

Most leatherhard modification is a development of work begun at the soft plastic stage. Partly because of this the possibilities of plastic and leatherhard modifications are linked but it must be clear that the firmer stage allows a quality of control and precision impossible at the softer stage.

*54* When a pot is to be tapped to a squarish cross section the basic shape can be begun at the plastic stage. The hands should be wet and clean. Pushing to flatten one side at a time may well make the pot lean and though this can be corrected it can cause unnecessary sagging at the base so it is much better when the intended shape allows it to modify the shape with two opposing pressures

*53*

*54*

55
56

57

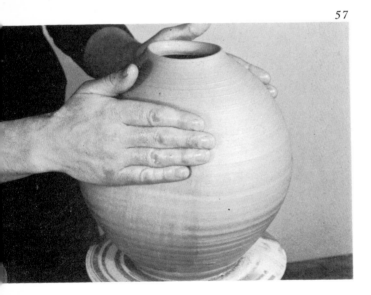

55 Using a gentle up and down stroking movement the sides can be increasingly squared but unless access to the inside is possible, which would allow the corners to be stroked outwards, the cross section cannot be made very angular at this stage

56 It is ideal if the pot being worked on can be kept an even consistency throughout. All pots once formed tend to dry out at the top edge first and the bottom last so either the top part should be loosely draped with a damp cloth leaving the lower part exposed or the whole pot, when possible, should be inverted to rest on its top edge. Unless the pot is of even consistency throughout it will be difficult to tap it to shape with control. The ideal consistency is early, rather than late, leatherhard and once this stage is reached the shape will respond quickly to firm tapping. It is best to work round a form several times progressively modifying it and, whether or not symmetry is intended, small incised marks can make useful reference points. Whenever a form is being tapped the opposite side should be supported both to prevent the pot rocking and, if the base is a little soft, to prevent a lean developing. If the wooden tool has a truly flat face and sharp corners it will tend to leave a texture of linear impressions on every beaten surface. This can be left as a feature or can be avoided if, as in the illustrations, the tool is planed to a slightly convex surface and the corners are planed off. There is nothing difficult about tapping and most clays can be readily formed to surprisingly angular shapes. If cracks do occur as angles are progressively sharpened it is probable that the clay has been allowed to become too dry, unless of course the clay body is a very short one

57 Angularity is not the only possibility with tapping and beating. It is just as possible to make softly rounded shapes. In this instance the intended oval shape is begun at the plastic stage

30

58 To achieve a regular oval cross section it can help initially to beat a number of equal planes and then to merge these into one another. The initial beating makes a wide flattened plane

59 Secondary planes are then beaten on either sides of the form. Even, or perhaps particularly, with a softly oval cross section guide marks are helpful. In this and the next illustration the small incised marks indicating the end of the longer dimension of the oval are clearly visible

60 The angularities of the planes are then tapped away to leave a continuously rounded form. Freer work of less symmetrical intention can be done more directly without the intermediate formation of planes

61 Work on rounded forms like this can be done with the clay somewhat softer than that for angular forms. Final work with a chamois may correct minor irregularities of form as well as finishing the surface

58

59

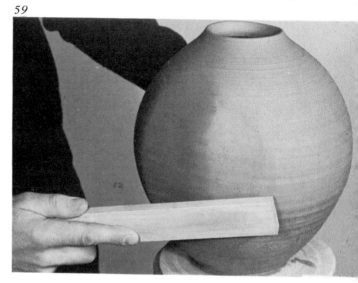

61

60

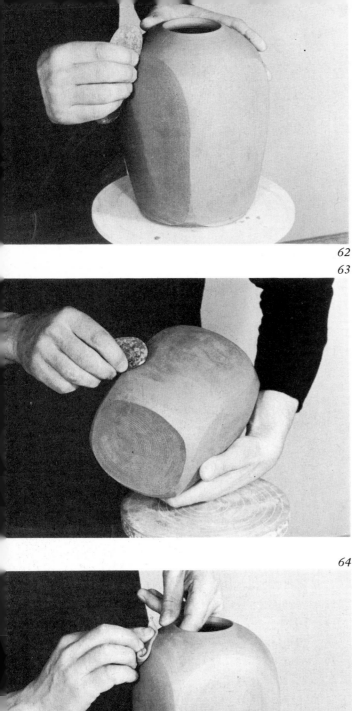

62

63

64

62 After stroking at the plastic stage and immediately after tapping at the leatherhard stage it is of course possible, with both angular and more rounded forms, to scrape the form. With rounded forms this will simply give a different quality to the surface but with angular forms it allows a subtly sharper, but importantly different, quality of precision to be given to the angles. Here a similarly squared pot to the one in the series 54 to 56 is being lightly scraped over the upper part of its body to give greater definition. Note the excess of clay at the base of the planes in this illustration. When pots are beaten the clay is readily displaced inwards except at and very near the base where the wall is restricted from moving inwards by the flat base. When a squared form is required right down to the base one solution is to pick up the pot resting it in one hand on its side and to beat the excess clay both downwards and inwards forming a beaten foot, figure 67

63 Scraping, however, as here allows the alternative of removing the excess clay at the base. This is the one place where scraping following beating needs to remove anything more than the smallest amount of clay

64 A scraped sharpness may be left as the finished surface but even if a chamois is used to soften angles the quality of angle will be quite different to that achievable by tapping or beating alone

65

66

*65 and 66* The two views of this pot by Bernard Leach show a fairly gently flattened shape. The use of beaten sides for decoration is fairly common practice with the process. *Craft Study Centre, Bath, England*

67

67 and 68 This angularly beaten bottle, also by
Bernard Leach, shows how considerably forms
can be modified. The detail of the base shows
how the clay at the bottom, rather than being
removed, has been beaten in and under to form
a foot. The sharpness of the form is cloaked
somewhat by the thick, dark tenmoku glaze.
The pot is a good example of a form which is
frequently not treated monochromatically but
in which each side is separately treated as an
area for decoration. *Craft Study Centre, Bath,
England*

# Agate

Agate is pottery made from a clay body containing at least two clays which are distinctly different in tone or colour and which are intermingled usually in quite a complex way. The configurations may vary from controlled formal ones to those which are completely random. With the exception that agate clay is occasionally inlaid into the walls of a pot agate-ware is distinct in that the intermingled clays comprise the fabric of the pot and are not, like marbling with which it is often confused, a surface treatment.

There are two quite distinct stages to the making of agate pottery: firstly there is the mixing together of two or more clays to make the agate body and secondly there is the forming of this into an object. Apart from its colour, deriving obviously from the chosen clays, the appearance of an agate object is conditioned both by how the clays are initially mixed and by how the mixed clay is formed into an object.

The processes most often used to form agate clay into pots are pressmoulding and slab building. Agate was made at different times by many cultures, and, historically, pressmoulding was the most commonly used process. Agate can, however, also be coiled, pinched or thrown. Thrown agate inevitably exhibits a pronounced spiral effect.

Concerning agate much is said and written about the need to use clays of compatible shrinkages. If 'compatible' is thought to mean 'identical' this can seem a rather daunting prerequisite. In fact identical shrinkage is not necessary. The most important factor in coping with differential shrinkage is to ensure good adhesion between the two clays. Providing the adhesion is good the tension of differential shrinkage can be easily tolerated.

To achieve the contrast necessary for agate the choice is either to use different bodies, which already have inherent contrast, or to colour, with oxides or stains, a single body usually light, often white, to create contrast. As well as being mixed from two clays of strong contrast it is entirely possible to make agate from clays which are closely similar in colour or tone.

The dampness of clays which are to be mixed for agate should be as similar as possible and adhesion will be easily achieved if they are mixed together when only slightly firmer than a sticky softness. They should not however be so damp that they intermingle too readily. The mixing of agate can be a very varied process involving a mixture of wedging, kneading, cutting and reassembling, rolling and folding. The mixing which occurs when any clay lump is kneaded, cut and rejoined, rolled or folded is a complex three dimensional phenomenon and, with experience, procedures can produce complex, clearly intended, predictable results. Even apparently random, irregular configurations can be the result of an ordered procedure.

Slab building and pressmoulding both require sheets of clay and when agate is being mixed it should be clear whether the sheets are to be made by cutting from a block or by rolling as these two alternatives very fundamentally affect the final configurations of the agate. When agate is pinched, coiled or thrown some of the effects possible and common in sheets are changed and some new possibilities are revealed.

A study of historical examples will reveal similar qualities occuring in contexts with little or no cultural connection. Few large objects will be found. The traditions of agate could certainly be built on and the process is open to fuller and thoughtful development.

The interest of any agate piece owes much to the methods used to intermix the clays and to the way the intermixed clays are prepared for forming. The examples which follow do not and could not aim to be exhaustive, for the possible variety of agate is immense, but they aim to show enough to convey some understanding of the principles and the possibilities.

Though the processes of actually forming objects are not the concern of this book, agate clay, while it can be used quite normally for slab building, can require particular handling when it is used with moulds so the section ends with some brief comments about this aspect.

In the first example two clays are carefully mixed to produce a striped agate. It is fundamental to all mixing of two, or more, different coloured clays to form an agate body that the clays used are of closely similar consistency.

*69* Two lumps of clay of a soft plastic consistency and of the same size are rolled out into thick slabs of the same shape. Care should be taken that no air is trapped between the two slabs as they are laid together to be joined

*70* The clays should be soft enough to be securely joined by a fairly gentle pressure of rolling. The slab should not be released from the cloth and, stuck to it, can be rolled a few times to ensure good adhesion right to the edges but care must be taken not to extend the top clay down over the edges of the lower clay as this would impair the definition of the subsequent stripes

*71* The slab is then cut into equal parts. For a really regular agate the rounded sides could be cut off and discarded leaving four rectangles

69

70

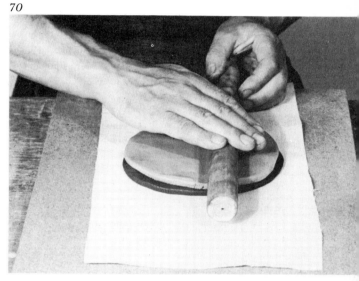

71

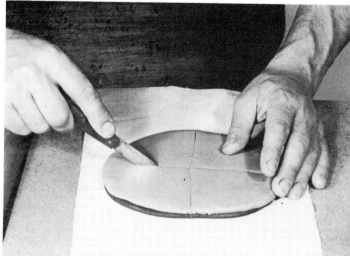

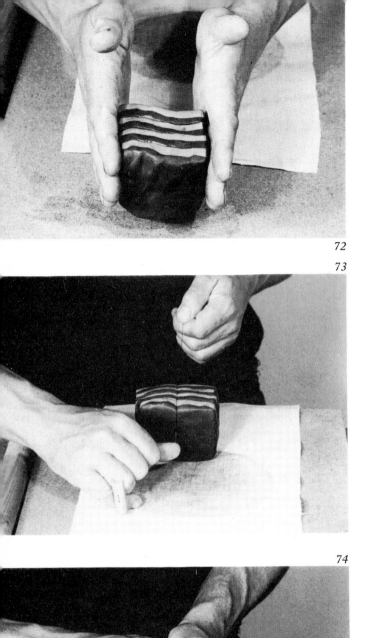

72 The four pieces are then neatly stacked, again taking care to exclude air, and are pressed and tapped into a regular block

73 *and* 74 The block is cut in half and the two halves are stacked doubling the number of layers

75 Initially by pressing and then by rolling this block is extended to a slab

72

73

74

75

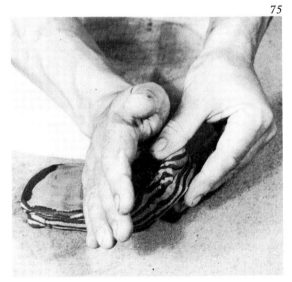

76 The slab is then cut up into strips of even width. The more that is discarded from the ends and sides of the slab the more even will be the final stripes but the care of each rolling out action is also very relevant to this. Observing what happens to agate when it is rolled out is immensely informative. Certainly the most even lateral extension of a slab occurs when it is released from the rolling cloth each time the whole surface has been rolled. If a thick slab is left stuck to a rolling out cloth and is repeatedly forcefully rolled the outer areas of the upper surface will actually become the outer areas of the under surface of the new slab. So with agate, when the aim is to retain the horizontal structure within a slab, rolling should be done with unusual care

77 The cut strips are then turned on their sides to reveal their section and are pressed firmly together to join them

78 and 79 This thick slab is then lengthened, halved and joined again

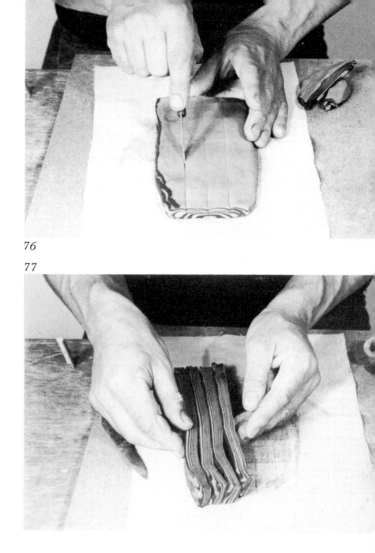

76

77

79

78

*80* The slab is then rolled out for use.

   This slab can be used as it is but it is also possible to cut the slab up and by overlapping and rolling to construct a new slab with additional or repositioned pieces. This process of addition and repositioning considerably extends the configurations possible with agate. It can be done in far more complex ways than the simple example shown

*81* Overlapped joins, which need be no larger than ¼ in. (6 mm), should be carefully positioned and pieces consisting wholly of one or other of the agate clays can be included. Providing the clay is still in a soft plastic state there need be no fear of non-adhesion

*82* Distortion will be least if the arrangement of pieces is not rolled until all are in position. Where further thinning is not intended the piece should be rolled from the edges inwards as far as the centre or it can have a rolling cloth placed on top of it to prevent spreading (see also figure 95)

*83* Mould-formed into a simple dish the slab made by the basic mixing procedure shown displays one aspect of the quality of agate clay. A more rigorously methodical procedure at each stage will produce a more regular configuration but to attempt to be over-precise with the forming of an agate clay is to deny and fight against the

*80*

*81*

*82*

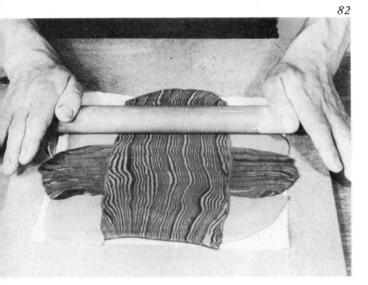

*83*

soft plastic nature of the material. The mixing and making of agate clays and slabs is perhaps best thought of as a process where a particular but only general control can be exercised over configurations which in fine detail are less controllable

The second example produces agate with a cell-like structure of repeated spirals.

*84* Two sheets of white clay and two of black have been thinly rolled out, the black sheets have been placed on the white and each has been further rolled out to extend and thin them and each black and white pair has been cut to a fairly neat rectangle. The edge of one sheet is being carefully turned over, taking care not to trap any air, as the beginning of rolling the sheet into a coil

*85* In rolling a sheet up into a thick coil care should be taken to ensure that the ends are kept fairly tight so that air is not drawn into the coil. With both coils note the extended, tapered and tightly closed up ends

*86* When rolling up is complete the tapered ends can be cut off the coils as these parts contain an ever diminishing spiral while in the remainder the black and white clays are distributed in a more or less equal spiral

*84*

*85*

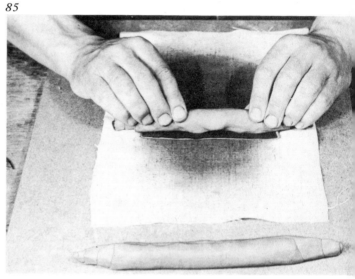

*86*

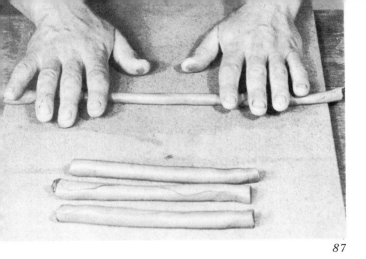

*87*

87 The thick coils can then be rolled out thinner and can be halved and thinned again. Note in the thinning that the white outer layer is unbroken and that the ends of the coils are not tapered. Rolling of this sort should be gentle and unrushed and throughout the rolling the round section of the coil should be distorted as little as possible so that the coil is extended sideways with as little internal displacement and mixing as possible. With care the coils could be considerably further extended and thinned than in this example with little loss of internal definition

*88*

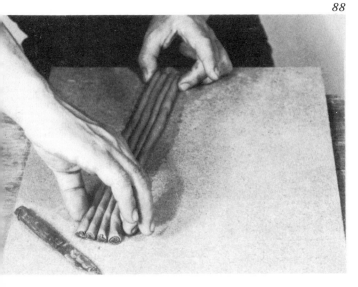

88 The coils are then laid side by side and pressed together and tapped down to form a long, narrow, rectangular block of clay

89 and 90 The block is then cut in half and one half superimposed on the other shortening and thickening it. The block is then tapped on its various sides to thoroughly join the coils and to give it a regular rectangular cross section

*89*

*90*

42

91 Short identical lengths are then cut through this block at right angles with a knife or a steel palatte

92 A steel palatte offers the slight advantage that the cut pieces stick to it and several can therefore be gathered together in consecutive motion. The cut pieces are laid on end on a rolling cloth revealing their section

93 Before they are rolled they should be positioned together and pressed inwards to effect an initial join

94 They are then firmly and steadily rolled to consolidate this join. To minimise the extension of the piece during rolling it should not be freed from the rolling out cloth

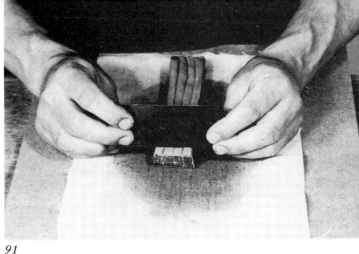

91

92

94

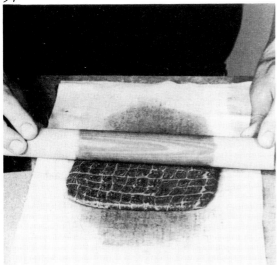

93

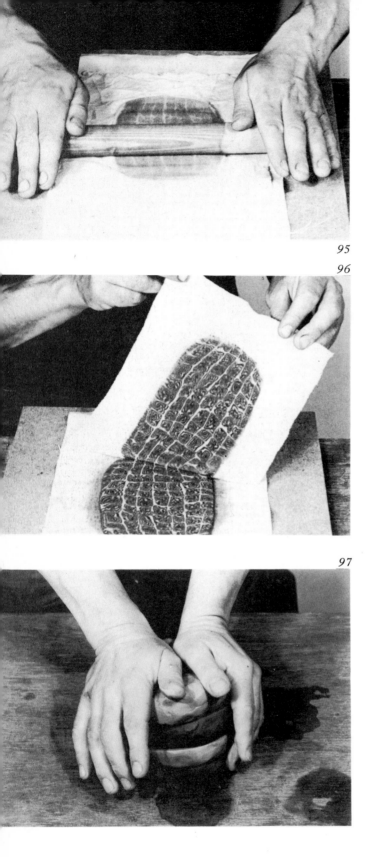

95

96

97

**95** An excellent procedure to minimise the extension of a slab of agate and to consolidate its joins is to roll it with a cloth placed over the top. If the cloth is slightly damp, as here, the dampness will be quickly transferred to the slab and will help the adhesion of the cut coils. Dampening a slab of agate formed from coils may well be necessary as repeatedly halving a coil and rolling it thinner, especially on absorbant surfaces, can have a considerable drying effect on the clay. When there is no need to dampen the clay a dry cloth on top of a slab can be used in the simple consolidation of joins

**96** When damp cloths are used they tend to take a fairly clear print of the agate and if this contains strong colouring pigments such as cobalt they clearly should not be used for rolling out plain clay. Indeed all cloths used for rolling out agate whether damp or dry should be kept for this purpose and discarded when the pigment can no longer be washed out thoroughly

Once the clay has been rolled sufficiently to close up all the gaps it can, if necessary, be extended to its final thickness and used. While striped agate can be extended by rolling along its stripes and therefore be little changed, cellular agate is inevitably enlarged and more altered by rolling. In this context, cutting working sheets of agate is inevitably enlarged and more altered by good alternative to rolling (see figures 100 to 104).

The third example of mixing produces an agate of random configuration.

**97 and 98** Broad and random configurations of agate can be simply produced by the incomplete wedging and kneading together of two clays. The amount of wedging done contributes directly to the evenness with which the two clays are distributed throughout the agate mass and the folding and rolling of kneading break up the layered effect, which wedging produces, into swirling uneven shapes

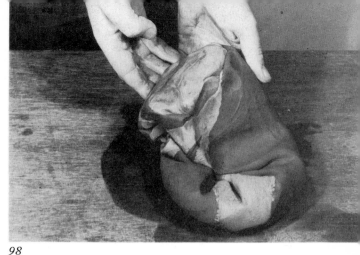

99 A block of random agate should be cut in half every so often while it is being mixed to ensure that mixing is not overdone and to see what sort of shapes are being made within the mass. Obviously mixing of this type does not and is not expected to offer a high degree of control but with experience, by increasing or decreasing the total amount of mixing done and by altering the balance between the amount of wedging and the amount of kneading, an element of predictability can be achieved

98

99

When a slab or block of agate has been formed which contains a fine scale of mixing which it is not intended to enlarge the use of a harp is a preferable alternative to rolling

100 and 101 Harps can be bought in a wide variety of sizes. The smaller one illustrated is only 2 in. (5 cm) wide and of limited use in this context; the larger is 14 in. (35 cm) wide. The cutting wires in harps are either located in grooves, as in the larger example, or through holes, as in the small. Harps should be provided with a number of grooves or holes on each side equally spaced from their ends so the distance of the wire from the ends, which governs the thickness of the cut slab, can be altered

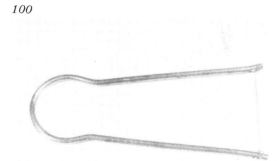

101

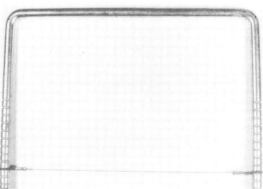

100

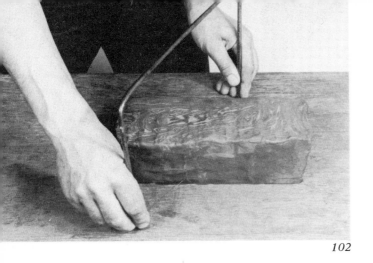

102 and 103 In use harps cut a slab of very even thickness by being drawn through a block or thick slab of clay with their ends resting on a level work surface

104 Like cuts through figured wood the bottom surface of each new slab has identical markings to the top surface of the previous one

102

103

104

*105 and 106* By drawing a sharp pointed tool through a soft mixture of agate and then rolling the incised grooves until the surface is again smooth marks very like those of feathered slip can be produced

*107 and 108* Both in the mixing of agate clay and in the formation of agate objects the surface can tend to become somewhat obscured by smudging. Many glazes will, in forming the interface layer which always exists between glaze and body, dissolve away this layer and reveal the crispness of the agate, but if strong oxides or stains have been used this may stain the glaze so it is normal to clean up an agate surface prior to firing. Most clays are cleanly scrapable at a middle to late leatherhard stage and, considering the health hazards of the airborne dust created when dry clay is scraped, this stage and not later is the time to clean agate. Moreover the clay is far less brittle at the leatherhard stage and with firm scraping with a metal kidney or similar tool the clay will pare away smoothly leaving the agate crisply defined. Except in an extraction booth, the use of wirewool and sandpaper on dry clay are practices considered to be hazardous to health and are banned in most educational and production contexts

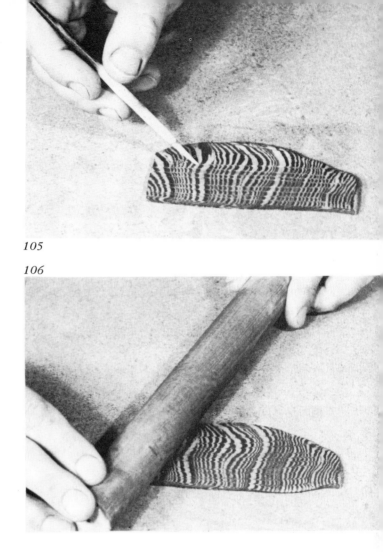

105

106

108

107

109

110

*109* Thrown agate inevitably displays a spiral marking (though by using a kick wheel in alternate directions something rather different would occur). Throwing obviously coats an agate clay with a mixed slip so thrown agate forms are invariably turned to reveal the agate. Note in this example that no agate is evident on the unturned top edge or inside. If a throwing rib is used in the final stages of throwing this will clear most of the slip from the surface and can eliminate the need for turning

## AGATE CLAY IN USE WITH MOULDS

When forming plain clay bodies in moulds a frequent sequence is to place the smooth rolled side of the clay against the mould surface, to peel away the cloth and, using a steel or rubber kidney to smooth sway the cloth texture. This treatment of a textured surface is obviously not advisable with agate.

The first thing to ensure is that the cloth texture is minimised. When pieces of agate are being rolled to consolidate them, as is often the case, a cloth with a pronounced texture is ideal to hold the clay from spreading but as soon as the actual use of the slab approaches it is sensible to transfer the clay to a smoother cloth for final rolling so the texture is minimal.

When agate clay is being formed over a hump dish-mould the smooth rolled surface is obviously placed on the mould surface and the cloth is peeled away leaving the back of the dish with a slight texture. Some people do a final rolling on polythene which, if it releases from the clay well, gives a very smooth surface, but with soft clay release is not always easy.

111

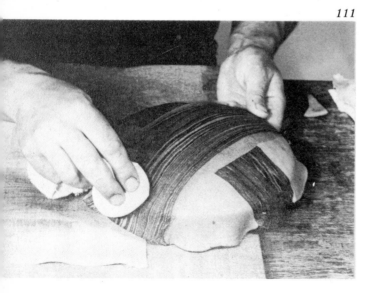

*110* Instead of the usual quick stroking with a kidney to press the clay against the mould and simultaneously smooth the back, the clay is pressed against the mould surface with the hands and fingers held very flat

*111* The back of the dish is then lightly tapped all over with a pad of soft clay wrapped up in a fine cloth. The edge can be trimmed as normal the cut, if necessary, being softened with the same pad of clay. This treatment will remove the majority of the texture and any that remains can be scraped away when the surface is scraped clean at the leatherhard stage

When forming dishes in hollow moulds the smooth rolled side is placed uppermost so the sheet of agate should be made as smooth as possible on both sides, if necessary by rolling directly on a smooth absorbent board and then turning it back onto a cloth. It is laid in the mould resting on a smooth cloth. When it has been positioned one edge of the clay is lifted up a little and one side of the cloth is folded back on itself and tucked under this edge

112 Then if the edge of the clay is held the cloth can be gently peeled out from between the clay and the mould. This procedure virtually eliminates any dents and grooves made in the back of the dish by the edges of the mould, the inside of the dish needs no smoothing and the outside should be sufficiently smooth not to need anything more than the slight scraping it receives to clean it

113 Though it does not need smoothing the inside surface has to be gently worked over with a pad of clay wrapped in a smooth cloth to ease the clay against the mould surface

114 The edge is trimmed normally

115 The pad of clay is then used to soften the cut angle of the edge simply by rocking it gently on the surface

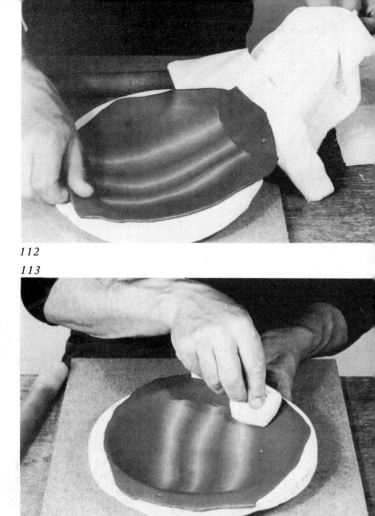

112

113

115

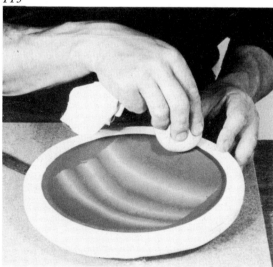

114

The descriptions so far have all been in terms of producing rolled or cut slabs of agate for use whole as slabs or in moulds. It is perfectly possible to assemble agate forms from smaller pieces, in the mould itself indeed historically this was undoubtably done extensively. In the production of agate slabs the overlapping of joins was described and these were rolled to effect a join and to close up gaps. Obviously rolling is not possible in moulds, figures 116 to 121 are not of joining agate in a mould but are simply a demonstration of an important factor which determines the appearance of such joins, not in terms of colour or tone but of relief, and ensures strength

116 As a demonstration a cut slab of clay is placed on part of a hump dish-mould. The right hand side is cut vertically and the left hand side is pressed or cut to a shallow angle

117 Two additional pieces of clay are then put in position, one on each side, with a slight overlap

118 and 119 The two overlaps are then firmly fingered down with equal pressure

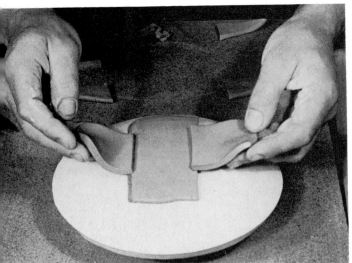

118

119

50

120 If the demonstration piece is turned over the left hand join shows as a bare hairline while the right hand one is an obvious groove. Provided the join is sound there is no right or wrong about the existence of a groove, indeed in some contexts obvious joins have a major quality to contribute. The point is that the existence or elimination of grooves is entirely determined by the outside edges of the clay already placed in the mould to which new pieces are added

It is of course entirely possible to make more enclosed moulded forms as well as open dishes with agate. Here again the conventional process of filling the pieces of the mould and then pressing them together can be varied with agate. If the conventional process was used with agate it is obvious that a very visible seam would be formed by the linear break in the configurations of the agate where the moulded parts met. By assembling the mould pieces when they are only partially filled and completing the filling in the assembled mould there is no need for any break in the agate markings that coincides with the mould joins.

121 For work of this kind to be possible the mould has to be held together securely so it can be moved about and worked in with absolute confidence that the halves are securely fixed together. Obviously the mould should be keyed as is normal. Each half should have at least one deep groove and with strong non-stretch string or cord the halves should be tied together. The tying should then be made absolutely rigid with folding wedges. Folding wedges are vastly better than a single wedge as unlike a single wedge, if they are tightened properly by moving only the inner one they exert only an outward pressure on the string, not an upwards or downwards one as well

122 Securely held together like this the joined mould can be tilted to any position to facilitate the addition of pieces of clay. The primary opportunity is to lay agate pieces across the mould join

120

121

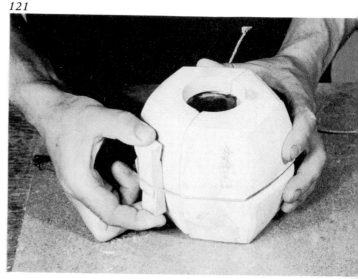

122

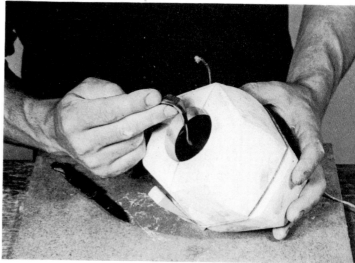

*123*

*123, 124 and 125* The two teapots and the chocolate pot shown in detail were all made in Staffordshire in the early part of the eighteenth century. All three are pressmoulded forms. In all three there is a clear interruption in the shapes of the agate where the handles and spouts are joined on but no break in continuity where the halves of the mould would have met suggesting that all three were completed in already assembled moulds. In all three, but most distinctly in the first, (figure 123) there is a remarkable consistency of repeated shapes within the agate underlining the degree of control which, with the practice inevitable in a production context, can be achieved. The two teapots are each just under 5 in. (12.5 cm) high and the chocolate pot just under 6 in. (15 cm) high. English. *Victoria and Albert Museum, London*

124

125

*126* Like the preceding three illustrations the cat is English and mould-made in Staffordshire in the first half of the eighteenth century. Unlike the preceding three there is a strong seam mark breaking the shapes of the agate and dividing front from back, showing that the parts of the mould were filled before being joined. There is also a deep groove (refer to figures 116 to 120) between the white of the neck and shoulders and the agate of the body. 4½ in. (11 cm) high. *Victoria and Albert Museum, London*

*126*

*127* This jug 8 in. (20 cm) high shows a typical version of the type of spiral marking common with thrown agate. English. Late eighteenth to early nineteenth century. *Victoria and Albert Museum, London*

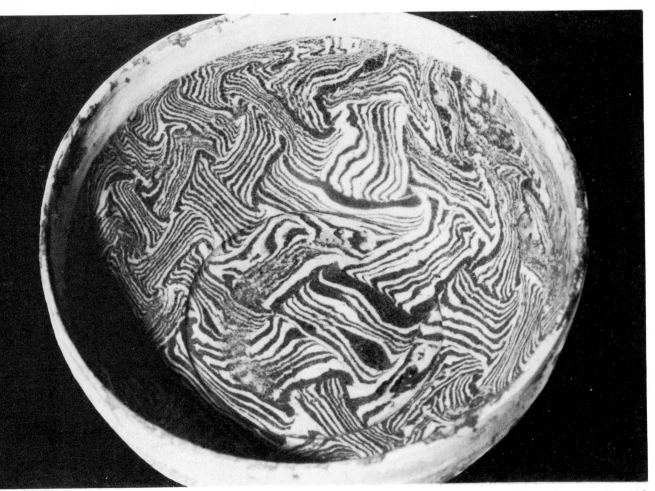

*128* This small bowl, just under 5½ in. (14 cm)
wide, was, from the crispness of the inside form
made over a hump mould. The rectangular
shapes of the striped agate were either individually placed and then rolled into a sheet or the
whole piece was made from strips of striped
agate woven together and then rolled. The idea
of weaving strips, whether it occurred in this
case or not, is an interesting possibility with
agate. China. Sung Dynasty. *Victoria and
Albert Museum, London*

*129* This bowl is slightly shallower and wider than the previous one. Though they are clearly agate the markings on a large part of it are very similar to feathering. Markings of this type are simply made by deeply pulling a needle or knife blade through a soft striped agate slab and then rolling the piece to eliminate the cuts. It is a more pronounced example of the process shown in figures 105 and 106. Chinese, Sung Dynasty. *Victoria and Albert Museum, London*

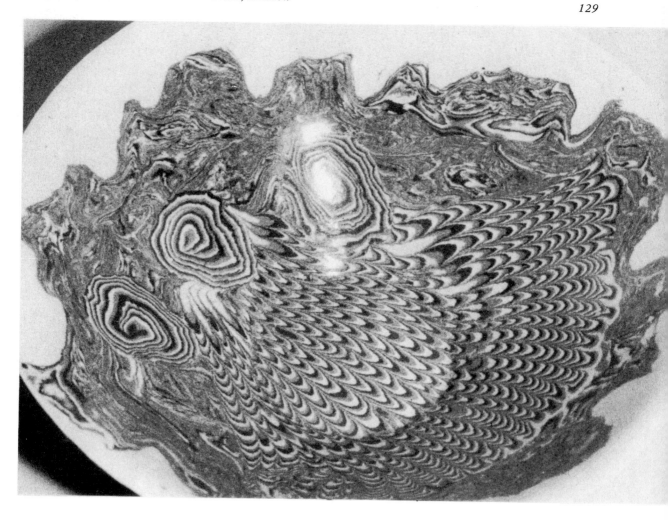

# Inlay

Inlay is the filling of recesses made in the surface a clay object with contrasting clay resulting in an object with a smooth surface in which there are lines or shapes which are visible solely by their colour or tone contrast. There are three possible processes of inlay: rolled clay inlay, scraped clay inlay and scraped slip inlay. Rolled clay inlay has rather different visual possibilities to the other two. The main difference between scraped slip inlay and scraped clay is the context in which each is the more convenient.

Inlay, in both mediaeval and Victorian times, was extensively used in the production of floor tiles and it has been finely and precisely used in pots from a variety of contexts. It offers a quite distinct quality which in its crispness and flatness of surface is unlike that obtainable by other means. A study of historical examples of inlay will reveal a surprising amount of cracking of inlaid clay. Whether this is tolerable or not is a personal question but it is not inevitable. It perhaps occurs in history through the desire to exploit the particular quality of crispness. The crispest marks are most readily made in firmer clay which leads to late inlaying, which leads in turn to cracking. Adhesion of inlay is the first thing to ensure, whether inlay is late or early, and both are possible. If cracking occurs the shrinkage of the inlay should be adjusted by non-plastic additions.

## ROLLED CLAY INLAY

Necessarily, rolled clay inlay occurs in sheets of clay so its uses are limited to tiles, slab-building and pressmoulding.

Of the three varieties of inlay it offers the most plastic possibilities though considerable control is possible.

Rolled inlay can be done at any stage between quite soft and quite firm. The clays used at any stage should be as similar as possible in consistency.

With soft clays the clay to be inlaid is simply cut from very thinly rolled sheets or is pinched out thinly to shape from small pellets or lumps. It is laid on the ground clay and rolled in. With large areas it helps to approximately depress recesses in the background clay. At this soft stage adhesion should be more or less instantaneous and no particular steps should be necessary. Rolling inevitably distorts and enlarges the inlaid clay to some extent, though this is minimised if a finely woven cloth is placed over the sheet as the inlay is being rolled.

With firmer clay much greater precision is possible especially if appropriate recesses are made to receive the inlay. As firmer clay is used the tendency to spread out excessively diminishes. To assist adhesion it is wise to use some slip, either applied or brushed out of the recesses in the background clay. While soft clay closes up fairly readily to present a flush meeting line between inlay and ground, firmer clay tends to be difficult to close up completely.

As rolled inlay is not scraped flat it enables grogged clays to be used without the problems of the creation, or subsequent time-consuming elimination, of rough texture.

130 The example in this and the following five illustrations is of rolled inlay done with soft clay. The thicker sheet in the background is the ground clay and the thinner, darker sheet in the foreground is the inlay clay. Both clays are of identical, almost sticky soft, consistency

131 The inlay pieces are cut out and carefully laid in position. Until all are in place it is best to simply lay them in position without attempting to fix them

132 When all are in the intended position they can be lightly pressed to help them to adhere. With firmer clay a brushing of slip under each piece will assist adhesion

133 The slab can then be gently and slowly rolled. Until they are adhering well to the ground the inlay pieces can, if they are sticky, wrap themselves round the rolling pin. Once adhesion between the two clays is achieved, and with soft clay as in this example it is more or less instant, rolling can proceed. The ground clay should be stuck to the rolling cloth so that rolling pushes the inlay into the ground and extends the whole piece only minimally. As the inlay clay is rolled into the ground it will spread and distort a little. The spreading will be most even if the original slab of inlay clay was rolled out to a very even thickness and the distortion can be minimised if a constant watch is kept on

130

131

132

133

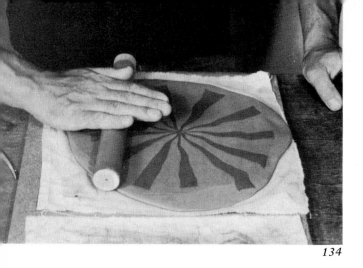

134

135

the effect of the rolling, and the direction of rolling is changed accordingly. With firmer clay it may help if a clean cloth is placed on top of the work as in figures 95 and 96 so that it can be firmly rolled with minimal extension until the surface is flush. Where strongly coloured inlay is used a cloth has the additional advantage that it eliminates the smudging that can be caused by rolling. Soft clay is so mobile that a cloth on top of the work is usually an unnecessary process in flattening the surface

134 Once the surface is flush the work can be released from the rolling out cloth and, if so wished, be rolled out thinner and larger. This should be done with care as considerable distortion can quickly occur at this stage

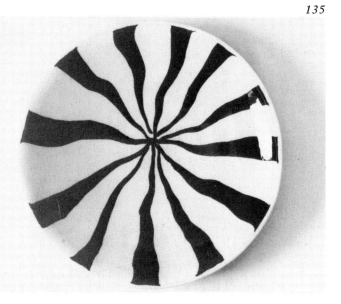

135 Done at this stage rolled inlay is seen in its most plastic form. Thin coils, pellets and thinly pinched flat shapes can be rolled into a clay ground just as easily as cut pieces. The possibilities are further extended if firmer clays are used. With firmer clays hollows can be pressed into the ground to receive the inlay clay and this can be cut or pinched out more or less to the intended final shape offering a much preciser degree of control and taking the process closer to that of scraped inlay. Though they can approach one another the possibilities of rolled and scraped inlay do however remain distinct

*136* This detail of a slab built pot shows an unusually controlled use of rolled inlay done at a fairly firm leatherhard stage. The initial impact is of the bold repeated shapes of the birds and of strong tone contrast. On closer inspection a more delicate quality is apparent. Each of the bird shapes is slightly different and each is surrounded by a slight hollow where the inlay and the ground clays have not been rolled flush giving the surface a plasticity of detail. This complementary combination of the differing qualities of boldness and delicacy is a very particular use of rolled inlay which would essentially differ in scraped inlay. There is little, if any, tradition of rolled inlay and the work is a good example of how processes can be modified and extended in pursuit of particular qualities. *Jill Radford, 1978*

## SCRAPED INLAY

In deciding how deep to make marks for inlay and whether slip or clay will be the more appropriate material three factors should be borne in mind: small marks and narrow lines are more easily filled with slip than clay; large areas are less likely to be scraped through if they are relatively deeply inlaid; deep marks are more easily filled with clay than slip.

### Scraped clay inlay

Marks for clay inlay may be impressed or carved into clay. They are best made relatively deep unless they are very narrow. So that edges of inlaid areas are not spoiled by the pressure of inserting the clay, inlay is generally done no earlier than soft leatherhard. With care the marks can be filled in so that a minimum of scraping is necessary or even (though this gives a different quality from the flatness of scraped inlay) so that no scraping at all is necessary. Slip is usually necessary to ensure a good adhesion between the inlay and the ground and if this is worked up out of the ground of the recessed areas, any that spreads out as the inlay is worked in, will be the same colour as the body of the pot and will not therefore complicate matters when scraping is done. The right time for scraping may vary considerably from clay to clay. Some white clays, which tend to be used frequently for inlay because of the ease with which they can be coloured, go through a stage when they tend to flake or crumble if they are scraped. This tendency moreover is exaggerated by colouring additions. The right state for scraping can only be determined by trial and error but broadly the more plastic clays are generally more easily scraped early and the less plastic ones later. When scraping is done early minor streaks are apt to occur and should be left once the surface is flush to be removed later. When possible the scraping of inlay should be done along, not across, the edge of areas — when inlay is small scale and complex this is clearly not possible.

### Scraped slip inlay

Slip for inlay can be applied into recessed marks in one of two ways. It can be poured on or brushed on. Pouring is the obvious method if a large area of small marks is to be inlaid with the same colour. Brushing is obvious if there are relatively few marks within a large area. Brushing has the additional possibility that in any area two or more slips can be inlaid with placing that would be impossible with pouring, but where divisions between areas of marks are simple then pouring may be possible and would be quicker. A slip trailer rather than a brush may sometimes be appropriate.

Marks for slip inlay should be relatively shallow; never deeper than can be filled with a single application of slip, and they should be made as even as possible in depth so that in scraping down to reach the slip surface of deeper marks, shallower marks are not scraped away.

Slip fit is as important with inlay as in other contexts and the measures taken to ensure it are the same.

Brushed slip is usually not applied before early leather hardness so the action of brushing does not destroy the edges of marks but in some contexts, like pressmoulded dishes or tiles, poured slip can be applied to soft clay. Slip is generally scraped flush at an early leatherhard stage.

### Scraped inlay, with clay

137 It is equally possible to use clay for inlay on freely drawn and on impressed marks but the example here is of carefully cut, hard-edged work. Once the areas have been decided and lightly drawn in, the edges can be cut with a pointed knife held at a steep angle. A further cut, at a shallower angle, as shown here, will lift out a piece of clay leaving the edge of the recess neatly defined

*137*

138 The remainder of the area can then be recessed with a cutting levering action of the knife edge. Once the edge is carefully defined this work can be quite fast, the clay being almost flicked out of the recess. The right depth for recesses obviously depends in part on the wall thickness of the particular pot. What must be avoided, with wide areas particularly, is to leave so shallow a recess that in cleaning up the surface the inlaid clay is scraped through in places. Equally, and obviously, the recess should not be so deep that there is any risk that, in pressing in the inlay clay, the wall of the pot will be distorted. A minimum depth is about $\frac{1}{16}$ in. (1.5 mm) and for larger areas $\frac{1}{8}$ in. (3 mm) is better but much depends on the nature of the work and the thickness of the pot

139 Lines can usually be recessed by levering sideways in the downward cuts which define their edges. Failing this a narrow chisel-ended wooden or metal tool has to be used, working within and across the width of the line

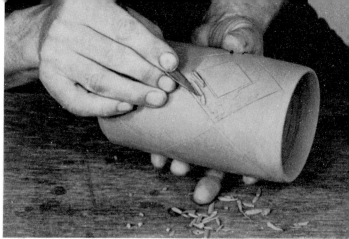

138

139

140

141

*140, 141 and 142* Recessed areas should be well prepared to receive the inlay clay. A good sequence is to rough up the surface with a suitable tool (figure 140), to brush this with water using a stiff bristled brush, working up a good slip from the surface right into the edges (figure 141) and then to key the surface again (figure 142). The clay of the pot should be no drier than medium leatherhard and softer if the shapes of the inlay recesses permit it. The inlay clay should be in a stiff plastic state. This difference of consistency between the body and the inlay clay may necessitate the addition of some non-plastic material to the inlay clay especially if the inlay is of large areas which are the most prone to cracking where there are differential shrinkage problems

*143* Each recess should be carefully filled while the slip is still sticky the clay being pressed down methodically over the whole surface. Edges of areas need to be carefully pressed so that a good adhesion at the visible join on the surface is achieved but pressure must be firm rather than excessive so that the shape of the edges is not distorted. The clay of the pot should be just soft enough for such distortion to be possible

142

143

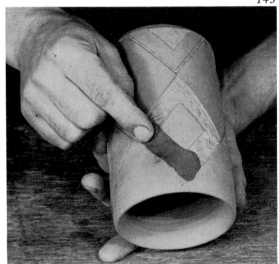

**144** It is usually convenient to fill larger areas with several pieces of inlay clay working each piece into place before beginning with the next. In doing this it is important that each new piece of inlay clay is first pressed down onto the previous inlay and then worked into the remaining recess. Failure to do this, working inlay clay across a recess to join up with a previous piece, can result in fine lines of the adhesion slip working out of the recess and showing at the junctions between inlay pieces when the work has been scraped down. This is a particular hazard when white clay is inlaid into a coloured body. In this illustration the inlay clay was joined onto the end of the previous piece, see figure 143, and is being worked along the recess from this join. When two edges have to meet as is the case working round an open diamond shape the piece of inlay clay is first laid and joined across the gap, bridging it, and is then worked down into the recess

**145** In fine lines keying with a toothed tool is difficult so these should be brushed twice rather than once and, in addition to the brushing, some slip may be applied

**146** Fine lines should be filled with a fine coil so that as the clay is pushed in it reaches right to the bottom of the narrow, steep sided recess

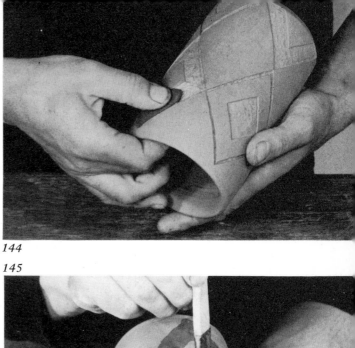

144

145

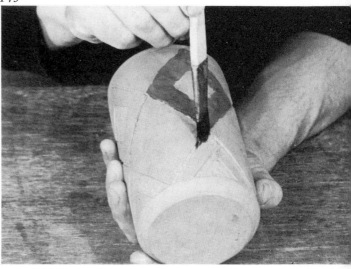

146

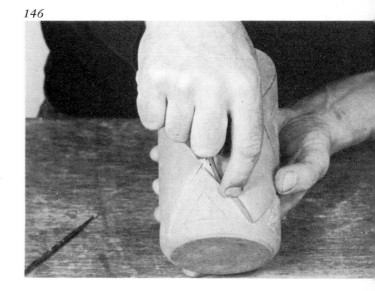

147

When all inlay is complete the pot can be wrapped up in polythene and put on one side for a day or so. Retarding the drying process allows the inlay and body clay to reach a more equal consistency and minimises the chance of cracking

*147* It is sometimes easier with narrow lines to pare away the excess clay with a palate knife than to scrape it away

*148* Scraping with a metal kidney is however the most usual procedure to make the surface of larger areas flush with the body. If all areas and lines of inlay have been filled neatly and slightly proud of the surface the inlay only will need scraping to smooth it and once the body has been reached the marks of the inlay will be evident. Scraping should be done with deliberate, unhurried movements. Poor, uneven filling of the inlay areas will necessitate further scraping which brings with it the danger of scraping right through any shallowly recessed areas. Wherever possible scraping should be along rather than across junctions between inlay and body

*149* Final cleaning up may be done by sponging but this should be done with some caution. When sponging is used it should be along not across edges, as much as is possible, and the sponge should be frequently washed and wrung out. Poor sponging can create rather than remove smears of clay and often the initial scraping is quite sufficient. With very smooth clays there may be a strong temptation to gently scrape, or even wire wool, the work when it is bone dry. If this is done precautions against creating airborne dust should be taken

148

149

**150** The finished work shows the flush, clean sharp quality which is the hallmark of inlaid work. Historically clay inlay is less common than slip inlay mainly because slip inlay is much quicker to do and allows equal definition on a very small scale and with greater complexity

## SCRAPED INLAY WITH SLIP

**151** Slip is commonly used to fill incised or impressed marks for inlay. That the marks are not too deep to be easily filled with one application of slip is more important than exactly how they are made. Here impressed marks are being rolled onto a simple concave dish with a roulette made of carved plaster. It is important, if the scraping of the inlay is not to be laborious and time consuming, that, however complex the inlay itself maybe, the surface which contains the inlay is even and simple enough to facilitate scraping

**152** The background of a roulette used for inlay should be cleanly cut back to give good clearance so that unwanted impressions are not made. It should be noticed that stamps and roulettes can have a very different effect whether used for inlay or as impressions. With impressions the sharpness at the bottom of the impression is usually the part which is visually strongest. When an impression is filled with slip for inlay that sharpness is hidden and the outline or the impression at the clay surface is

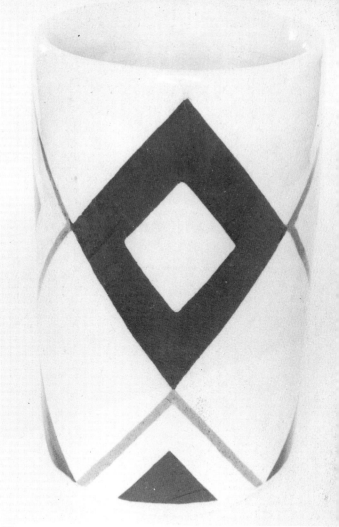

*150*

*151*

*152*

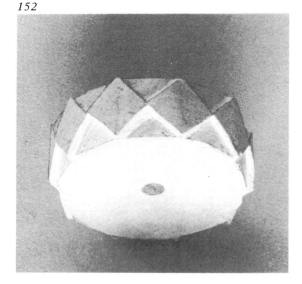

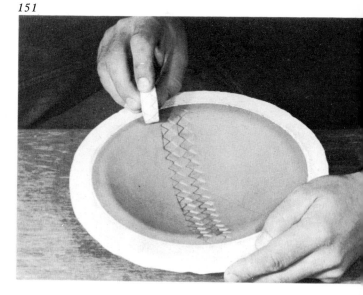

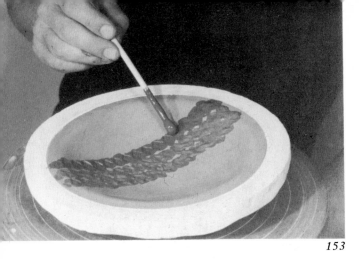

seen. Thus the meeting points of the chain of squares in this roulette becomes overlapped, not touching, squares as inlay (see figure 155) as it is the section of the roulette below its own surface which becomes the inlaid surface

153 Slip can be applied as soon as the recesses have been completed. Two slips of slightly different colour have been applied. It should be easily possible to fill the marks adequately with a single brushing but here the furthest line has first been painted with a thin coating, well worked into the recess, and is being filled up with thicker slip spread on from a well filled brush

*153*

*154*

154 Early to medium leatherhard is the usual time to scrape away the excess slip which can usually be done quite quickly with a firm, steady action. The slight bumpiness on impressed surfaces caused by the sideways displacement of clay can sometimes cause slight problems during scraping and these may be exaggerated by the bumpiness of brushed slip if the scraping has been left rather late. If this occurs the remedy is to scrape the inlaid areas using a metal kidney in a crisscross manner, in this way each new scrape of the kidney removes any high points left by the previous one rather than exaggerating high points into a ridged unevenness. Whether as a corrective measure when unevenness has occured or, in normal cases, with softish leatherhard slip using a kidney with a crisscross action is an efficient way to produce a smooth, even surface but with the danger of scraping through the slip, scraping should never become too fast or mechanical

*155*

155 The finished dish clearly shows the difference between the inlaid shapes and the initially apparent shapes of the roulette. The dish also shows two errors which can occur. Both of these are in the middle line on the left hand side of it. At the bottom edge the last mark has been scraped right through. In the middle of the row there are marks where the recessed edge of the roulette has left an impression where it has tilted over to one side. The marks left by this tilting are evident in figure 151. The work could have been scraped more deeply to remove these marks but this would have entailed the risk of scraping through less deeply impressed adjacent areas

156 This illustration shows a distinctly and carefully inlaid jar. The feel of the pot is of robust country pottery and the materials are those found in such work. The carefully spaced inlaid ornament is unusual though not incongruous in this context. The products of eighteenth and nineteenth century English country potteries are more usually notable for a quality of speedy freedom than of deliberateness but named and commemorative pieces do often have a different careful quality not least perhaps because they were a break from routine. The letters are clearly impressed with a printers metal type face and the stars are therefore almost certainly printers ornament. In places where the stars are less distinct either the impression was too deep and did not register the star crisply on the clay surface or the metal ornament was clogged up with clay. Work with as many and as fine marks as this is inevitably inlaid with slip not clay. 6 in. (15 cm) high. English. The full inscription is Mr T. Gutsell Senr. November 3 1803. *Craft Study Centre, Bath, England*

157 Mediaeval inlaid tiles are probably the most quoted examples of inlay. They are thought to have been formed in moulds which simultaneously formed the tile and the impressions which were then inlaid. Broken inlaid tile fragments often show considerable depth of inlay suggesting that clay not slip was used in some cases but other tiles are so complex that it seems unlikely that clay would have been used. Probably, as broken pieces show so considerable a variety of inlay depth, slip and clay were both used when their differing qualities were appropriate. As substantial flat objects tiles were obviously a very suitable context for inlay as the slip or clay could be quickly and simply cleaned off with a simple wooden or metal straight edge. Because available red firing clays are much more common than cream or white firing clays the tiles were invariably made of red clay and inlaid with creamy white clay. Mediaeval English. *Victoria and Albert Museum, London*

156

157

158

158 This detail is from a Chinese tomb pillow. It is unusual in that it combines clay and slip inlay. The circular and triangular shapes are clearly inlaid clay, cut from carefully arranged agate clay. The crescents, small circles and triangles in darker clay, some of which impinge into the agate areas were clearly done after the agate inlay and are of a complexity and scale only sensibly possible with slip. Sung Dynasty, China. *Victoria and Albert Museum, London*

159 This detail from a piece of what is sometimes known as 'Henri Deux' ware is of work impressed by very fine metal stamp ornaments, possibly those used by bookbinders. The unevenness of the incised lines which border the impressed inlaid ornament detracts from what would otherwise be an even more extraordinarily fine quality. The sharp definition of the marks is heightened by the contrast between the dense, dark-toned inlay and the bright white clay of the dish. Unquestionably this is slip inlay. 'Henry Deux' ware occured and ceased without direct antecedants or successors and it is now accepted that it was made in the mid-sixteenth century in France. Only slightly more than sixty pieces are known. *Victoria and Albert Museum, London*

159

160 Here white and black slips have been inlaid into a pale grey stoneware. This is a fairly simple example of a type of inlay known as mishima which originated in Korea and later spread to both Japan and China. The use of inlay is widespread in oriental stoneware and porcelain and, given the reverence accorded to this by western potters, it is surprising that the inlaid work has not attracted more attention. Korean. Koryu Dynasty thirteenth to fourteenth Century AD. *Victoria and Albert Museum, London*

160

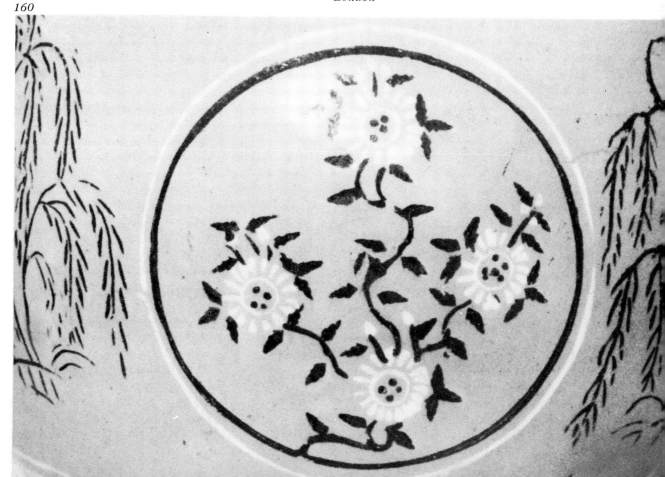

*161*

*161* This crisp, clean work consists of incised lines and marks, inlaid with white slip, glazed with a pale celadon. Rather as with Geometric Greek painted pottery this work shows a quality of detail which can too easily be missed in the context of the whole pot which has a rather cold severity. Work of this type is as much part of the Oriental ceramic tradition as its better known more gestural manifestations. Japanese in the Korean style. *Victoria and Albert Museum, London*

*162* This detail is from an Oriental storage pot over 20 in. (50 cm) high the entire surface of which is inlaid by filling rouletted impressions with slip. By treating the entire pot in this way an ambiguity between inlay and ground is created which extends the idea of inlay as marks on a ground. *Victoria and Albert Museum, London*

162

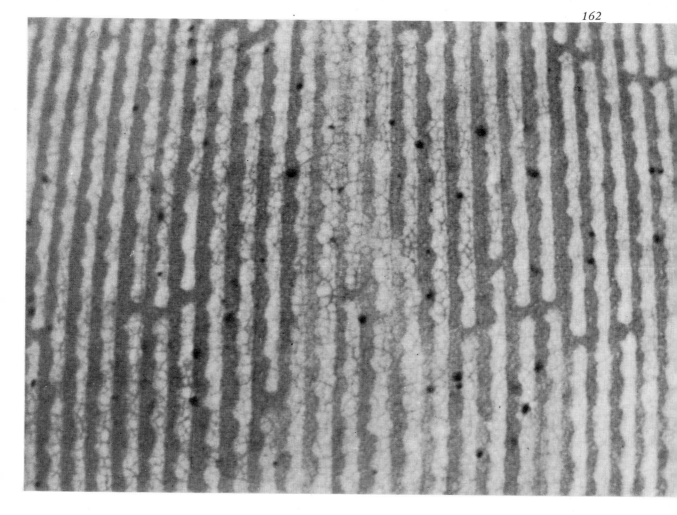

# Sprigging

Sprigging is the application of pressmoulded relief units, called sprigs, to the surface of a pot. The two stages of the process are the initial making of the sprig moulds and the subsequent making of the clay springs and the application of these to the pot surface.

The two major possibilities of sprigging are the exact repetition of relief units and use of a fineness of relief quality which would be actually and economically unrealistic working directly by modelling or carving on a pot. An important production possibility, which made sprigging a much used process in some periods of history, is that relatively unskilled labour can be used to mass produce pots of fine and controlled quality — the application of sprigs is clearly not completely unskilled but the skill is of a different order to that needed to model or carve the initial moulds.

Moulds for sprigging can be made of fired clay or plaster of paris. Plaster has the disadvantage that the mould surface will wear relatively quickly and as fine clay will accurately accept detail as fine as it is offered this is a serious draw back. Where plaster is used it is normal to have a master mould from which to cast working moulds so that these can be discarded and replaced when they begin to wear. In the past metal moulds were sometimes used which were oiled to prevent sticking.

There is of course not a large step between moulding relief units and applying these to a pot and making the entire pot form, including its relief, in a mould. In Hellenistic times 'Megarian' bowls were wheel formed in moulds which formed relief on their outer surface. The Romans subsequently refined this process and used it extensively to produce bowls with intricate and finely formed relief.

In the eighteenth and nineteenth centuries much pressmoulded and slipcast industrial production in England closely echoed earlier and contemporary sprigged work.

Sprigging, however, has the possibility of applying relief units in a different colour of clay to the body of the pot. Even this can be copied in pressmoulding or slipcasting by filling relief area of a hollow mould and neatly cleaning these off to neat edges before pressing the body of the vessels or by painting coloured slip onto relief areas of a mould before casting. In both these cases however the results are not wholly satisfactory and processes which were evolved for their simplicity are made more complex. With sprigging it makes little difference whether the sprig mould is filled with the same or a different clay to that of a pot.

One limitation of sprigging is that while it is simple to cover a pot with many small sprigs it is rather difficult to apply very large sprigs. A sprig of say 16 sq in. (100 sq cm) would be exceptionally large. Larger ones than this have certainly been used but examples showing cracking tend to underline the problems of ensuring good adhesion and controlled placing. An alternative practice is to build up large areas of relief from a number of smaller, related units.

The problem of large areas is related to that of curvature. Sprig moulds are flat so that excess clay can be easily and quickly scraped off the back. While small sprigs can be bent sufficiently to adhere to almost any curve the larger a unit is the more difficult it becomes to make it fit onto a surface which is curved. It is notable that much of the German salt-glaze work which was sprigged from very large moulds was usually confined to cylindrical forms, often tall tankards, where the sprig had to bend in one plane only.

Except in the industrial reproduction of eighteenth century prototypes sprigging has been little used either inside or outside the pottery industry for some long time. Outside the industry it may well be that it suffers from historical or industrial associations which are misunderstood. If this is the case it is a pity for it has varied and unique possibilities.

## THE MAKING OF SPRIG MOULDS: NEGATIVE AND POSITIVE STAGES

This brief section does not aim to describe the actual modelling or carving which is necessary to form a sprig mould but to outline the possibilities created by transferring the relief from negative to positive state and back.

Sprig moulds can begin either as positive modelling done on a smooth surface and subsequently cast in plaster or as negative carving done into plaster cast on a smooth flat surface.

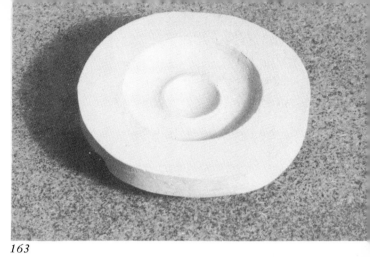

*163*

*164*

*163* This mould was carved into plaster. An initial model could have been modelled, or with this example, a more precise version of the same from could have been turned in clay and then cast to form a plaster mould. With a selection of filed metal shapes carving is actually surprisingly quick. In itself this mould will form a simple sprig but in this state the possibility of scratching lines into the mould exists. Such lines, sunken in the mould, would be raised in the sprig, see figures 168, 176 and 177. Such marks could not be easily modelled in clay nor carved by reserving in plaster in the positive state

*164* The progress of carving into plaster can be observed at any stage by taking a clay pressing. If several pressings are cast a number of plaster negatives can be made to be developed differently by further carving. The important possibility exists of modifying the clay pressings by impressing or incising to create a recessed relief which could not be easily carved by reserving in plaster in the negative state shown in figure 163

*165*

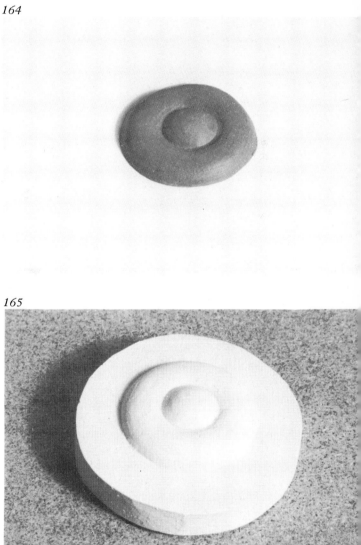

*165* From the carved plaster mould it is also possible to make a positive plaster cast. Because plaster expands very slightly on setting, taking a cast from a negative mould is a little more difficult than taking a cast off a positive mould. Deep, steep sided casts in expanding tend to grip the sides of the hollow mould but with shallow casts the expanding cast can actually push itself out of the mould a little. The mould must be well sealed with soft soap to ensure a clean release and casts should be made in a hard dense plaster

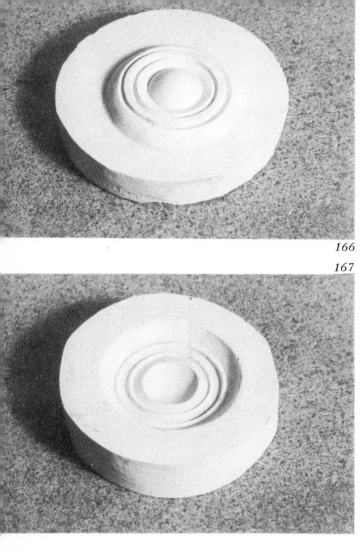

166

167

**166** Some aspects of a carved mould are far easier to modify, and to see, in positive than in negative. Here for example the junction between the inner bump and the outer ring is easier to make more precise by carving in the positive state than the initial negative. Additionally, incised lines can be carved which could not have been reserved in the initial carving. Work may of course proceed from this state with further complete cyles of transferring work from positive to negative with modifications in each state. If a large number of sprigs are needed the final state should be a positive cast in hard plaster to function as a block mould from which to cast working moulds

**167** The casting of working moulds from a block mould is facilitated by the slight expansion of plaster

While the quantity production of sprig moulds is a somewhat unlikely exercise it should be clear that the possibility of the transferance from negative to positive states and the differing materials of clay and plaster allow the progressive modification and refinement of relief work which would be impossible working in one state only. This principle is of relevance to all work involving relief in models and moulds.

168

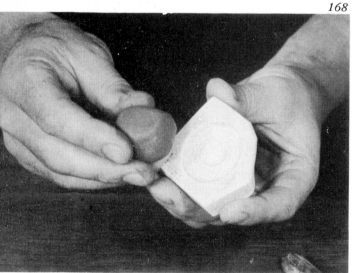

## THE MAKING AND APPLICATION OF SPRIGS

**168** The clay from which sprigs are formed should be soft enough to readily take up any detailed relief in the sprig mould. The ball of clay should be slightly larger than is needed and should be smooth and even, entirely free from folds and dents

*169 and 170* Though larger than necessary the ball should be so shaped that when placed in the mould centrally it does not touch the edges. It is then pressed down in the middle and the thumbs or fingers then walk round it pressing it down over the whole surface. If, as the clay is being pushed into the mould, the sprig can be felt releasing itself then the mould is too dry and work should be stopped and the sprig removed and the mould briefly immersed in water, for a few seconds only, to reduce its porosity. If the clay does release itself the action of pushing the clay into the mould will move it around on the mould surface resulting in unclear, shadow impressions of the relief. While a very dry mould is useless, so is a saturated one as the clay will stick in this. A slightly damp mould will grip the clay sufficiently for a crisp sprig to be made and will allow the sprig to be released. If a mould becomes too wet it can be dusted with talc, applied with a dry brush — in all types of casting and pressing when a moulded form will not release readily from the mould a dusting of talc usually corrects the problem

*171* As soon as the clay has been well pressed into the mould the back can be scraped flat with a straight edge. An old wooden ruler or a straight edged hardwood tool is best for this — terracotta moulds quickly wear steel rulers and steel rulers tend to remove pieces and dust from plaster moulds which then find their way into the clay. Sprig moulds should be scraped from the centre outwards because a single edge to edge movement tends to roll the sprig out of the mould. Scraping from the centre outwards pushes the clay against the mould edges giving a well defined pressing of the mould outline

169

170

171

172

173

*172 and 173* Sprigs can be applied directly from the mould onto the pot and in this case, unless the sprig clay has had some addition to reduce shrinkage, there is bound to be some difference in consistency and in shrinkage. For this to be tolerated, which is entirely possible, the place where the sprig is to be positioned must be prepared by scoring and with brushed or sprayed water until a sticky slip has been worked out of the clay. In this way a sufficiently good adhesion to tolerate the differential shrinkage can be created

*174 and 175* The sprig can then be applied directly to the pot, usually in a single deliberate rolling motion, in this case from left to right. Firm pressure should be used though obviously not so great that the pot is distorted. Note that the inside hand is supporting the pressure of application. Small sprigs, because of the quickly diminishing effect of a given pressure as area increases, are easier to apply directly like this than large sprigs. When direct application is done it is sensible to mark the edges of the sprig mould so that its precise position is known — though with a round symetrical sprig, as in this example, that is not so necessary. If directly applied sprigs have to be placed near each other, as well as marking the mould edges, which becomes essential for accurate placing, the flat edge of the mould can be cut down until it is sufficiently narrow to allow the

174

175

intended spacing. If the mould edges are cut very narrow then the pressure of application will need careful control as the edges can start to impress the clay around the sprig. It is clearly not possible for directly applied sprigs to touch each other

176 Any slip squeezed out during application should be removed immediately with a brush

177 Simple sprigs with simple sharp detail can effectively break through otherwise opaque glazes though where a more finely modelled or carved relief exists opaque glaze should be used with restraint

---

178 and 179 Just as with sprigs of simple outline those of more linear character should be filled in the middle first and then the clay should be pushed out to the ends of the lines

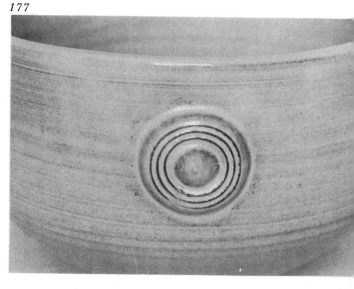

176

177

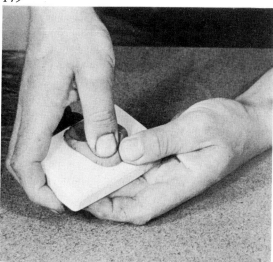

179

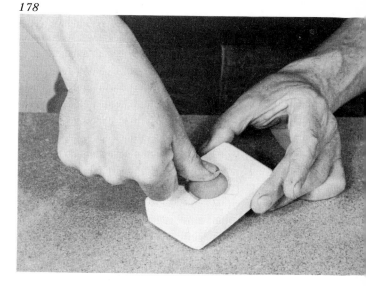

178

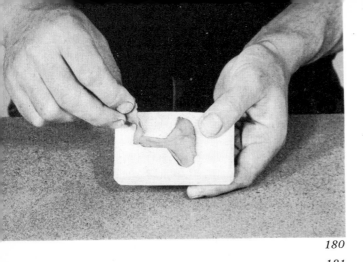

*180* When sprigs are quite narrow it is often possible to remove most of the excess clay by tearing but only if it breaks easily at the edges

*181* Tearing can only remove the bulk of the excess and the remainder has, as usual, to be scraped away as this also makes the back of the sprig flat. Linear sprigs are especially prone to be lifted out of the mould by scraping the back so moulds should have the right degree of porosity to hold the clay quite positively. It can also help if the scraped parts are gently held in the mould while the unscraped parts are cleaned off and flattened

*182* If the sprigs are positively held by a dampened mould they will need freeing so they can be lifted out of the mould easily. This is best done by pressing a palatte knife on the flat back, which will grip through suction, and by lifting the sprig gently upwards starting at the edges or the ends of lines first. As soon as the end of the sprig releases, the knife is lowered to return the sprig to the mould and is slid off the clay by moving it away from the middle. The other parts are then similarly released

*183* In this example fine molochite, to reduce shrinkage, has been added to the sprig clay so although the pot is quite firm and the sprig soft only a thin slip is needed to achieve a strong adhesion. This is brushed onto the pot

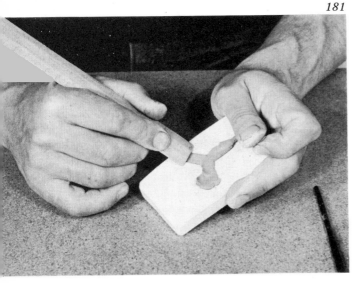

*182*

*183*

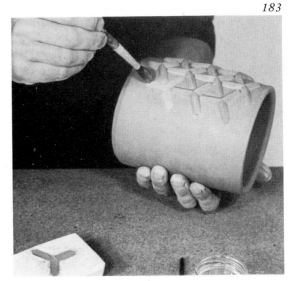

*184* A thin layer of slip on the sprig back, both means it will not stick too suddenly and makes it easier to lift the sprig from its mould again using the flat of the palatte knife

*185 and 186* The slip on both surfaces makes it easy to place the sprig in a position and then adjust it a little if necessary. It also makes it easy to withdraw the knife. The sprig is then gently pushed onto the pot surface and excess slip is removed with a brush. Exactly how any sprig is pushed against the pot depends a lot on the detail of its surface. Sprigs with fine detail should be pushed down at their edges with a suitable tool and if there are depressions in the relief a blunt pointed tool can be used at such points. Sprigs without fine detail can be fixed with finger pressure alone. Providing the materials and the states of the materials are right little pressure should be needed as the slip will ensure adhesion as long as there is not too much slip and as long as the whole of the sprig surface contacts the slip on the pot

*187* The use of sprigs of contrasting clay introduces an additional visual element but if unintended smears and spots of colour are to be avoided it demands a more meticulous care. Excessive use of slip must be avoided. A thin slip has been applied to the pot surface and a thin slip of the pot clay, not the sprig colour, has been painted on the back of the sprig avoid-

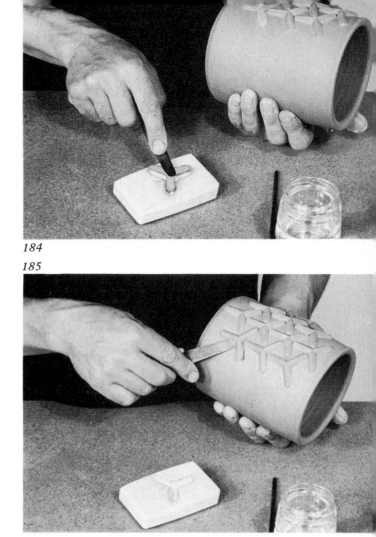

184

185

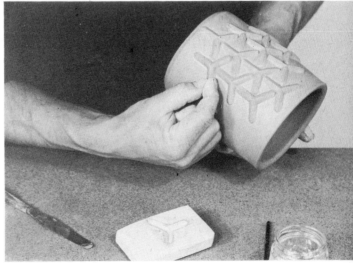

186

187

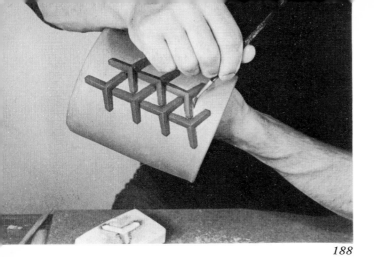

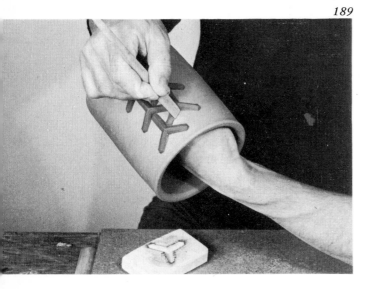

188

189

190

ing the very edges. The sprig is lifted from the mould and placed in position as normal. Fingers should be kept clean

188 There should be little if any excess slip. Any there is should be carefully removed with a fine brush

189 In some contexts a fine stiff brush can be used to secure the sprig in position by brushing it firmly along the edge with half the brush on the sprig and half on the pot. In this way smears of one clay do not go onto the other but the brush should be cleaned and squeezed out dry frequently. A flat rather than round brush is better for this purpose but the process is not possible in all contexts. An alternative, as here, is to gently push downwards and inwards on the sprig edge with a modelling tool

190 Sprigs are not always fixed in position immediately. A possible alternative where production is large or repetitive is to make a stock of sprigs and fix them onto the pots only when a large stock exists. The process offers the advantage that the sprigs can be placed on plaster of paris to bring them closer to the state of the pots and the plaster can be dampened so they do not become too firm too quickly. To fix them in position the process shown between figures 178 and 186 is used except that as this is not accessible no slip is put on the back of the sprig. The sprig is picked up by sliding a palatte knife under it — a touch of slip on the end of the knife will safely hold the sprig. As the entire sprig has had some time to stiffen up it is relatively easier to press it into place than when the whole sprig is soft

191 This extraordinarily fine work shows part of a very large panel of sprigging which is one of several applied to a tall salt-glazed tankard. The vertical lines of the joins between this panel and the next can be clearly seen. There can be no mistake, the piece, and this type, is sprigged not pressmoulded. The tops, bases and insides clearly demonstrate the thrown basis and though the sprigging technique is admirable the occasional crack, as to the right of the main figure here, indicate the problems that have been virtually overcome. Exceptional work of this type was done at several centres in the Rhineland in the late sixteenth and early seventeenth centuries. 18 in. (45 cm) high. Dated 1580. Siegburg, Germany. *Victoria and Albert Museum, London*

191

*192* This jug is about a hundred years later than the previous example. The material is a similar whitish grey saltglaze but while the relief on the Siegburg piece, figure 191, compares in quality with the finest contemporary work in cabinet carving, silversmithing and architectural decoration this relief roundel depicting William of Orange, though an admirably crisp impression, is in a different category. An interesting technical aspect is that while the sprig in figure 191 is simply bent in one plane to fit the curve of a cylinder this sprig is applied onto a far more spherical form. 8 in. (20 cm) high. About 1690. Westerwald, Germany. *Victoria and Albert Museum, London*

*193*

**193 and 194** Of somewhat contrasting quality these two sprig moulds are both over 4 in. (10 cm) wide and made of fired clay. Both are late sixteenth or early seventeenth century from the German Rhineland. Both are in the *Victoria and Albert Museum, London*

*194*

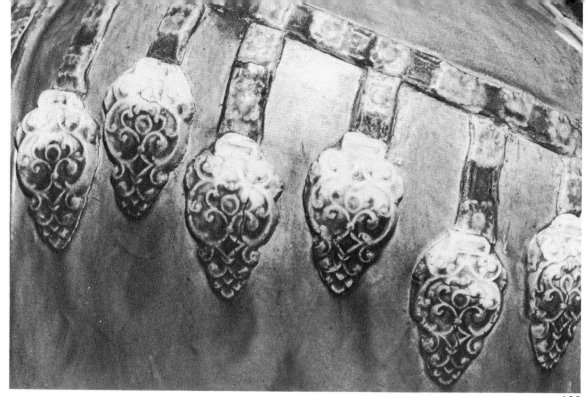

195

*195* In this detail of a large modelled figure of a horse, about 3 ft (100 cm) high, sprigged units are used to represent details of harness ornament. Chinese tomb statuary contains many examples of sprigged details among its richly modelled and moulded work. Chinese. Tang Dynasty. *Victoria and Albert Museum, London*

*196* Sprigged units are extremely common on eighteenth century creamware as a neat device to cover up the ends of extruded handles and lugs. English. *Victoria and Albert Museum, London*

196

*197*

197 This detail is from a thrown and turned jug made at the beginning of the nineteenth century and is typical of much of the classically inspired work of that time and slightly earlier. The jug is 8 in. (20 cm) high and the sprigged vase on it is just under 3 in. (7.5 cm) in height. Two points are of particular interest: firstly the openwork scrolls which flank the sprigged vase are each composed of over a dozen units breaking down what would clearly be an impossible arrangement to sprig in one piece; secondly in the vase and the horizon, both applied as large units, there is considerable evidence of cracking, though no parts of the sprigging have actually cracked off the pot. This type of cracking is surprisingly common in work of this period and seems most common in sprigging where the actual thickness of the applied clay is thin. Strong tone contrast between sprig and ground, as here, always and inevitably shifts the emphasis from the quality of relief to the quality of profile. English. First quarter of the nineteenth century. *Owned by Gilbert Harding-Green*

198

198, 199 and 200 The sprigged unglazed redwares produced in England and Holland at the very end of the seventeenth century and in the early part of the eighteenth show some fine and interesting work. The pots are distinct not simply for their sprigging but for the delicate controlled precision of their form and the refinement of their bodyclay which was ideal for fine moulding. Much historical writing refers to this work as impressed but it is clearly

199

sprigged, not impressed, for the relief is above, not within, the surface. The history of the work is ill defined and conflicting reports exist but it does seem certain that two Dutch brothers, the Elers brothers, were among the first to produce this work in England, firstly at Fulham and later in Stoke-on-Trent, and that their work was much emulated. Both in considering the pots and their sprigging it is interesting that they were silversmiths originally. In this context it should be mentioned that though it is not now thought of as a material for clay moulding (except in dust pressing) metal was used in the past as a mould material for plastic clay. If the metal is thinly oiled clay will release from it easily. In the first two examples, 198 and 199, the imprint around each sprigged unit suggests a direct application from mould onto pot and the narrowness of the surrounding impression suggests the use of metal as the sprig mould. In the right hand panel of the third example, 200, the bottom left hand corner where the sprig is very thin is missing and, interestingly, there is no mark of any scoring or any slip where the piece is missing. The quality and content of redwares varies considerably but examples do emphasise the suitability of fine unglazed vitrified clay as a finish for sprigged pots with finely worked relief. Figure 198 late seventeenth century, made in the Bradwell Wood works of the Elers Brothers. Figure 199 late seventeenth century marked in the base with a stag in a circle, Elers Brothers. Figure 200 about 1760 showing George III and Queen Charlotte, Staffordshire, England. All three in the *Victoria and Albert Museum, London*

200

# Modelled relief

There is a long and continuing tradition in pottery of vessels which are modelled in their entirety and formed by coiling, pressmoulding, slip casting or sometimes by the assembly of thrown parts. In vessels of this type it is impossible to separate the modelling from the forming of the vessel itself so they represent particular use of a forming process rather than a subsequent separate action performed on a formed vessel. For this reason neither vessels of this type nor modelled figures or other modelled objects made in fired clay are described here. The concentration is solely on relief modelling added to complete forms.

In the history of ceramics there is an impressively clear demarcation between the traditions of modelled figures (and other modelling), modelled vessels and modelled ornament on vessels. The traditions of figures and other modelling exploit the full three dimensional plastic possibilities of clay; those of modelled vessels represent a considered compromise between the full possibilities of modelling and the requirements of function; those of modelled ornament are surprisingly restrained and are confined largely to relief work. This may be a slight oversimplification and certainly there are exceptions. The modelled extravaganzas of some European porcelain factories, especially in the nineteenth century, when modelled ornament, often floral, was liberally applied to vessels could never be called restrained but these vessels were ornamental rather than functional in intention. Possibly some of the restraint of modelling work is due to the fact that sprigging and impressing both offered quicker ways of applying relief ornament and involved less skilled labour.

Restrained though traditions are the possibilities of modelling are wide and rich and could certainly be more fully exploited, particularly in an age when potters are not solely required to make readily repeatable vessels as economically as possible.

As a process there is very little to describe about modelling. The quality of plastic clay invites manipulation and that very manipulation is modelling. Modelling onto the surface of a vessel is certainly a limitation as the clay has to be manipulated on the surface rather than freely, three dimensionally. Consideration of the nature and function of the vessel may demand other limitations. But all that has to be done is to manipulate the clay with ones fingers and any appropriate tools into the intended form and relief.

Technically two things have to be ensured. Firstly the added clay must adhere to the walls of the vessel and neither crack within itself nor crack off during subsequent drying and firing. Secondly the relief which is built up should not be so great that the thickness or weight of it leads to problems in the firing. Both these conditions are easy to meet. The first can be met by ensuring that work is done while the clay of the vessel is still soft enough or alternatively a little non plastic material can be mixed into the added clay to lessen its shrinkage. The second can be met by making any exceptionally deep modelled forms hollow rather than solid. What constitutes 'exceptionally deep' depends partly on the wall thickness and size of the vessel and varies from clay to clay. A relatively slight addition on one side of a porcelain bowl could well cause it to warp considerably. Substantial additions to a grogged, large earthenware pot would be better hollow not because warpage would ever be likely but solely because an exceptionally slow biscuit firing would then be unnecessary.

While it is clearly best to stick the additional clay to a pot at an early stage it is unnecessary to complete the modelling immediately. Finely detailed modelling is easier to do and to finish with modelling tools when the clay has stiffened somewhat. Modelled additions may be subsequently impressed or carved.

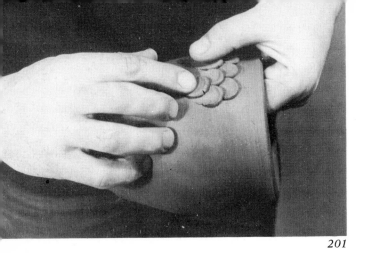

201 Much of the simplest relief modelling involves pressing small pellets of soft clay onto the surface of a pot. Providing the clay surface is no drier than soft leatherhard it is unnecessary to use any slip to assist adhesion. Frequently the pellets, as well as being pressed onto the clay, are stroked down either singly or in simple arrangements or repeated units

201

202

202 Small coils are also a frequent element in simple modelling. They are often simply stuck in position by gentle pressure and, if necessary, a wipe of slip and left as lines of relief

203 They can also be stroked into narrower relief lines either smoothly with the fingers or a flat tool or, as here, more texturally with a toothed tool

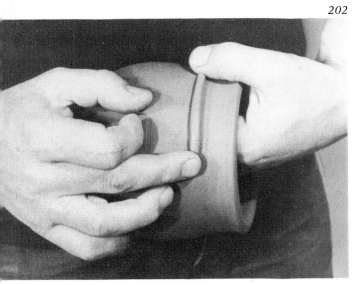

204 If the clay of the pot is any firmer than soft leatherhard the areas where soft clay is to be applied need preparation. First the area should be scored lightly

203

204

205 Water can then be sprayed onto the area with a hand sprayer or be brushed on. The scored lines serve two purposes: firstly they hold the water on the surface where it is needed and secondly they increase the area of clay surface which the water can soften

206 After a minute of two a sticky slip can be worked up out of the surface by further scratching with a knife. If the clay will not work up into a slip a second scoring and application of water may be necessary

205

206

207 Clay can then be added to the prepared areas and modelled into shape. The best adhesion is achieved if the clay is gently pushed into place and then very slightly moved from side to side until it grips

208 Subsequent work can push the clay onto the vessel and further define the form of the relief. Any differential shrinkage between the clay of the pot and the added clay can be tolerated very easily when the areas of contact are as small as in this example. If the whole of the area covered by the ten bosses was covered with a single piece of clay with a modelled surface then the differential shrinkage might be a problem and when this occurs the applied relief may, in drying or firing, develop cracks which generally occur across the greatest length. Providing the area was well prepared and good

208

207

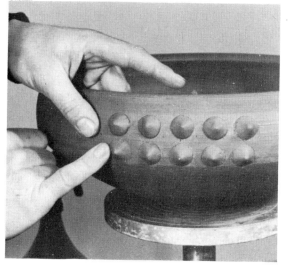

adhesion was achieved the relief will not crack off the pot, or even tend to, as cracking of this type is a sign that the join is stronger than the tensions set up by different rates of shrinkage. The cure in this eventuality is either to apply the relief at an earlier stage, or to apply slightly stiffer clay for the relief or to add some fine non plastic material to the applied clay to reduce its shrinkage

Modelled work may require no tools. It is pointless to buy expensive, beautifully shaped tools that are never used. It is most sensible to start with two or three of the basic types of wooden modelling tools and to add to these only if, and when, necessary. It should always be remembered that the work should determine the tool not the tool the work and that to reshape the end of a tool may vastly improve it for particular work.

The tools shown here, all about 6 in. (15 cm) long, are a small selection of types which may be useful. All are tools which may be used for modelling but some duplicate as tools which may also be useful for incising, sgrafitto and carving

*209, 210, 211 and 212* These four tools are fairly typical of the variety which can be bought. 209 is thin at both ends. 210 is a much sturdier tool having a full, rounded section throughout. Both 211 and 212 have one thin knife like end and one more pointed end that of 211 being round in both section and profile. Except for 212 which is German and comprises two hardwoods the tools are made of boxwood. If used frequently with water all wooden tools benefit from an occasional wipe with linseed oil which helps to prevent brittleness and surface deterioration

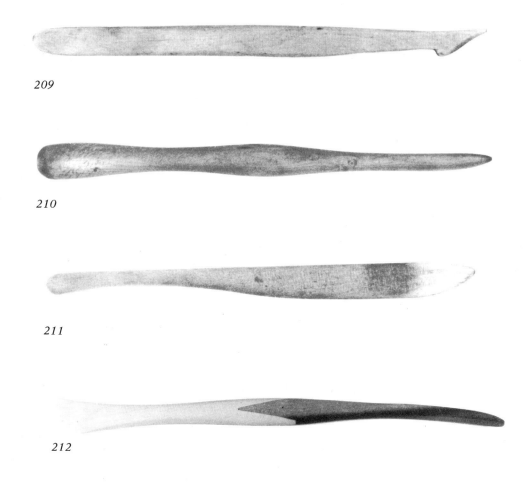

*209*

*210*

*211*

*212*

*213* This thin tool has been sharpened and re-shaped at both ends

*213*

*214* This knife-tool is home-made from split bamboo and only the pointed end is intended for use

*214*

*215* An immense variety of metal tools is available. Though primarily intended for plaster work they can be useful for precise work with firm clay

*215*

*216* Wire loop tools can also be bought in a variety of shapes and sizes and with much smaller narrower ends than those illustrated. They are primarily intended for the removal of clay but as the wire loops are very rigid they can equally be used to model the clay

*216*

217

218

*217* This detail is from a Roman cup no more than 5 in. (12 cm) in diameter. The soft plastic quality of the work suggests that the small pellets with which the scale like relief was stroked were extremely soft. *Verulamium Museum, St Albans, England*

*218* This cup is also Roman and is 4½ in. (11.5 cm) in diameter. The process is similar to the previous example but here the finger stroking of the pellets has left the work ridged and somewhat angular, reminiscent of a pine cone. Again the quality of the work suggests that the clay was in a very soft plastic state. Roman. Second century AD. *Archaelogical Museum, Granada, Spain*

*219* This example of modelling is interesting in that the applied modelling is done in a clay which contrasts with that of the vessel. This colour and tone contrast diminishes the possible effect of the relief which, in understanding of this, is done in bold shapes and strong simple lines. The texturing of the applied clay with a serrated tool gives a graphic rather than a three dimensional quality to the applied clay. The outline shape of the horse is either cut from a thinly rolled slab or pinched out from a sheet of clay. Most of the rest of the clay is applied as pellets or coils. The use of impression, glaze and the additional coloured clay in the eye and mane of the horse make this piece more complex than straight forward modelled work. The use of contrasting clay for modelling is an important possibility. Chinese. Probably nineteenth century, *Victoria and Albert Museum, London*

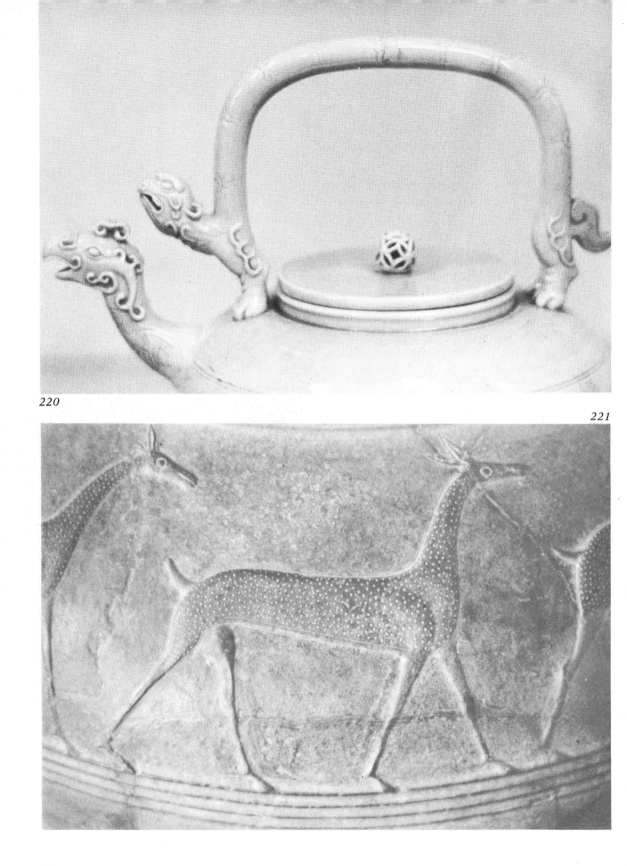

222

**220** Handles and spouts can hardly be classed as applied decorative modelling but the handles, if not the spout, of this pot can be distinguished from its modelled additions. The details of the head of the creature which forms the handle are finely finished — in fact the work is a good example of a type which needs to be formed and finished in a number of stages. It is notable that the modelling of the head on the handle is strong enough to have been enhanced, not negated, by the way the pale glaze has behaved on its relief — it reads not graphically, as can so easily happen if glaze is unsympathetically applied, but as form and relief. Chinese. Ming Dynasty, period of Tung Cheng 1723-1735. *Victoria and Albert Museum, London*

**221** It could perhaps be said that to extol the virtues of unglazed modelling is to avoid the challenges and ignore the possibilities of the full range of ceramics but it is surely true that, as pure relief, revealed by shadow and light alone, the finest modelling in ceramics whether of objects, or modelled vessels or relief on forms, is unglazed. This frieze of deer about 6 in. (12.5 cm) high on a large pot just over 4 ft (120 cm) high is very sensitively modelled. Despite its stylised flatness bone and muscle beneath the soft surface can be perceived and each animal is subtly different from the others. The impressed dots introduce a more decorative element but serve only as a focus towards the form and reveal, rather than destroy, the slight but controlled relief within the animal forms. Greek. Late Geometric period. *National Museum, Athens, Greece*

**222** The actual relief of this piece is simple. Its complexity is largely repetitive and is minimised by the matt opaque glaze. With a translucent and shiny glaze it would have been impossibly confusing. Despite the serene simplicity usually associated with that time it is nevertheless from Sung Dynasty China. *British Museum, London*

# Pouring and dipping; slip and glaze

Pouring and dipping are both standard ways of applying an even, overall layer of slip or glaze to a pot so it may seem odd to list them among processes of decoration. However anyone who has tried will be aware that with both processes it is all too easy to apply a layer which is neither even nor overall. It is the considered exploitation of this which gives these processes their decorative possibilities.

Of the two processes the possibilities of pouring are more varied. Bold, simple areas and more random, complex shapes can both result from pouring. The form of the pot, the angle at which it is held and the downward flow of the liquid are obviously fundamental factors but if varied experiments are fearlessly made it will be found that within the limits of the process a diversity of effect and a surprising degree of control are possible. Linear effects are just as possible as areas. As well as a jug, a ladle or a spoon may be used for pouring. The container used for pouring will always, to some extent, condition the effect. The quality of shape, made by suddenly slopping the contents of a small flat dish on the side of a pot will, for example, be quite different to that made by applying the same quantity of liquid from a jug with a well defined pouring spout. When smaller quantities are being used rather deliberately the process becomes closer to trailing — indeed a trailer, with or without its nozzle, can be useful to add smaller marks to larger areas.

The decorative content of pouring lies in the nature of the shapes produced and in the colour or textural contrast between poured and unpoured areas. The possibilities are extended, especially with glaze, even when only one glaze is used, when one poured area extends over another thereby producing whatever is the result with particular glazes of an additional thickness. The use of more than one glaze further extends the possibilities. With slip, where there are overlaps, the top layer is the one which will be dominant unless it is thin enough not to be completely opaque but with glaze an overlap of any two glazes will almost always produce a distinct third colour.

One particular technical problem to watch when overlapping glazes is to be aware that if the second layer is poured directly onto the first with force the strength of the stream of liquid can, if it is concentrated on one part for too long, wash away the first layer in that area.

While pouring offers varied and random qualities and possibilities those of dipping are more formal.

The most common and the simplest possibility is where the upended pot is dipped into the glaze normally and vertically but for less than its full height. The resulting division into glazed and unglazed areas (or slipped and unslipped) is, in terms of proportion, a basic element of decoration.

But there are also less common and more variable possibilities. Simple areas of slip or glaze can be made by immersing pots in some particular way. Bold crisp areas can be made by dipping the side of a pot — the depth of the dip, the angle at which the form is dipped and the form of the pot itself are the three factors which condition the shape produced. Subsequent dipping, with or without overlap and in the same mixture or another one, extends the possibilities. Rolling or rocking the pot while it is immersed, holding it steady and then raising it introduces a different type of possibility.

One particular technical point to watch with dipping is to ensure that the slip or glaze is thoroughly stirred and is kept thoroughly stirred. The crispness of dipped outline which is a major quality of the process is clearly lost if there is water on the surface of the mixture.

An important technical point to watch with both processes is that excessive thicknesses are not created where overlaps occur: excessively thick slip will tend to flake unless it is a perfect fit;

excessively thick glazes will tend to crawl, or peel prior to firing, or simply run. With glazes the only consideration is not the overall thickness, for timing and time are also factors. If the first layer is too dry when the second is applied the moisture of the second can cause the first layer to bubble up and lift immediately.

It might seem that pouring and dipping are rather different processes to describe together, that pouring might appeal to the carefree and dipping to the careful. In fact it is true that the two processes do offer separate, distinct qualities but both, however, require fluent, confident work, both can be done spontaneously and both, once experienced, allow broad planned intentions within the range of their qualities. Dealing as they do with fluid material neither pouring nor dipping allow opportunity for correction or for hesitant decision making. A sensible condition is to have quite a number of pots to work with — this will allow experiment to proceed with greater confidence and freedom. In most cases it is possible to sponge off the decoration and begin again but having a number of pots to work with allows more rapid learning through sequential experience.

As with most processes involving speedy or spontaneous execution it is important that intentions are clarified, as much as possible in the light of experience, before the work is done and that when it is complete the resulting quality is rigorously assessed both against the original intentions and, importantly, against what actually occurred. A happy accident is rarely an effective aim but an aim should never be so rigid as to preclude a happy accident.

## POURING WITH SLIP

When slip is to be poured two factors condition what is the best time for slip application. The pot must be firm enough for it to be held with confidence but it should not be so firm that there is any danger of slip flaking through late application.

223 Upright forms with tops which are not narrower than the hand are easy to hold at almost any angle

224 On a fairly cylindrical form which is held horizontally the poured slip can tend to gather a bit thickly at the lowest part. The pot can be shaken gently to remove excess or can be rotated which will spread out the thickness. Most of any excess slip will, as the pot is rotated follow back the paths taken by the poured slip but some new lines may also be formed and by tilting and shaking these can be extended

223

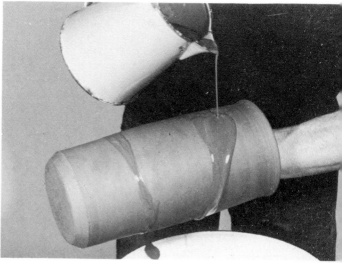

224

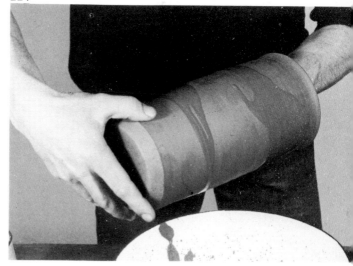

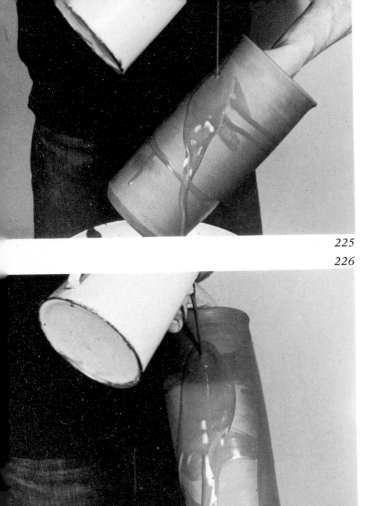

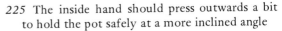

225 The inside hand should press outwards a bit to hold the pot safely at a more inclined angle

226 With a softish pot trying to hold it more vertically, right way up, may risk distortion if this is attempted by spreading the inside fingers very firmly. It should with care be safe enough to hold it by gripping the wall between the fingers and thumb. If the edge is very thin and the pot softish it may be necessary to hold it with the base resting in the palm of the hand but this means cleaning the hand before the pot is again lifted. The pot can of course be easily held vertically upside down with the hand inside supporting the base. Really vertical poured lines and areas can only be made with the pot vertical. Slip should be kept off the inside as it makes the pot impossibly slippery to hold by the inside and slip on both inside and out has a considerable softening effect on the wall

227 Vertical pouring leaves less slip on the pot than horizontal and there is less opportunity for extending shapes by tilting and shaking though a few lines can usually be extended. Quite a bit of slip may gather on the base of the pot and as much of this as possible should be removed before the pot is set aside for the slip to become touch dry. As soon as the slip is touchable any final cleaning up work on the top edge and the base should be done

225
226

227

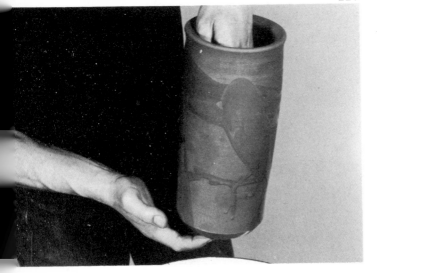

No leatherhard pot has even remotely comparable porosity to normal biscuit fired clay so slip pouring does not need to be completed as quickly or as directly as glaze pouring. The process with slip can be more leisurely and more considered as there need be much less concern about the sudden creation of potentially troublesome excess thicknesses.

228 The finished example is glazed only on the inside and the clay body at stoneware temperature has begun to burn through the slip. Not all slip coatings are completely opaque nor are they always intended to be, in either stoneware or earthenware, glazed or unglazed. The knowledge of the effect of the thickness applied in the intended finished context is of great importance and is developed only through experience.

229 The inside of a bowl, unless it is very shallow, cannot be poured across in the same way as the outside of forms. Some slip is therefore poured into the bowl and this can be tilted about the bowl to make areas

230 The slip has been tilted back across the bowl covering the top of the original poured mark and the bowl has now been returned to the position in which it was poured. By tilting the bowl and moving the small volume of slip about areas can be made with some control

228

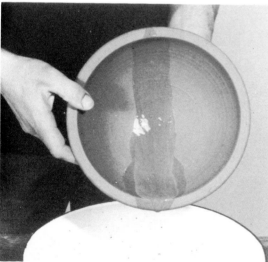

230

229

*231*

*232*

*231* Apart from areas the other alternative is to tilt and shake the bowl to produce much more random and more linear configurations. To aim at too controlled effects will probably only result in rather contrived freedom. With all pouring, whether of slip or glaze, spontaneous execution of fairly simple areas and lines is probably the most effective aim to pursue initially

## POURING, WITH GLAZE

It would be possible to make poured areas and lines on a high biscuited pot but this would probably be limited to a single glaze giving a body to glaze contrast. In this context the application of a second glaze would be almost certain to wash through those parts of the first layer onto which it was poured. The most likely context for the various possibilities of poured glaze is a fairly porous biscuit

*232* The simplest possibility is a single glaze giving a glaze to body contrast. If work is done quickly and there are not overlaps of poured glaze over already dry glaze there is no need to alter the normal consistency of a glaze. If there are overlaps then the glaze may need thinning somewhat so that excessive thickness does not develop. Once they become touch dry many glazes will retain a thicker layer of a second glaze pouring than is retained directly on biscuit. The possibilities of this simplest manifestation can be extended by using a glaze which is markedly different in colour and tone at different thickness and by pouring in two stages allowing sufficient time between pourings for the first to dry. This would rarely be more than about a minute

*233* A second very similar possibility is to completely glaze a pot, as normal, and then, when that is touch dry, to pour areas of a second glaze over that. It is important to ensure that the first layer is firm enough not to be disturbed by the pouring of the second. This disturbance is most likely to occur when the biscuit is relatively non-porous because once the wetness of the second glaze has rewet the first the biscuit is not actively retaining it. To avoid excessive thickness of glaze where the biscuit is freely porous the second glaze certainly and perhaps the first as well should have some water added before use. Obviously with an appropriate glaze this process can be done with a single glaze giving a thin to thick contrast but greater contrast is obviously possible if the second pouring is done with a different glaze. If the pouring of the second glaze is delayed too long it can cause the first layer to lift away from the surface which sometimes will lead to crawling

233

*234* A third possibility is to pour freely with one glaze and when that is touch dry to use a second glaze. This divides the surface into four finishes: the two glazes where they are alone, the overlap of second glaze over first and the unglazed areas. With restraint in planning, and this is not incompatible with the spontaneity of execution which gives pouring its best qualities, it is perfectly possible to pour with many more glazes than two. This should however be done with some caution both visually, for more is not always more effective, and technically, for excessive thicknesses of overlaps lead fairly predictably to problems of crawling or running or both. Visually the overlapping of glazes deserves testing because results in terms of tone, colour and texture are not entirely predictable. In this pot, for example, the middle toned glaze where it overlaps the pale glaze produces not an intermediate tone as might be expected but a darker one

234

235

236

## DIPPING, WITH SLIP

*235* Whether dipping is done with slip, as in this case, or glaze, it is very important that the suspension is of even consistency and is well stirred. Even a thin watery layer on the surface of the suspension will make an ill defined area with either material and the lack of definition may well only show after firing. Dipping into slip can be a little more carefully controlled than into glaze as additional time in the slip does not lead to excessive thickness. It is harder than it may seem to dip to a specific point

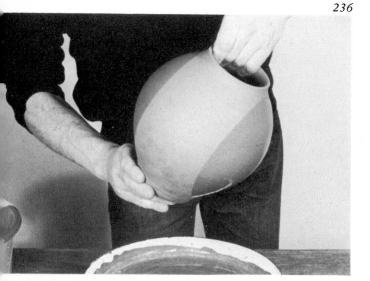

*236* Before a pot is put to one side for the slip to stiffen and before it is even returned to a vertical position excess slip should be shaken off and the pot should be inspected to ensure that the slip will not run and destroy the dipped shape. A fairly firm state of leatherhardness ensures both that the pot is easy to handle and that the slip will quickly be held in position

## DIPPING WITH GLAZE

Working with glaze is rather different and dipping must be completed speedily. There is little time for modification so the intention should be quite clear.

Dipping to contrast dipped glaze against body is the simplest possibility visually and presents fewest problems technically. Because of the nature of the processes of glazing and the different absorbancy between a layer of touch dry glaze and of unglazed biscuit it is less usual to partially dip a pot in one glaze and then completely glaze it with a second glaze though this does depend on the particular context. The best procedure for each case should be judged on merits

237

*237* An already glazed bowl is dipped into a second glaze. It is held still for a second or so for the glaze to form a distinct shape

238 It is removed from the glaze and gently shaken to remove excess drips. Both the immersion in and the removal from the glaze should be done with smooth, sure movements. As soon as it is clear there is no excess to run back from the edge and form lines the bowl can be put aside to dry

239 Here the pot which was slip dipped in figures 235 and 236 has been glazed all over and is being glaze dipped at right angles to the slip dips. A line pencilled across the base before the first glaze was applied indicates the locations of the now concealed slip shapes and therefore allows fairly accurate overlapping of glaze dip over slip dip. Providing care is taken not to create excessive thicknesses it is perfectly feasible by dipping in this way to make a series of overlapping glaze areas around a form

240 This vertical pot has been dipped twice from both top and bottom in the same glaze. There is an obvious contrast between glaze and body and a lesser, though still clear, difference between the single and double dipped areas

238

239

240

*241*

*242*

*241 and 242* In both these examples the poured areas of glaze contrast simply in colour and surface with the body. Though in the bottle there are small areas of overlap at the top the more important impact is the shapes made and left by the poured areas. The bottle has been broken and rather than hiding the mend it has been emphasised by the use of gold lacquer

# Slip trailing

Where it is thin, slip has a tendency to be dissolved into a glaze and either virtually to vanish or to begin to reveal the underlying body clay. There are obvious limitations to the amount of slip a brush can hold and therefore to the length of mark which a brush can make with slip. Slip trailing is, in fact, a good example of a process that has developed out of demands imposed by the nature of materials.

The consistency of slip used for trailing is usually slightly stiffer than that used for pouring and dipping.

What should never be forgotten with slip trailing, both technically and visually, is that one is dealing with a liquid material. An uninterrupted fluency of working can give trailing a quality which is usually appropriate and sometimes a technical necessity. A good slip trailer is essential. In the past, when many tools were homemade, slip trailers were made in a variety of forms from various materials, and worked on a number of principles. Cut hollow quills were often used to form the nozzle. Containers were usually rigid and the slip flow could be stopped with air pressure by putting a finger over a hole in the body or simply by tilting it. Whatever form the trailer takes to be effective it must be easy to start the flow of slip smoothly, easy to maintain a steady unbroken flow, and easy to stop the flow of slip. In addition, the whole trailer should be easy to clean and both easy and quick to refill. The type most commonly available now is a flexible rubber bulb, usually fitted with a detachable nozzle and occasionally supplied with nozzles of varying sizes. The best of these are very efficient tools.

Trailing may be done onto soft leatherhard forms, onto dishes in hollow moulds and onto flat sheets of clay prior to their being formed on hump moulds. In that slip is a fluid material, flat sheets offer the widest scope but to aim for over-precise control or very complex content is arguably in-appropriate for the process.

The three material contexts for trailing are into a wet, freshly slipped ground, onto an unslipped ground (usually of soft leatherhard consistency) and onto a touch dry slipped ground. The latter two are so similar they can be considered together.

The former context — trailing into a wet ground — allows the work if the clay is supported on a workboard, to be tapped, or slightly lifted and dropped which makes the trailed marks sink to the level of the ground and spread slightly giving a fluid, completely flat quality. This is mainly relevant to work on shallow dishes or on flat sheets. Untapped trailing may stand up in slight relief but has a similar fluid quality. It is this that is the particular quality of trailing into a slip ground. If the clay to which the ground slip has been applied is approaching leatherhard, then the drying effect which this has on the ground slip may impose a time limit on trailing. If the limit is exceeded and the ground slip begins to dry, the overall quality will be uneven with some trailed marks sunken fluidly into the surface and others sitting on the surface in a soft relief.

The latter context — an unslipped ground — inevitably involves a less fluid quality than the former and offers the possibility of relief. Whether the relief is considerable or slight the absence of a wet ground allows more deliberate working. 'Piping' is a term occasionally substituted for 'trailing' and while, with its associations with cake decoration, it may seem an inappropriate term for wet ground work it does seem more appropriate for some manifestations of trailing onto a touch dry ground.

Whether in the former context or the latter the visual elements of trailing are lines and dots. Lines may, by altering pressure on the bulb or by varying the speed of the hand, be made wider or narrower and dots of very varied size may be made but the elements of line and dot are fundamental.

On unslipped grounds areas can be built up with trailed slip which is brushed or tapped to form an even thickness. Such areas can be relatively precise. With wet ground work controlled but less precise areas can be made prior to trailing by pouring.

One other important quality deserves mention. It is the quality of line and shape which, uniquely in wet ground trailing, may be left around trailed marks. If lines are trailed close together and then the clay is tapped the lines spread but the gap does not close over and a crisp fine line is left, finer by far than could ever be trailed. The quality is inherent in the fluidity of slip and within limits it is controllable. Similarly when dots are trailed in close proximity a fine cell-like tracery is formed when the clay is tapped.

Trailing is not subject to any particular technical pitfalls but exceptional thickness may bring out a weakness in the fit of a slip which was not obvious in more normal contexts. Care should therefore be exercised when trailing with considerable relief on a touch dry ground or when tapping trailing into a wet ground on bowl forms which always tends to make a thick pool of slip in the base.

## TRAILING INTO A SLIPPED GROUND

*243* The important point to remember when trailing into a wet slip ground is to keep the nozzle of the trailer just above the surface. The nozzle end in this illustration is $^1/_{16}$ in. (1.5 mm), or slightly more, above the surface and only contacts the surface through the slightly raised trailed slip line. The slip used for trailing is usually a little less fluid than the ground slip.

Trailers of this type should be kept well filled. They work most easily if, before trailing, they are filled, held right way up and squeezed to expel all air until slip is just emerging from the nozzle. They should then be inverted and the pressure on the bulb relaxed just enough to hold the slip in the nozzle but not enough to allow air into the bulb. When trailing is started the trailer is held in position and squeezed very gently until slip emerges. A gentle squeezing pressure is enough to keep the slip flowing steadily and a fractional reduction of pressure will stop the flow. It is sensible to practise on a clean board to acquire the feel of the action and the slip can be gathered up with a rubber kidney for re-use. Holding the slip by greater or lesser air pressure in the bulb and working with a

*243*

*244*

nearly empty trailer is to court disaster because as the slip runs out there is a miniature eruption from the nozzle as air rushes into the bulb and the hand responds to the changed pressure. This invariably results in a splash of slip in the wet ground. Quite simply the trailer should never be allowed to become nearly empty.

*244 and 245* Obviously trailing has to be done in a slip which contrasts with the ground but it is entirely possible by pouring to have two, or more, colours of wet slip ground in which to trail. So that there is no interruption to the flow of work there should be as many trailers as there are colours of trailed slip. Provided it is done while the slip is still wet, trailers are easy to clean simply by squeezing them repeatedly in a bowl of clean water

If the trailer nozzle does touch the wet slip surface it will pick up ground slip and tend to merge this with the trailed slip. The nozzle end should be wiped clean immediately. If the nozzle touches the surface where trailed lines cross a rather crude sort of feathering results.

*246 and 247* If trailed lines or dots are placed very close the ground slip is left in lines far finer than can be trailed. If the board holding the work is tapped this gives the ground slip an even sharper quality

Slip trailing done on slabs of clay on boards can be tapped to flatten the relief of the lines and to spread them a little by lifting the board an inch or two (a few centimeters) and dropping it. Flattening the relief of trailing inevitably involves spreading the lines as well. The relief of trailing can be very slight and it does not always need flattening — indeed a slight, soft relief can be a positive quality. When flattening and spreading are done the effect of tapping should be considered for while slip on rolled sheets of clay on workboards can be spread very evenly, the movement of slip on forms is fundamentally affected by the nature of the three-dimensional surface

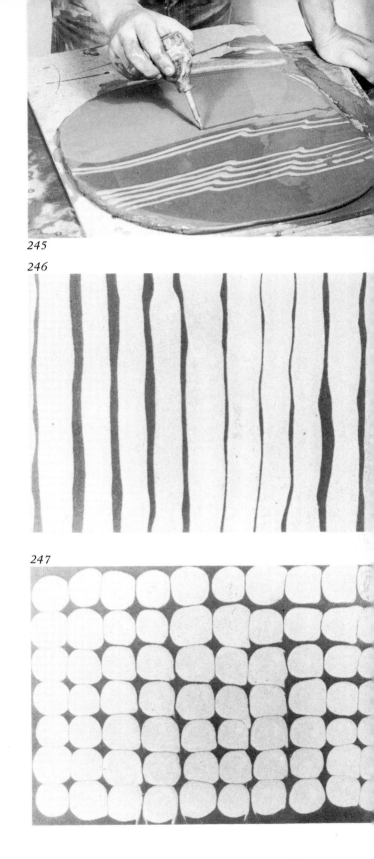

245

246

247

109

248

249

## TRAILING ONTO A TOUCH DRY GROUND

This is usually done at an early leatherhard or late plastic stage and may be either onto a previously applied layer of slip or directly onto a clay body.

*248 and 249* Slip trailed onto a touch dry ground has little tendency to spread and any there is depends on the consistency of the slip. In a wet slip ground more trailed slip leads to bigger dots or wider lines; on a touch dry ground it does this too but also leads to higher relief

*250* Too often earthenware is thought of as the inevitable finish for slip trailing. Here a stoneware glaze has been used over the trailed slip which, being based on a red clay, has fused and burnt through the dark glaze. The thick glaze and the fusing of the slip have left a flat surface quite different to the relief at the trailing stage

*251* On a banding wheel with good momentum trailed lines can be made as easily as painted lines. This can also be done into a wet slip ground

Trailing can be in quite prominent relief, indeed it may be in the same clay as the body so the entire quality of the work is dependent on relief not tone or colour contrast.

250

251

252 When trailing of distinct relief is done on surfaces which are not horizontal, the form should be held horizontal during trailing to eliminate any immediate tendency of the slip to run. Work of this sort is generally done with thickish slip mixtures which contain an amount of nonplastic filler, such as molochite or flint, and the clay body can be drier than usual. In these conditions work can proceed without undue delays as the slip stiffens quite quickly allowing the form to be turned around almost immediately each trailed mark is completed

252

253 The trailing here is done on a white slip ground either near or at the touch dry stage. The relief of the trailing is evident in the light reflections within the trellis border. The naive, somewhat crude, robustness seems slightly incongruous in a royal commemorative piece but the directness is very typical of much contemporary work of this kind. Diameter 20 in. (51 cm) approximately. Last quarter of the seventeenth century. England. *Victoria and Albert Museum, London*

253

254

255

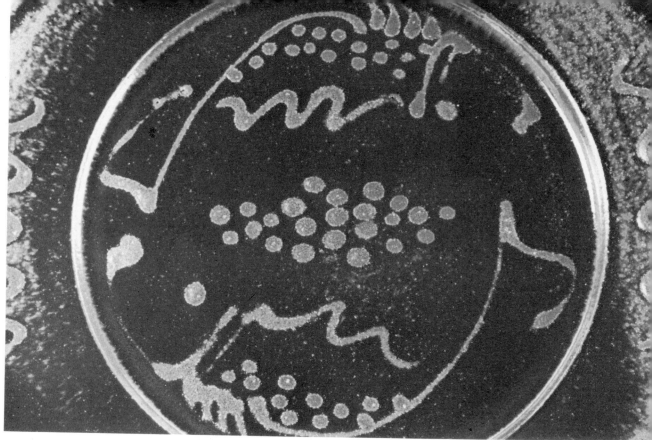

256

254 The clear relationship between the border of this dish and the previous one makes an interesting comparison. Though precise and controlled in comparison to the previous work the trailing here has a softening effect on the angular forms of the dish. Trailed on a flat sheet and subsequently formed over a hump mould it is a good example of the degree of control over placing which, somewhat surprisingly, can be achieved with this method. A subtle and interesting quality is the way the high points of the relief, where the white lines cross the black, have been flattened and therefore indented slightly as the clay was pressed over the mould. *Mark Henderson, 1978. England*

255 Similar in technique and feel to figure 253 the content here seems more appropriate to the handling. The work has the rich direct simplicity of folk art traditions. The infilling of the flowers and leaves is of thin painted slip. The fluid glaze has dissolved some colour from the slip which has begun to flow softening the bold silhouettes of the trailing. Dated 1688. England. *Victoria and Albert Museum, London*

256 This detail shows the centre of a large stoneware plate in which a fusible red clay slip was trailed directly onto the clay body. The technique is that shown in figures 248 to 250. The work shows a free calligraphic quality more usually associated with a brush than a trailer and yet entirely possible and appropriate, especially with trailing on a touch dry ground. The centre of the plate 10 in. (25.5 cm) in diameter. *Wayne Hathaway, 1977, England*

*257* Here fluently trailed relief lines have been used, cloissonée fashion, as barriers between different areas of coloured glazes. Chinese. Sixteenth century AD. *Victoria and Albert Museum, London*

*258* The trailed lines here both serve as barriers between some glaze colours but also, as in the trees, leaves are left as trailed marks for the transluscent glaze to emphasise tonally. The combination of sunken, incised marks and raised, trailed ones both emphasised, but differently, by a single coloured glaze is an effective one. Chinese. Late fifteenth century AD. *Victoria and Albert Museum, London*

*259* For sheer quality of relief some of the most remarkable trailing is Roman. This is sometimes referred to as barbotine ware. This detail is from a small beaker less than 4 in. (10 cm) in diameter. Quite clearly all the foliage and the legs and ears of the hare are trailed. Exactly how the hare's body was made is not clear, it could have been an applied modelled pad of clay but from the fluent outline it seems possible it was made up from a number of trailed marks of slip subsequently brushed or modelled to shape. Any doubt about the body should not detract from the relief quality of the remainder. Technically too the work is controlled as there is no sign at all of cracking. The feat is not

258

simply to mix a slip which does not tend to crack when applied in high relief but more to mix one which both does not tend to crack and permits such control of breadth and narrowness of line, and of relief form. The entire pot is coated in a thin iron bearing separated slip which has a dull sheen and being reduced fired is a grey black colour. The sharper parts of the high relief break through this slip in a lighter tone. Roman. *Verulamium Museum, St Albans, England*

259

# Marbling

The first thing to say about marbling is that, as a process, it is completely distinct from agate. Agate is a specifically prepared clay body from which objects are made. Marbling is a surface treatment of clay, comprising a layer of intermingled slips. The distinction is fundamental and the fact that the visual manifestations of the two processes may sometimes be superficially similar or that agate can occur in contexts, for example as inlay, where it is not strictly forming an object, should not be allowed to confuse the issue that agate is a clay process and marbling a slip process.

Too often marbling is seen as a process which may be tried to save slip trailing which has become a lost cause. On occasion it may well do this but it should also be seen as a process in its own right with its own unique possibilities. It is not a wholly haphazard process. Aspects of its qualities are inherent in material and process but it does allow more control than might at first sight appear.

Marbling offers fluid, swirling qualities of line and shape quite unlike those achievable in any other way. It exploits the possibility of moving the whole layer of slip by gently shaking, tilting, tapping or turning the slipped object. For marbling, the layer of slip can be slightly thicker than for trailing. For trailing the slip layer should be just thick enough to allow trailed marks to sink in and thin enough to inhibit overall movement of the slip layer. The greater thickness for marbling facilitates this subsequent movement of the layer. Marbling can begin from poured areas but finer lines are obviously more easily extended from trailed lines. It is probably best to start experiments with the relatively simple basis of a few trailed lines. The process of moving the slip around — marbling — produces complexity quickly and easily enough. Initial practise might well aim at achieving increasing control over the complexity and distribution of the inter-mingling of the slips and increasing understanding of exactly what marbling can be developed from simple or more complex beginnings.

The contexts for marbling are the same as for trailing but while trailing usually aims to eliminate or minimise the overall movement of a slip layer, marbling aims to exploit that movement. To this extent the particular context exerts a comparatively greater influence on the nature of possibilities. Some forms may inhibit possibilities considerably while others may give particular shape or direction to the marbling. Because marbling involves the movement of the layer of slip leatherhard objects, with their tendency to stiffen slip relatively quickly, do impose a time limit. For this reason and for their lack of concavity or convexity to influence movement, rolled sheets of clay for subsequent forming on hump moulds, or as slabs, do offer the most open possibilities.

While marbling is being done it will be noticed that movement is greatest where the slip is thickest and least where it is thinnest. So far as is possible a technical consideration should be to keep the layer relatively even in thickness. On forms, as opposed to flat sheets of clay, this is only possible within limits but thick pools of marbling in the bottom of concave forms should be avoided. The limits of thickness should be discovered, for even if the slip has excellent adhesion to the clay body it can, in excessive cases, develop cracks within its own thickness. Such thickness should be avoided. It is far better to clean the slip off with a rubber kidney and sponge and to start again, but here there are limits. Both plastic and leatherhard clay can only stand a renewed layer of slip two or three times at the most before it either develops a very messy surface or starts to develop cracks.

260 In this example a round dish has been formed in a hollow plaster mould and has been quickly and simply trailed. In moulds slipping, trailing and marbling should be completed as soon as possible because as time passes the tilting, shaking and jogging which accompany marbling are increasingly likely to dislodge the dish if it begins to release from the mould. To overcome this danger at least partially it is a sensible practice to liberally dampen moulds in which marbling is to be done. A physically thicker layer of slip than for simple trailing facilitates marbling so the slip should be less fluid than for trailing. This will stay mobile longer than a thinner slip. For marbling the trailing slip can be the same consistency as the ground slip.

261 With concave marbled surfaces, as in bowls and dishes, jolting or tapping with the form in a horizontal position simply makes a pool of thick slip in the base. In the initial stages at least, horizontal bumping should be avoided. If the dish is tilted and shaken, lines parallel to the tilt are straightened and narrowed and those at right angles are unevenly broadened. The curvature of the dish makes those lines parallel with the direction of the tilt converge

262 Further shaking and tilting in various directions will effect further changes. Throughout marbling the slip layer is most mobile where it is thickest. If excess slip is shaken over the edge of the dish marbling can continue to the point of obliteration or until the slip is no longer mobile. An important aspect of marbling is knowing when to stop

260

261

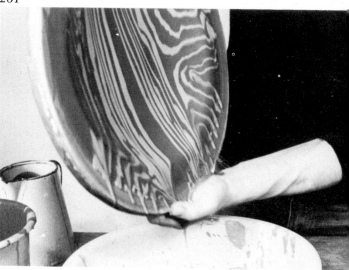

262

In any attempt to do marbling it should be noticed that a number of factors directly affect the end result: (1) the fluidity and thickness of the slip; (2) the original trailed or poured marks; (3) the type of marbling movements used; (4) the extent of the process and (5) the influence of the particular form. In each instance the nature of the form can be decided and in every instance the first four factors are all controllable and variable. Contrary therefore to its reputation marbling has content which, within limits, is controllable. Its distinct quality is inherent

263 This detail is from an English eighteenth century dish. It is interesting when considering examples of marbling with pronounced distinctive markings to try to deduce the original markings from which the work developed and the movements used to do it. It can usually be seen that richly swirling strong movements have come from quite particular beginnings. *Victoria and Albert Museum, London*

263

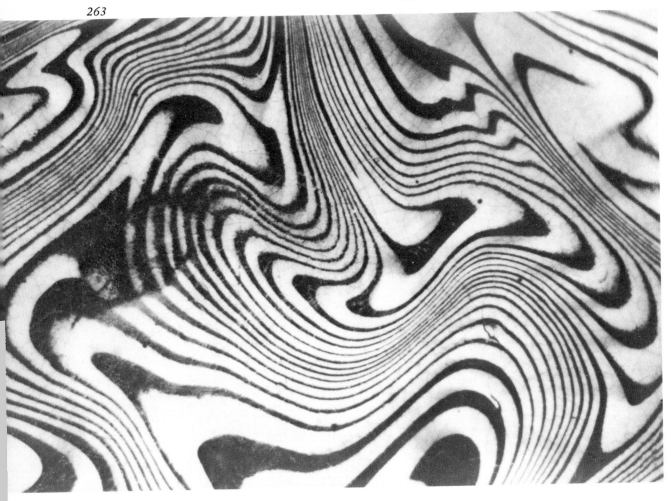

# Feathering

Feathering is a treatment of wet slip. It consists of the drawing out of a fine line of one slip into another slip of differing colour. It may be done wherever two poured areas of slip meet or from or across any trailed dot or line. As the process relies on the fluidity of slip it is done as soon as the application of slip is completed. The name derives from the use in the past of quills to do the actual feathering. Either end of a feather may be used. If the thicker quill end is used it should be sharpened to a fine point, if the finer end is used it may or may not require some trimming. A pin, a needle or a fine-bladed, sharp-pointed knife are, however, just as effective but a hard feathering tool should be used with care. The feathering tool whether soft or hard should penetrate well into the thickness of the slip as it is drawn through it but it should not mark the clay surface itself for such marks will become more pronounced as the slip dries. A steel tool should never be allowed to cut into the clay surface as such cuts allow the moisture of the slip to penetrate and may encourage cracks. Whether soft or hard the feathering point should be kept clean of any build up of slip or the feathered lines will become progressively thicker.

Feathering may be used to add to marbled and poured slip work as well as to trailing. It may be done on dishes as soon as they are moulded in hollow moulds, on harder vertical forms to which slips have been applied (though in this case work needs to be completed quickly for the firmer clay tends to quickly reduce the fluidity of the slip), and it may be done on flat sheets of clay prior to their being formed into dishes over hump moulds. This last context was the commonest traditional application of feathering. Most frequently lines were trailed parallel to each other and the feathering crossed these at right angles, often in alternate directions, giving a quick all-over decoration. Even within this relatively narrow context the scope for variety and invention is considerable.

264 Much of the final nature of feathered work is determined by the pouring, trailing or marbling which precedes it. In this series a sheet of rolled clay has been covered with a poured layer of dark slip and is being trailed with parallel lines of white slip. Note as always with trailing, that the nozzle of the trailer is above, not in, the wet slip surface

264

265

266

267

268 and 266 To flatten the surface the sheet of clay, supported on a board, is tilted and shaken in alternate directions. This tends to spread the trailed slip a little leaving thinner crisper lines on the original dark ground slip

267 When working with slip on sheets of clay on boards it is important to wipe excess slip off the board so that the edges of the sheet do not stick to the board and are free to shrink when the sheet begins to stiffen. As the slip can tend to creep under the edges this is best done as soon as the application of slip is complete

268 and 269 Either end of a feather may be sharpened to a point for feathering. The flight end, in figure 269 is a useful tool on strongly convex or concave surfaces as its rigidity is springy enough to be held against the clay surface and to follow it, but not stiff enough to cut into the clay

268

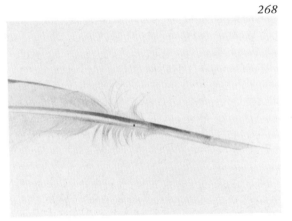

269

270 A fine needle, securely mounted in a cork, makes an excellent feathering tool provided care is taken not to allow the point to cut into the clay

271 A common treatment of trailed parallel lines was to feather at right angles to these

272 Feathered lines in the opposite direction to the first set were often inserted in the spaces. Note the shallow angle of the needle which is held very gently as it is drawn through the slip. At the end of each stroke the needle is wiped clean otherwise a progressive build up of slip may produce thicker, less defined feathering. Feathering of this type, as well as more broadly spaced, occured commonly on English country-made dishes of the eighteenth and nineteenth centuries

273 The trailing and feathering of this dish are controlled but the control has not inhibited the fluid quality which is so fundamental with trailed and feathered slip. Too often response to tradition is insensitive to quality and uninventive in context. Here an awareness of quality and thoughful approach to context have combined to produce a very distinct object. The trailing and feathering were done on a flat sheet of clay subsequently formed, with careful placing, on a hump mould. *Mark Henderson, 1978*

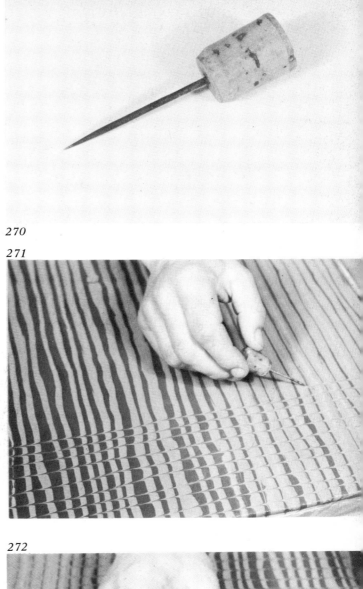

270

271

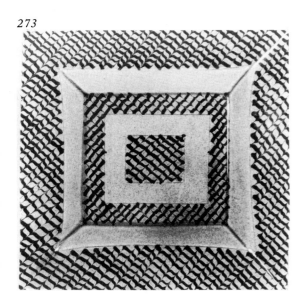

273

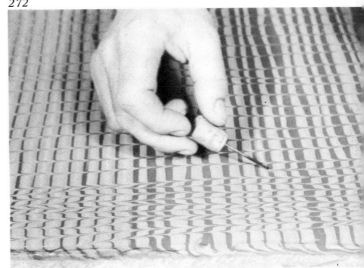

272

274

274 This detail of a nineteenth century English dish, also trailed and feathered on a sheet and formed over a mould, shows work of a different quality. The irregular somewhat random quality of the trailing is held together by the swift straightness of the feathering

275

275 This example shows a more complex textural use of areas of feathering. The horizontally trailed lines were first feathered vertically and then feathered horizontally producing an intricate but still distinct quality of mark. English, dated 1701. *Victoria and Albert Museum, London*

276

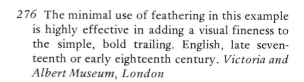

276 The minimal use of feathering in this example is highly effective in adding a visual fineness to the simple, bold trailing. English, late seventeenth or early eighteenth century. *Victoria and Albert Museum, London*

# Glaze trailing

Glaze trailing is a very convenient way of applying small areas of glaze and is probably more often thought of as an occasional alternative to brushing, for work such as this, than as a process in its own right. As a graphic process it has unique possibilities which, surprisingly, have been largely unexploited.

Glaze trailing on biscuit cannot be feathered or marbled because the nature of glaze is so different from that of slip and in most cases the porosity of the biscuit anyway absorbs the water from the glaze within seconds of its application, making such treatment impossible. It is possible that worthwhile experiment could be done with raw glazes but even here the difference of the quality of fluidity between raw glaze and slip would make comparable quality unlikely. In any case, the sharp definition which is part of the nature of feathering and marbling is inherently possible with slips and well nigh impossible with glazes as these always tend to merge where they meet or overlap.

The consistency with which glaze is trailed is important and exerts a strong influence over the type of marks which are possible. The tendency is to think of a glaze as being too runny for trailing and to thicken it up. This can, to some extent, be done but unless the surface on which trailing is done is vitrified, or nearly so, this usually tends to be overdone. The relative porosity of the surface is the other factor which plays a large part in determining the sort of mark which is possible. On a strongly porous surface quite fluid glaze can be trailed with control. Any adjustment to the consistency of a glaze which is to be used for trailing must be in relation to the particular porosity of the biscuit.

Trailing onto vitrified biscuit is an unlikely and difficult operation except on flat surfaces.

Whole surfaces can be glazed entirely by trailing with a number of different glazes and glaze can be freely trailed into marks scratched through a poured or dipped layer of glaze. Of the many possibilities the two most direct are trailing onto biscuit giving a glaze to body contrast, and trailing over an even layer of poured or dipped glaze giving a single to double glaze contrast.

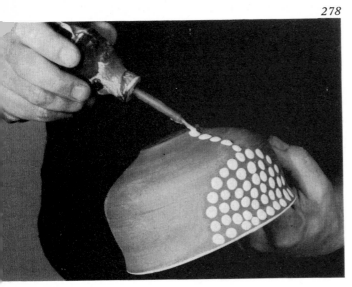

*277*

*278*

*277 and 278* As glazes used are generally more fluid than slip the pressures on the trailer bulb used to control the flow are slightly more delicate though the principles are exactly the same as described for slip. When trailing dots it can seem that too thick a glaze is being applied but as the water is absorbed into the biscuit the relief diminishes. It is very much easier to trail onto soft biscuit with a ready porosity than onto only slightly porous biscuit. To minimise the chance of accidental runs any object being trailed with glaze should be continually turned and tilted so that the working surface is as nearly horizontal as possible

*279* The contrast here is between a strong warm brown earthenware clay and a white glaze. Obviously the possible contrast ranges from this to far subtler contrast where the tone and colour difference is minimal and the trailing is more evident simply as a shiny surface against an unglazed clay. Except for solely decorative work, trailing using a glaze to clay contrast normally occurs only on bodies which become vitreous, or nearly so, in the glaze firing

*279*

124

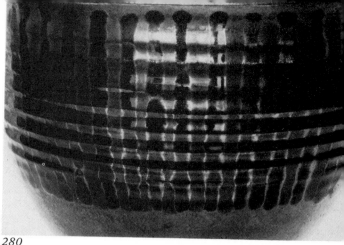

280 Trailed lines of matt and shiny black glaze have been alternated in this example glazing a whole area of the surface. Where the matt and shiny glazes meet and merge a highly reflective, metallic linear effect has occurred. This is one example of a considerable diversity of effects which occur at the edges of trailed glaze lines if they are over, or touch, another glaze

281 A touch-dry layer of glaze usually possesses a very strong porosity, even if the ground glaze is thin, and exerts an almost instant drying effect on the trailed marks, quicker than even a very porous biscuit. While this does lead to a more confident trailing it tends to make lines and dots stand up in rather high relief and subsequent handling of the work has to avoid touching any trailed marks as these are fragile and easily dislodged

282 Unless the trailed glaze is very viscous the lines and dots will flatten down in the firing, spreading a little. The unpigmented trailed glaze has formed a strong dark outline in reacting with the ground glaze. In addition to any outline effect, the colour, texture and tone which occur when one glaze is trailed over another are variable. It is worth preceding work of this kind with tests of various ground and trailed glazes for the effects are unpredictable in both earthernware and stoneware

280

281

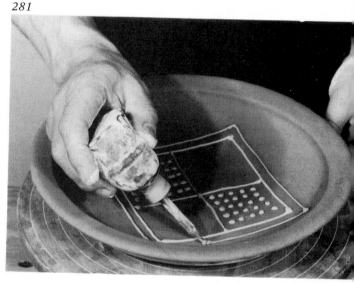

282

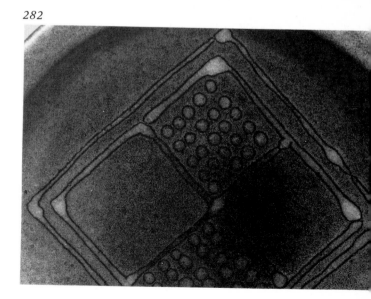

# Combing: slip and raw glaze

Combing is more usually done with slip. The comb is passed over the surface of the slipped clay and its teeth remove or displace slip revealing the clay body underneath.

The quality of mark made depends on several easily controlled factors. Obviously the width of the teeth and the spaces between them are fundamental. The relative softness of the clay and the slip, when combing occurs, is also important. A third factor is the material of the comb itself, whether it is soft or hard — this not only affects the hardness or softness of the mark but also governs whether all or only part of the comb edge can touch curved surfaces.

Combing can occur in many contexts and at various stages of dryness.

In the context of soft clay which has just been slipped, combing can have a softness of quality which is not possible at a later stage. In this context slip stiffens only slowly. Pressure on the comb must be gentle if it is not to dig into the clay. Marks of combing done at this stage rarely have a crispness of quality, which is much easier to achieve with clay of leatherhardness. Indeed until the work is fired and glazed the combing may show only slightly. The glaze will dissolve the residue of slip from the teeth marks and reveal the movements of the comb as it displaced the slip. Work on clay of this softness is possible with rolled out sheets for tiles or subsequent forming over a hump mould and with sheets pressed into hollow moulds but is not possible with thrown pots.

When leatherhard clay is slipped and combed the effect is generally more distinct. The clay itself has more positive resistance to the comb so firmer pressure can be applied resulting in cleaner combing. Work can be done immediately or the slip can be allowed to stiffen for a few minutes. The longer the slip is left the more will be the tendency of combing to remove rather than displace the slip. The fluency of the process does in fact rely partly on the wet slip lubricating the movement of the comb across the clay. If the slip is allowed to become touch dry there is no lubrication and the process, though it can still work with a rigid comb, becomes closer to carving or sgrafitto.

The actual nature of a comb depends partly on whether it will be used on soft or leatherhard clay. Hard combs can tend to produce an unpleasant burr at the edges of teeth marks in soft clay. The softness or firmness of the slip being combed has a considerable relevance to the width and spacing of teeth. Firmer slip is removed rather than displaced sideways, so teeth spacing can be close. But with wetter slip, whatever the width of the teeth, the spaces between them must allow the displaced slip to pass through. Combs can be cut from thickish hide, from rubber kidneys, or other suitably rigid rubber, or from thin wood or hardboard (though this latter will not be long lasting). Temporary combs can be made from thickish card and for initial experiments to understand the effects of different teeth widths and spacings this is a very suitable material.

Finger combing is, obviously, done with the fingers and as the fingers displace slip sideways more effectively than they remove it, it is best done with fairly wet slip. Finger combing is inclined to be visually softer than other types.

Simple wave movements are a common traditional manifestation of combing. While it is true that combing does not lend itself to over elaborate intentions the possibilities of the process are wider than traditional manifestations might suggest.

While it might not strictly be called combing there is no reason why a single finger (or a single toothed 'comb') should not be used to draw in wet slip. The quality would not be paralleled in any other process. Such drawing could be combined with work done with more conventional combs. Such extentions of traditions in combing are not unknown but are rare.

The processes of combing can be applied to pots which are raw glazed, especially those to which the glaze is applied when the pot is still in the leatherhard state. As even raw glazes tend to have considerably less plastic clay content than slips they tend to stiffen more quickly, so if uniformity of quality is important, work cannot be too leisurely.

When combing on thrown forms involves some concentric work, the first action is to centre the form on a banding wheel as soon as it had been slipped or glazed.

*283 and 284* The process of finger combing could hardly be simpler — the fingers rest on the leatherhard clay surface and are drawn through the wet layer of slip or raw glaze. There is little difference in practice in working with the two materials — 283 is raw glaze and 284 is slip. In fact raw glaze does stiffen somewhat faster than slip but combing is a fast enough process for this hardly to matter. Pots which are raw glazed when bone dry cannot usually be combed because in this case the glaze does dry too quickly. In both these examples the additional thickness made as the material is pushed to one side is clearly visible. The thickness of the over-all layer, be it of glaze or slip, will determine the exact fired effect of this additional thickness

*285* It is perfectly possible to do combing on vertical surfaces. The only difference between work on horizontal and vertical surfaces is that with the former the material displaced sideways is displaced more or less equally to each side of the combed line whereas with the latter more material is displaced downwards than upwards. This is evident as slight relief here and with many slips and most glazes will show tonally in the fired result

283

284

285

*286*

*287*

*286 and 287* Combing tools allow a different and finer quality of mark to be used. The combs illustrated here are both cut from cowhide slightly over $\frac{1}{16}$ in. (2 mm) thick. This combines a degree of give with a degree of rigidity. Some people prefer to cut combs from old rubber kidneys. Teeth cannot be spaced very closely as the gaps have to allow the displaced material to pass through

*288 and 289* The finer scale of mark which combing tools make possible is immediately evident. As in figure 288 broad tools need supporting near the working end so that the full width is effective. A degree of flexibility is essential with wide tools for rigid cambs cannot accommodate curved surfaces and on concave surfaces either do not register in the middle or dig in at their edges. To make banded marks as in figure 289 the wheel should be revolved steadily and not too fast. Note that on the far side of this dish the two-toothed comb forming the concentric circles has closed up the combed divisions of the wave marks where it has crossed them. Slip or glaze should be wet enough to be as mobile as this for the fluent marks which are the particular quality of combing to be possible

*288*

*289*

*290 and 291* To be slipped or raw glazed thrown forms have necessarily to be at some stage of leatherhardness. Work on tiles, in press moulded dishes and on rolled sheets of clay for subsequent forming can be done before the leatherhard stage though slip, not raw glaze, would be normal for this. In these two illustrations the only difference is the state of the clay, figure 290 being leatherhard and 291 being plastic. Both illustrations show a nearly completed movement of tool combing to the right of which is a completed mark of finger combing. The conclusion to draw is not that combing is only possible on leatherhard clay but is simply that the state of the clay makes different qualities possible. Combing done on soft clay, in contexts where it is possible, will have a far softer quality than combing on leatherhard clay. Though the marks shown in figure 291 only show as relief in the raw state, when glazed and fired they will be clearly evident for the glaze will dissolve the thin slip left by the fingers or the comb teeth. The distinction obvious between work at leatherhard and plastic stages exists, but in subtler ways, within the various states of leatherhardness — the crispest marks occur at the firmest stages of leatherhardness with stiffening slip, until the point is reached where the process ceases to be combing and the displacement of slip and becomes sgraffito and the removal of slip. Flat sheets whether firm or soft offer one possibility not available on curved surfaces, that of using relatively wide combing tools. In both illustrations a wooden tool is held against the back of the comb to stiffen it and thereby keep all the teeth on the clay

290

291

*292* This detail is of a combed plate slightly over 12 in. (30 cm) in diameter by Michael Cardew. The clay is a warm coloured red earthenware and the white slip coating is only of medium thickness, allowing the clay to burn through a little. Each combing mark is flanked, as always, by thicker slip which is distinctly more opaque. The proportions of the work were established by the banded concentric marks which were applied first, as can be easily seen where the marks of subsequent combing meet and cross them. The piece is more formal and elaborate than most examples of the English peasant traditions from which it derives and as such is an extension of tradition. Made in the 1930s at Winchcombe. *Craft Study Centre, Bath, England*

292

293

*293* This smaller plate is 8½ in. (20 cm) in diameter. It shows an exuberant almost flamboyant use of combing. The materials are the same as in the previous piece, a warm red earthenware clay and a white slip. But on most of this piece the ground slip is thin and is tonally closer to the areas wiped clean by combing than to the light toned lines of displaced slip. The use of a plain untoothed comb has contributed to the distinctness of the lines of displaced slip. The plate has a simple directness of material and execution which is wholly traditional. Made in the 1930s at Winchcombe Pottery. *Owned by Andrew Crouch*

# Mocha work

Mocha work is done by dabbing an oxide mixture onto wet slip with a brush. If the liquid of the oxide mixture is chemically right in relation to the suspension water of the slip the two react and the water of the oxide mixture spreads out rapidly from the original mark carrying the oxide with it and forming the distinct fern-like shapes which comprise mocha work. Mocha is a phenomenon which can be made to occur rather than a variable, highly controllable process.

In the context of cylindrical mugs and containers of fairly unsophisticated, utilitarian quality mocha work was fairly extensively produced in England, and possibly elsewhere from the late eighteenth century until the first decades of the twentieth century. The story is that those who produced this work chewed tobacco and mixed their oxides with saliva. Whether true or not the story gives the clue to the principle underlying the phenomenon.

The oxide for mocha work must be mixed with water which is either distinctly alkaline or acidic. In differing water regions and with differing slips one or the other will work more readily. A liberal squirt of washing-up liquid, gently stirred into water to avoid frothiness, will provide an alkaline mixture and a vinegar and water mix an acidic mixture. Differing strengths of both these can form the basis of simple, speedy experiment to discover a suitably reactive mixture.

The oxide used should be really finely ground so it can be readily carried out from the applied mark by the reacting liquid.

Historically mocha work was limited mainly to rows of marks confined in bands by inlaid borders or turned beadings. It is a little surprising that it has not been more frequently combined with other slip processes or with subsequent underglaze painting.

The brush used to apply the dabs of oxide should not be heavily loaded. Even with a well-wiped brush the growth starts to spread out rapidly as soon as the tip touches the surface. As the reaction is between liquids it only occurs on freshly applied slip.

294 The two dabs on the right are from a well wiped-brush while the larger shape on the left is from an only slightly wetter brush. The main direction of growth is entirely governed by gravity. The main growth of each mark occurs in seconds and once it has ceased there is no further tendency for it to move so it is entirely possible to make shapes in opposing directions. The water of the oxide mixture tends to spread out a little further than it carries the oxide forming a shadow-like surround but on drying and firing the unpigmented mark vanishes

*294*

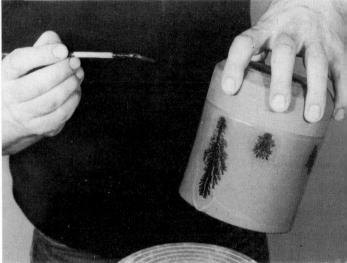

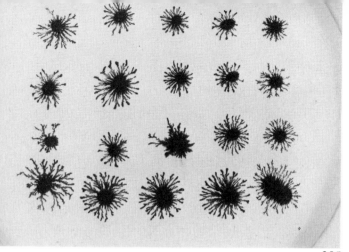

295 Dabs applied to a horizontal flat surface grow radially.

295

296      297

*296 and 297* These two photographs show different views of a mocha ware mug. Though manganese was the most commonly used oxide many others were used. The oxide here is cobalt which has given a more fluid mark than is often found. In this example the simple convention of a row of marks has given way to a more elaborate intention demanding quite careful control. In both these photographs the effect of the shape of the pot and the angle at which it was held when the oxide was applied is clear. The chequered band is of inlaid clay. English about 1800. *Victoria and Albert Museum, London*

# Burnishing

Burnishing is the rubbing of leatherhard, or harder, clay with some smooth, hard tool. The aim of burnishing is to give the clay a fine, smooth finish. This smoothness is inevitably modified by marks of slight relief left as the tool is rubbed over the surface. Sometimes, though not always, burnishing, as well as making the surface smooth, can give the clay surface a high gloss.

Burnishing can be done with different materials at different stages and in different ways but the principle underlying it is always the same.

The principle of burnishing is most easily understood if a common process not throught of as burnishing is considered. When grogged leatherhard clay is scraped with a metal kidney a rough, scratched texture results as the edge of the kidney catches on the grog dragging some of it along on the clay surface and lifting some of it right out of the clay. If the scraping is stopped and the kidney is again used to work over the surface, but this time at a shallow angle, trailing and pushing on the clay surface but not removing material, then the pits and furrows left by scraping will be closed up more and more as the firm, stroking action is continued. What is actually happening is that the grog in the clay is being pushed into the clay and the finer clay particles are, through the pressure exerted on the surface, being brought to, and moved sideways on, the surface to fill small concavities. This, on a large scale, is exactly what occurs on a much smaller scale in burnishing.

The action of burnishing is very simply to take a smooth tool and to rub it firmly on the clay. The tool may be a glossily smooth rounded pebble or a hardwood tool or a metal tool. Indeed clays which burnish readily can be burnished with the flat of ones thumb or fingernail. As long as it is hard and smooth enough the material of the tool does not matter but what is important is that the size and shape of the tool allow it to work easily over the whole surface which is being burnished.

No particular action is necessary. The tool may be rotated in small circles as it is worked over the whole surface or it may be worked in a simple linear way.

Virtually all clays can to some degree be burnished whether they are grogged or not. What is far more important than the visible texture of the clay is the proportion of it that is really fine.

The stage to commence burnishing is leatherhard. If the clay is too readily impressed by the pressure of burnishing then either it is not yet firm enough or the pressure is too great. Simple tests will determine the right stage. A clay burnished at a leatherhard stage may lose its burnish at two stages: it may lose it as it dries (few burnished finishes do not dull a little as they dry) and it may lose it when it is fired. Dry or almost dry burnished clay can generally have its shine restored by a further light burnishing if it is not quite dry or simply by rubbing with the hands if it is dry. In both cases this should be done with care for any coarse particles which are dislodged will scratch the surface. If the shine is dulled or vanishes during firing this may have occurred because of too high a firing or because of the inherent nature of the clay body. Temperatures much over $1000°C$ are excessive and, depending on the body, less may be better. Some clays simply do not retain a good shine. Whatever the causes of dulling in particular cases, whether temperature or the nature of the clay, the reason for the loss of shine is the same and is that the smooth, continuous, fine surface made by burnishing has been broken up in the firing and though still basically smooth to the eye is, under magnification, minutely granular.

While it is possible to burnish a clay body directly, and while some burnish very well, most of the burnished pots produced by cultures who used or use burnishing extensively are not the result of the direct burnishing of a body. It is possible to coat any clay body, which has been worked to an appropriate surface, with fine slip or with oxide mixtures and then to burnish this applied coating. Such coatings are rarely thick but their fineness is of vital importance for it is this which enables them to closely fill the clay surface during burnishing so that an enduring shine is produced. Fine suspensions of slip decanted from the top of watery slip mixtures often greatly facilitate burnishing. Indeed some such suspensions can dry to a shine without burnishing. Various forms of iron oxide, especially haematite, have traditionally been used extensively for burnishing but other oxides, not traditionally used, and even some body stains, either alone or added to slip, many, perhaps surprisingly, be burnished. With less conventional mixtures it is obviously wise to test these thoroughly in the intended context. Such testing is worthwhile for a much wider colour range is possible than traditions might suggest.

Probably because of its great antiquity traditions in burnishing seem strong. While the frequent association of burnishing with pinching and coiling has its roots in traditions which originated before other forming methods were known and while that association can be strongly argued to be appropriate it is not inevitable — it is for example perfectly possible to burnish thrown pots and even slipcast pots. The connection between burnishing and rudimentary firing processes also stems from the traditions of objects made when there was no alternative. Again, it can be strongly argued that the uneven colours which result from rudimentary firing are appropriate to the qualities of a burnished surface but it is of course entirely possible to fire burnished pots in electric kilns.

One aspect of the traditions of burnishing is however now often forgotten. Though a few were made specifically for burial in cultures where that was the custom, the majority of the burnished pots of antiquity were made for use. At the temperatures achieved the clay bodies used were mature enough to form completely serviceable vessels. The burnished surface, whether or not it was thought of as decorative or beautiful, was applied because it was the best available ceramic means of sealing the surface of a pot. A good burnished surface is never non-porous but it is always much less porous than the clay body it covers — any test on a chipped or broken burnished pot will confirm this. Most clay bodies marketed now do not mature sufficiently to develop usable strength at temperatures suitable for burnishing though as few burnished pots made with such clays are intended for use this is not a great drawback.

Bodies used in antiquity were, through generations of empirical knowledge, made from clays which would probably now be dismissed as low grade and too fusible for the common range of temperatures now used. In the few cultures still making unglazed slip coated pottery for daily use clay and slip blending is precise. The technology is not scientific but it is effective. The academic reasons for the behaviour of the different materials used may not be understood but the knowledge of the practical uses of those materials in their context of use is certain.

The process of burnishing is a small and rather isolated aspect of pottery but it is particular. The small and softly reflective undulations of a burnished surface are a unique possibility and the relationship of this surface to a form is, in subtle ways, open to interesting variation.

*298* Coatings intended for burnishing can either be poured or brushed onto clay forms. If a slip is to be used as an all over coating it can clearly be poured more quickly but as only a thin layer of material is needed and as burnishing material is not always slip, brushing is the more usual process. For an all-over coating full-bodied brushes should be used and should be well filled. If the creamy consistency of the mixture and the firmness of the leatherhard clay are

*298*

right in relation to each other it is easy to brush on an even layer of controlled thickness. The alternative is to use a thinner mixture and to brush on two layers allowing the first to become touch dry before the second is applied. The material in use here is a fine grade of iron oxide and a separated slip. The iron gives strength to the colour and the slip contributes to the gloss of the burnished surface. The mixture of the slip and oxide is easier to apply evenly than either of the two would be alone

*299* The burnishing can usually begin as soon as the brushed coating is touch dry, but the clay and the coating must be firm enough to be polished by the soft burnishing action. If the clay is indented or the coating rubbed off then the whole object must be allowed to dry a little longer. The stage when burnishing can be done most easily does vary considerably from clay to clay and from mixture to mixture and can only be discovered by experiment. Burnishing is sometimes done with a small circular motion covering each part of the surface several times and slowly working over the whole surface. Here the burnish is instantly achieved with each stroke. The type of surface made by burnishing is governed by the tool used, by the form of the clay surface and by the direction and nature of the burnishing movement

*300 and 301* By using a well-rounded tool, such as the back of a spoon or a smooth pebble, concave surfaces can be quickly given a more even, less linear burnish than strongly curving convex surfaces. Both for ease of holding and for access into deeply concave shapes the bowl part of the spoon may have to be bent upwards towards the handle

299

300

301

302 Whether forms are thrown, pinched, coiled or made in some other way the edge itself should present no particular problem for burnishing, though very sharp or thin edges are clearly not easy. With edges it is particularly important that the clay is not too dry or the pressure of burnishing may chip the edge or make it crumble. If this occurs the burnishing has been left too late

303 This example was fired to 1040°C which has given the body a durable strength and has not diminished the gloss of the burnish. Some mixtures will stand higher temperatures while others lose their gloss as much as 100°C lower. Such research as has been done on burnished and similar surfaces involves technical resources not available to individuals who, in testing materials for their burnishable quality, must rely simply on the methodical testing of likely materials bearing in mind that fineness of particle size is of great importance. When slip constitutes part of a burnishing mixture water-borne separation invariably improves the quality of shine

304 It is entirely possible to paint with two or more mixtures and to burnish these without marring the definition of the painted marks, providing these were applied with sufficient thickness

302
303

304

*305*

305 The darker marks in this example were painted with the same mixture of iron oxide and a separated slip as the rest of the form but with the addition of a little cobalt and manganese oxides. While the outside shown in figure 303 was burnished with straight radial marks this example was burnished with a small circular motion giving a less distinctly marked softer surface. The edge was simply polished by rubbing with a finger, both when leatherhard and dry, and the surface therefore has a completely unmarked smooth shine.

306 and 307 The combination of burnishing and incising is typical of the pots of many primitive cultures. It is a temptation when considering artifacts of primitive cultures to directly apply personal experience and to reach a definite conclusion about the process used. The danger is the ignorance of some factor which, at a different time in a different place, was fundamental and is not part of modern experience. Keeping an open mind in such matters is not purely a matter of academic or historical accuracy but is also of practical relevance for an altered procedure can make different possibilities emerge now. With all historical work, but particularly with that of primitive cultures from which modern experience is furthest removed, it is important firstly to observe the evidence of objects and only then, and with some caution, to see how far this can be related to personal experience. In both these examples the incised marks have slightly rounded edges and are closed up slightly in places suggesting that the marks were cut into the clay surface before the burnishing mixture was applied and polished and that the initial burnishing was at an early leatherhard stage. In both, the convex surface is unmarked with any linear marks from a burnishing action suggesting more of a polishing action and that the mixture was readily made shiny. The perceptible thickness of the burnishing mixture at the chip on the shoulder of the bottle tends to confirm that the process aimed to shine an applied layer rather than to polish a thin mixture into the surface of the clay body. Two other points to note are that the bottle has a form with finely detailed definition not always thought possible with burnishing and that the top ¾ in. (2 cm) of the bowl is reduced black, probably from resting upside down in

*306*

137

*307*

hot ash and embers, while the rest of the form is oxidised reddy brown. The bottle is just under 6 in. (15 cm) high and the bowl is 5½ in. (14 cm) wide. Both early third millenium BC. Figure 306 *Victoria and Albert Museum, London.* Figure 307 *National Archaeological Museum, Athens, Greece*

*308*

*308* Burnished pots have been and still are produced in quantity in Africa. The range of African burnished work shows the range of burnishing processes very fully and includes the use of graphite. Graphite powder can be mixed with water alone or with a fine separated slip. It will produce a high gloss on a smooth clay surface by soft brushing when dry, polishing with a cloth or rubbing between the palms of the hands. The problem with graphite burnishing is that graphite, being pure carbon, when heated combines with oxygen and burns away. Exactly at what temperature this occurs depends partly on the atmosphere of the firing and the fact that graphite burnishing is retained so effectively on Aftican pots is the result of the low temperature, the duration and the atmosphere of firing. In an atmosphere of firing which is reducing the combustion of carbon is inhibited so in the fast, smoky and relatively low-temperature firings which are typical of much traditional African work graphite burnishing is entirely feasible. The use of what in Europe would be considered as low grade fusible clays ensures that African pots have a serviceable fabric at low temperatures. The lustrous gloss of a polished graphite surface is quite unmistakable from the black of reduced iron bearing clays and iron oxide. From Uganda. About 1910. 13 in. (33 cm) high. *Horniman Museum, London*

# Separated slips

The phenomenon and use of separated slips is clearly related to the process of burnishing. Separated slips were an ancient discovery probably made through the experimental use of different clays for burnishing. A separated slip is the finest fraction of a natural clay which, either by virtue of its mineral constituents — the mineral illite is said to be an important constituent — or by virtue of its actual physical fineness, when applied as a slip coating develops a highly glossy surface on drying. The slip may develop its shine entirely unaided or it may need to be lightly polished when dry. Polishing will never detract from the shine and usually considerably enhances it. As few individuals are in any better position than the prehistoric potter for discovering if a particular clay sample has a high proportion of illite or contains exceptionally fine particles there is no substitute for trying out different clays to see if the separated fraction does develop a shine. Some clays will do it readily and some simply will not.

Slips are separated simply by mixing them to a watery consistency and decanting the top portion containing the finest clay. Suspending agents can be used to help the separation.

Separated slips of varying colours and varying degrees of gloss were used extensively in pre-glaze cultures. Like burnishing, which they tended to supercede, they were simply the best known way of giving functional vessels a finer and more impervious surface. Greek and Roman pots constitute the best known examples of the use of such slips. While the Greeks decorated their pots with different colours, the Romans used the slip as a thin overall coating on thrown, turned and relief moulded pots. It is an interesting example of the way one culture has difficulty in viewing another, except in its own terms and experience, that, throughout the nineteenth century and well on into the twentieth, writers on Greek culture referred to the glossy finish of its pottery as Greek 'glaze'.

The important thing to stress about the use of separated slips is the need for absolute cleanliness of hands and containers so that the finely separated slip is not contaminated by the coarser particles of ordinary clays, slips or other materials.

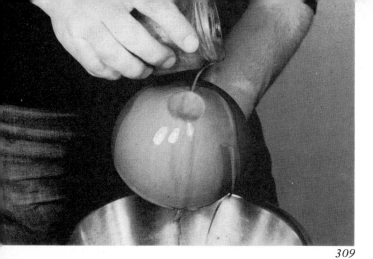

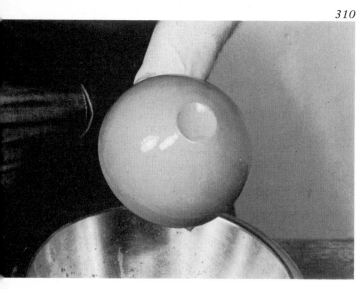

309 and 310 Initial tests are usually with small quantities of material so to minimise waste as few containers as possible of appropriately small size should be used. The slip can be poured in the usual way but it should be noted that, while thinner coats than with normal slip are needed, separated slips tend anyway to deposit thinner layers than normal slips of apparently similar consistency. On leatherhard clay separated slips tend to dry rather slower than normal slips. Separated slips can also be applied as brushed coatings

311 The shine developed by separated slips on drying is usually enhanced by firing but, just as with burnished surfaces, overfiring will cause a dulling of the surface. This particular example was fired to 1120°C without any loss of gloss, and tests of the same material surprisingly only began to dull and to blister at 1160°C. Each slip will have its optimum firing temperature and few mixtures start to dull much before 1060°C. The majority of Greek and Roman pottery was probably fired in the range from 1000°C to 1060°C the actual temperature being far more crucial to the hardness of the body clay than to the gloss or imperviousness of the slip coating. Being a much thinner layer than ordinary slips, separated slip does reveal very clearly the exact nature of the clay surface, a fact acknowledged by the Greeks in the meticulous finish of their turned surfaces and used by the Romans with their relief

312 and 313 The painted decoration in both these examples of Greek work with separated slips shows the marks of application and, though thin, has sufficient intensity to be well defined. In both, the darker slip shows a markedly stronger gloss than the paler background slip. Later, Classical Period painting shows a further refinement of the gloss and intensity of the dark slip see page 195. The black of the iron-bearing, separated slip painting is not a warm reddy brown because firings were reduced at or just before the point the slip was sintering. The higher iron content of this slip and the greater fluxing power of reduced iron oxide accelerated the sintering. In the oxidising cooling of the firing the partially sintered dark slip was unable to reoxidise while the paler unsintered slip reoxidised to a warm straw colour. Figure 312 is

312

a detail from a Mycenean period pot about 15 in. (37.5 cm) high, the upper band of painting being just under and the lower just over 3 in. (7.5 cm) high. Thirteenth century BC. Figure 313 is a detail from a very large

Geometric period krater (stem bowl form) just over 4 ft (122 cm) high the painted band depicting a funeral cortège being 7 in. (18 cm) high. Eighth century BC. Both from *National Archaeological Museum, Athens, Greece*

313

314

*314* This detail, from a moulded cup about 3½ in. (9 cm) high, shows the use of a separated slip over relief. The waxy shine is evident and the colour is a decidedly reddish brown. Older books refer to this type of pottery by various names — Samian ware, Arretine ware, Terra sigillata — but the accepted term now is simply Red Gloss ware. Throughout the Roman empire red gloss ware was red, fired in a clean oxidising firing. The slip is the same material the Greeks used for painting and its density, even in thin coatings, made it an appropriate finish for small moulded cups and bowls. Roman. *Verulamium Museum, St Albans, England*

# Wax resist

The principle of wax resist is that when a layer of wax is applied to parts of a pot any further application of waterborne material to those parts is prevented. The wax volatilizes in the early stages of the subsequent firing.

Two common uses of wax resist are in the application of glaze. It can be used to resist glaze on the unglazed feet of pots, eliminating the need for scraping and sponging and it can be used to assist in achieving a neat glaze join at the edge of a pot where different inside and outside glazes meet.

Quite distinct from these two simple, formal applications of wax resist the use of painted marks and areas of wax and of sgraffito through a wax layer both open up more variable possibilities and these are the subject of this section.

Painted wax can be used at both unfired (leatherhard and dry) and biscuit stages with any of the waterborne materials normally used at those stages. Sgraffito through wax resist can be combined with painted wax whenever the material on which the wax is painted is scratchable. It is not therefore possible to scratch through wax applied directly to biscuit and because the only way wax can be removed from biscuit is to fire it, it is important when working on, or near, biscuit to avoid unwanted splashes of wax.

Two types of wax resist mixture are in common use: cold wax and hot wax. Cold wax is a water based wax emulsion specifically prepared and sold as a resist material. Hot wax is a mixture of some type of wax with some form of light oil and has to be mixed and heated for use. Both types have their advocates.

Some points in favour of cold wax are: unlike hot wax it is ready mixed; unlike hot wax its use involves no fumes and only a slight, not unpleasant, smell; unlike hot wax there is no element of fire risk; unlike hot wax brushes can be cleaned in water provided they are not allowed to dry. (Brushes used for hot wax can be cleaned in hot paraffin but this causes rapid deterioration and is anyway never very satisfactory so in practice some brushes are kept for sole use with hot wax.)

Two points in favour of hot wax are: unlike cold wax it dries on the pot almost immediately and resists instantly (cold wax does not resist until it is dry and on damp surfaces it dries very slowly); unlike cold wax the thinnest of wax films can be relied on to resist positively.

One further point against hot wax is that until experience has been acquired it can be tricky to achieve the right blend of wax and oil at the right temperature.

Despite all the factors against it hot wax, well mixed, is the superior material — it has far more flexible mark-making possibilities and its superior quality of resist both make it preferable. In fairness though it must be stated that some workshops use cold wax exclusively. In the end personal preference and the particular nature of the work involved are important factors.

Candles or paraffin wax and paraffin, light lubricating or heating oil are the usual ingredients of hot wax. It is little use to give precise amounts as these depend on the type of wax (the wax content of different brands of candle varies) and on the type of oil used. As with most things it is sensible to record the materials, amounts and procedures used so that mixtures can be repeated.

The wax content can be added to the oil as pieces or lumps but melts and mixes more quickly if it is shredded with a surform tool or a coarse cheese grater. A rough guide for an initial mix is to lightly press down the shredded wax and then to barely cover this with oil. Once the initial mix is heated and melted it can be tested for quality and the wax or oil content adjusted accordingly.

In use hot wax should stay fluid long enough not to inhibit work. If it hardens before it reaches the pot or can only be applied in a thick broken-textured layer or, when set, is completely un-

*continued on page 146*

143

**Plate 1**

a **Slab built pot made of agate clay.** *Felicity Aylieff, 1980*
This slab built pot is made of unglazed vitrified clays. The coloured clays were made by mixing body stains into a white clay. The full tonal value of body stains only becomes evident when the clay is fired to the point of vitrification. The uneven, undulating stripes of colour in the agate contrast with the angular yet asymmetric precision of the form. Over complexity has been avoided in the simple, controlled mixing of the coloured clays. The unglazed, vitrified clay sharpens focus on the agate body and on the crisp edges and surface of the form

b **Slab built pot with rolled clay inlay.** *Jill Radford, 1978*
The coloured clay used for the rolled inlay of this slab pot, like (a), is made by colouring a white body with body stains. Vitrification gives the colours their tonal strength, and clear glaze has added brightness and richness to the colours. The colour vibrancy of the smaller areas of mauves, pinks and yellows is balanced by the tonal contrast between these shapes and the larger areas of rich, deep blue giving the work complementary levels of complexity and simplicity

c **Detail of underglaze painted tiles.** *Topkapi Sarayi Museum, Istanbul, Turkey*
This detail shows a small area of tiles from the exterior of one of the rooms, the Sunnet Odasi, in Topkapi Palace. The significance of what is not painted, as well as what is, is underlined by the importance, visually not just figuratively, of the smooth, brilliant whiteness of the only unpainted areas which form the flowers. That same whiteness gives the blue of the background, the mauve of the stems and the turquoise of the leaves' brightness and translucency. The inevitably uneven marks of the blue background area are used to give an additional aspect of movement to the work. The centre of each flower is painted with Armenian bole, a natural earth. The centres stand up in slight relief as Armenian bole has to be used thickly to give its characteristic colour

d **Detail of a Chinese enamel painted plate.** *Topkapi Sarayi Museum, Istanbul, Turkey*
European traditions of enamel use have developed in a particular way; use of the possible diversity tending to be narrow and concentrated mainly on thinly and precisely applied colour. This detail shows the glaze-like translucency and richness which can be a quality of enamel work. The work in fact comprises different qualities of enamel, the thicker areas of more freely applied colour being outlined with thinner, more opaque enamel

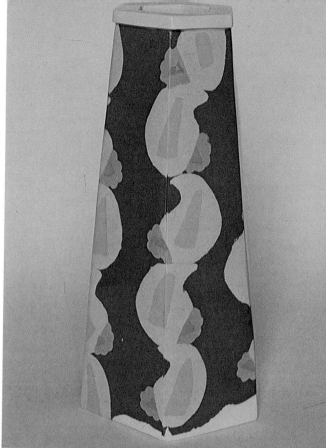

a   b

**Plate 1**

c   d

a   b

d

**Plate 2**

c

Plate 2

a   **Handbuilt pot, graphite burnished and incised.**
Uganda, about 1910. 5 in. high. *Horniman Museum, London*
The range and quality of black which can be achieved in ceramics is extremely diverse. This shiny black has an unusual quality of depth. The exact procedures used in the production of African pots are rarely clear. A variety of polishing and burnishing processes and materials are used before firing and are sometimes combined with treatments during cooling. These treatments include rubbing with leaves and other parts of plants, the sap and resins from which fill the clay pores reducing porosity and imparting additional and permanent gloss. The combination here of closely worked surfaces of high gloss and precisely scratched fine incising is highly effective giving two levels of surface interest: firstly the contrast between the plain and the incised areas and secondly the relief within the incised areas

b   **Coiled pot, treated with coloured slips and smoked.** *Judy Trim, 1980*
Carbonising can be accomplished in a number of ways which offer differing degrees of control but it is important to realise that the marks and placing of carbonising are controllable. The precisely applied areas of colour inside the rim are softened by slight carbonising and the precision of that part contrasts with the large area of carbonising on the outside of the form. The traditional association of the earth colours of red clays with the uneven colour effects of the varying atmospheres of primitive firings is refreshingly broken in the combination of body stain colours and carbonising

c   **Roman pot, slip trailed, coated in a separated slip and reduced fired, of a type known as 'Castor' ware.** Made in second and third centuries AD near Castor in Northamptonshire. *Verulamium Museum, St Albans, England*
A quite different quality of black to the carbonising of 2(b), and the burnished gloss of 2(a) is evident here. The matt black slip which breaks thinner on the high points of the relief is the same type of separated slip used on Roman red-gloss ware, but here it has been reduced. For control of slip trailing and fluency of quality, by any process, the work is distinct. The different tonality of the thinner parts of the slip is a strong contrast but it does not detract from the relief of the trailing

d   **Detail of Ming dynasty garden seat, with trailed slip and coloured glazes.** Chinese. *Victoria and Albert Museum, London*
Though like 2(c) this example also has relief, lesser but distinct, formed by trailed slip the intention of the relief is different. It performs two functions : firstly it acts as a barrier between the different areas of coloured glazes and secondly, within some of those areas, it serves to break up the tonality of the glaze

responsive to the warmth of finger pressure then the mixture needs more oil. If, on the other hand, it is slow to harden after brushing and spreads readily under the warmth of finger pressure then more wax is needed. The test of the wax's response to the warmth of finger pressure is a good one because it is relevant regardless of the temperature of the mixed wax. Ideally the wax should give just slightly from finger warmth. If it does this but is difficult to apply then the mixture should be made hotter. A good hot wax mixture should allow a thin film of wax to be fluently applied and the brush should become empty of wax before the wax stiffens.

Most brands of candles will make excellent wax resist but so does paraffin wax which is cheaper. Paraffin wax is less readily available but some hardware stores and chemists stock it. Light lubricating oil is more expensive than paraffin or heating oil but it is much better. It makes the least volatile mix and therefore has the least tendency to evaporate and give off fumes. Paraffin mixes are very prone to make fumes and if kept hot for long periods tend to need thinning from time to time with additional paraffin.

The best and safest way of heating hot wax is to use a modern waterless electric glue pot in which the glue pot (the wax container) sits in a dry container which heats it. In the best of these the heat can be regulated by adjusting the thermostat. The next best way is to use a double boiler in which the wax pot sits inside the water container. A tin can or a small saucepan in a larger saucepan works adequately but an old fashioned cast iron glue pot has the advantage that steam is not constantly rising around the wax container. For safety an electric ring is preferable to gas as it has to be remembered that wax resist mixtures are inflammable. Wax containers should never be heated directly either with electricity or gas.

For hot wax mixtures to be used efficiently the wax must be at the right temperature which will vary from mixture to mixture. In whatever way the wax is heated the heat source should be controllable and the heat should be contolled. Too little heat makes the wax awkward and wasteful to use because thicker layers than necessary are deposited. Too much heat makes the oil content evaporate thickening the mixture and creating fumes.

Brushes used with cold wax should be washed out immediately after use or they will not be useful for this or anything else again. If a long brush is used with cold wax for long periods the wax can tend to dry in the fixed ends of the hair reducing the mobility of the brush so it is a sensible precaution to wash out the brush every so often.

Brushes used with hot wax have to be kept for this. In use hot wax brushes should never be rested in the wax pot even briefly or they can be badly deformed. For precisely this reason glue pots are provided with a rod fixed across the top on which to rest brushes. It is a complete mistake to imagine that any brush will do for wax resist. Both where the application of waxed areas has to be precise and where the quality of mark is important the quality of the brush has to match the nature of the intention.

It is possible to pigment wax resist mixtures with metal oxides. This was done extensively in Moorish Spain in a process called 'cuerda seca', which translates literally as 'dry cord'. Its main, though not sole, use was in decorating tiles. The pigmented wax was painted directly onto the unglazed clay the wax acting as a barrier between areas of different coloured glazes and the pigment acting as an outline to these areas. Finely ground dry pigment is easy to mix with hot wax mixtures. If too much pigment is added the resisting power of the mix is badly impaired but in fact very little oxide is needed to make a strongly toned line. The only guide to amount in mixing is that pigment should be added to the mix little by little and as soon as a painted mark looks opaque in the raw state that should be sufficient.

Whenever a kiln is fired which contains any quantity of wax resist the kiln should be well ventilated, with spy holes and vents left open, in the early stages of the firing. Fumes will take care of themselves in flame kilns, except for muffle kilns, and in muffle kilns and electric kilns ventilation should continue until all fumes have ceased. All kilns should anyway be sited in well ventilated rooms but the need for this becomes particularly apparent when wax resist has been used.

## WAX RESIST ON LEATHERHARD CLAY WITH SLIP

*315* The least watery material with which wax resist mixtures are used are slips, and a good test of the resist power of a wax mixture is how quickly and positively it will clear slip from its surface. In this illustration slip is being poured from a leatherhard bowl which has been broadly painted with wax. The resulting contrast will be between the clay body colour in the waxed areas and the slip colour in the unwaxed areas.

Use of wax resist on leatherhard clay is a little more difficult than use in other contexts simply because the clay is damp, which gives the wax poor adhesion. The one precaution to take is to avoid delay between application of the wax and application of the slip. If the clay is only a soft leatherhard the wax can tend to lift off if slip application is delayed

*316 and 317* Scratching through waxed areas just into the leatherhard clay underneath introduces the possibility of fine lines of slip within resisted areas. If the line depth of the scratching and the slip thickness match the work can take on an inlay-like quality. In scratching through wax to produce fine lines of slip it is important that the colour and tonality of the slip are considered carefully. A pale slip which may contrast adequately as an area against a clay body may well not be visually strong enough as a fine lines

315

316

317

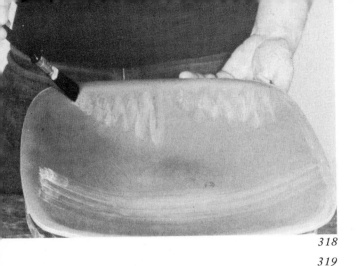

318

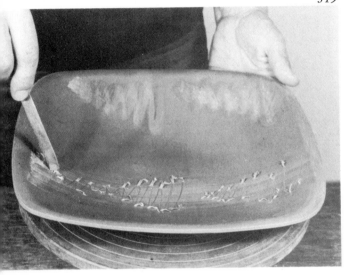

319

## WAX RESIST ON DRY UNFIRED CLAY WITH SGRAFFITO AND BRUSHED PIGMENT

The next six illustrations are a simple demonstration of marks that can be made with brushed wax, brushed oxide and sgraffito used with both of these.

318 A broad band of wax has been painted across the dish and two freely painted marks are being completed

319 Two freely drawn marks are being scratched through the wax band

320 Somewhat foreshortened by the angle, two marks have been painted on the near edge of the dish and oxide is being brushed over the scratched wax band. The pigment only takes in the scratched lines of the band and where the brushing goes over the ends and edges

321 The third band is plain brushed oxide owing nothing to wax and the last band of oxide, nearly completed here, clearly reveals the two wax painted marks

320

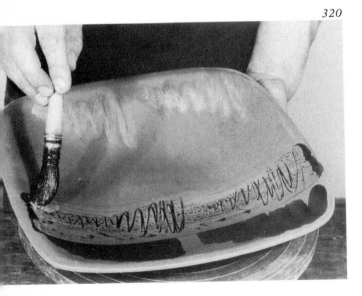

321

**322** The sgraffito treatment of the plain oxide band owes nothing to wax. Large droplets of pigment can be clearly seen on the waxed band and in the two waxed marks. These can be left but with some pigments such droplets can be rather strong. As they stay wet for a long time they can be easily cleaned off simply by lightly touching them with a well wrung out damp sponge

**323** The demonstration has here been glazed with a semi-opaque earthenware glaze. From the top the first and third bands owe nothing to wax resist while the second and fourth, reversing the marks of the third and first, are uniquely possible with wax

## WAX RESIST ON BISCUIT WITH GLAZE

**324** Just as wax can be applied by banding to protect the feet and bases of thrown pots so it can be used to define and contain areas of brushed wax

**325** Holding a brush well away from its working end, as with all painting, gives a much better sight of the whole work and allows for more considered placing. When working directly on biscuit like this wax cannot be scratched away so correction of accidental splashes is not possible

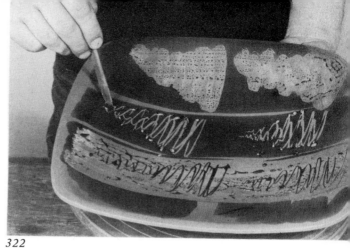

322

323

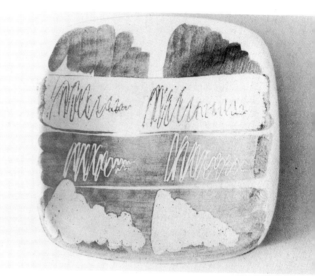

325

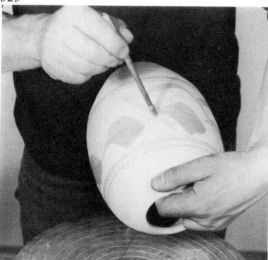

324

326

327

328

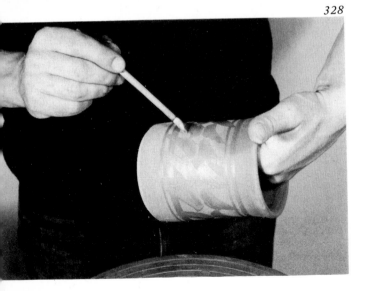

*326* Sometimes the divisions of a form into areas by brushed wax may facilitate glazing but in all cases the general procedure is similar to that which would be used in normal glazing. Here the top of the pot has been dipped into the glaze and held steady for a few seconds for sufficient thickness to build up

*327* It is then quickly turned right way up and the glaze is poured into the still wet coating on the top part so it can flow down over the rest of the form leaving an even coating all over. In all painting the spaces between marks should be considered. This often becomes dramatically evident during the glazing of wax painting for it is the spaces which accept glaze and the negative of the painting suddenly is made manifest. Painting directly on biscuit prior to glazing is a stark experience for while the overlap of oxide painted marks can bring a bonus in changed tonality or colour or texture, an overlapped wax mark on a clay body still only leaves the clay body. As wax resist on biscuit becomes a body to glaze contrast, work of this type is usually restricted to bodies which become well vitrified in the glaze firing

## WAX RESIST ON GLAZE WITH PIGMENT

Work in wax resist over a glaze whether it is to be treated with brushed oxide, as in this case, or a second application of glaze can commence as soon as the glaze is touch dry and, to avoid the problems of lifting and bubbling which can occur when a dry glaze coating is wetted, should not be delayed too long

*328* Because there is none of the suction which occurs when waterborne pigments are painted onto an absorbant unfired glaze surface, wax can be brushed onto touch dry glaze more smoothly and fluently than pigment. To avoid splashes and runs brushes should not be overloaded and a single brush filling of a good hot wax mix will go much further than one of pigment

*329* Whether by banding, as here, or freehand a reasonably large mop brush is ideal to brush a pigment mixture over wax resist on glaze. Mop brushes combine softness with volume. No more than two passes over the surface should be necessary and one is usually sufficient for most pigment mixtures. The tendency to brush on too much pigment should be avoided. On a vertical surface there is much less tendency for droplets of pigment to settle on waxed areas than with horizontal surfaces

## WAX RESIST WITH TWO GLAZES AND WITH SGRAFFITO

The next thirteen illustrations show three related examples of different uses of painted wax resist and sgraffito through wax with two glazes.

*330* Involving only painted wax the first example is the simplest. Lines and areas of wax are painted on a white glaze in preparation for the poured application of a second glaze

*331* If, as here, the form can be held by its thickness between the thumb and fingers with fingers on the back and thumb on the front, within a waxed area, this will make glazing much easier. In this case the dish can be rotated so that an even layer is poured all over and that a minimal amount of glaze goes onto the back of the dish. As with all applications of a second glaze layer it is important that the consistency of the glaze is adjusted so that an excessively thick layer is not created. Unless they contain a high proportion of ball clay, or some other plastic clay, most glazes, even when only touch dry, have a stronger porosity than an average biscuit surface so it is usually essential to water down the second glaze

329

330

331

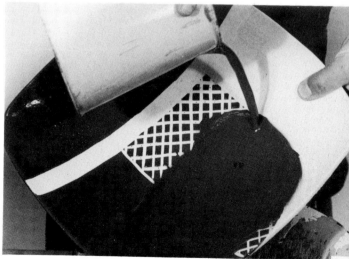

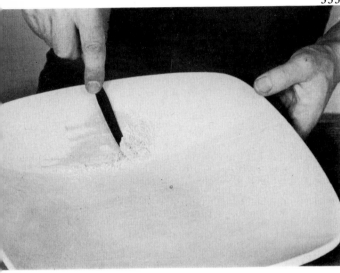

332

333

334

*332* The detail of the fired surface shows the typical mottling which occurs when a dark earthenware glaze is applied over a white one and shows the clearly defined areas and lines of wax resist

*333* A second possibility is to paint wax over the whole of a glazed surface and then to scratch through this back to the biscuit in lines or areas so that when a second glaze is applied all the remaining areas of the first glaze are resisted. This results in areas and lines of two glazes which meet with no overlaps. In practice, as here, when the intention is to have large areas of the second glaze it is not necessary to wax these areas. A flexible palatte knife will quickly remove large areas of glaze

*334* Areas are best defined by scratching through the wax with a point

*335* The palatte knife can then again be used to remove glaze up to this precise line. Any glaze which is contaminated with wax should be put to one side for cleaning. The wax can be removed very simply by putting the contaminated glaze into a bowl with excess water and stirring it about momentarily before putting it to one side to settle. When the glaze has settled the wax on the surface of the water can be floated off with the excess water and the glaze returned to the main batch

335

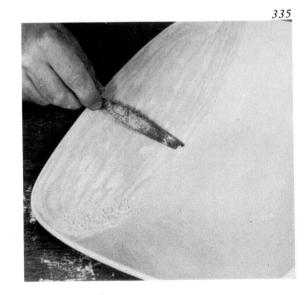

336 The residue of scraped glaze can be removed from large areas with a well wrung out sponge, taking great care not to dampen the area too much

337 Linear sgraffito can be done through areas of waxed glaze. Clearly it is hardly practicable to meticulously clean all the fine lines with a sponge but the work should be shaken or brushed to remove all loose pieces of wax and the lines should be quickly and lightly sponged over with a damp sponge. This is more to reduce their strong porosity than to clean them. The reason that the second glaze may take rather thickly in lines is partly that the glaze is dispelled sideways from the waxed areas to the lines and partly that each line beneath the cut through the painted wax contains two exposed edges of glaze which usually have very strong porosity. For the same reason a glaze is usually depositied in a slightly thicker line adjacent to the edge of resisted areas but here there is only one exposed edge of glaze so the build up is not usually excessive

338 To keep glaze off the back it is always preferable to pour glaze onto a dish with it held so the glaze leaves the dish across rather than along edges. Here the top part of the scratched grid has been glazed with the dish held the other way up. With the fingers supporting the lower edge from the back the remainder is being poured as the dish is rotated through an arc starting with the left hand corner down and ending with the right hand corner down pouring across from left to right

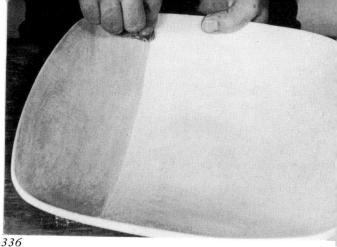

336

337

338

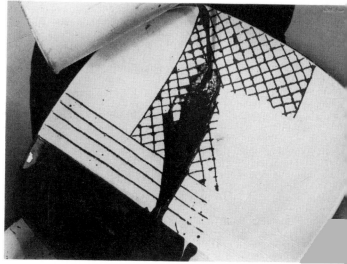

*339*

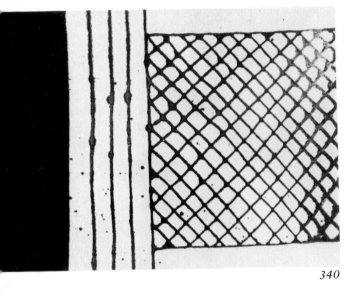

*340*

*339* As soon as glazing is complete the dish should be shaken sharply to remove large droplets of glaze from the waxed surface, the lines which tend to hold droplets and the lower edge of the dish. A dry line of mattness is immediately and clearly visible where the poured black area meets the white and is caused by the strong porosity of the exposed edge of the white glaze sandwiched between the wax above it and the biscuit below. With opaque glazes this thickening at edges does not show and with translucent glazes it can contribute a tonal change which adds interest to the edges of areas

*340* It is notable in this detail of the fired dish that the edge separating the areas is crisper in quality than the lines. This is because, as mentioned above, lines tend to take a thicker layer of glaze than areas. The dots of black on the white glaze and those enlarging the black lines correspond with the droplets evident in the previous illustration. Just as with brushed pigment on wax these can in fact be removed very simply by wiping the surface with a damp sponge straight after glazing

In work of this kind it is usual to use unpigmented or paler glazes first and pigmented darker glazes second because with pigmented glazes it is difficult to remove all traces of pigment from scratched areas if the darker glaze is applied first. Sgraffito and wax resist used in this way offer very distinct possibilities with glaze which are not paralleled in other processes. It is, however, a mistake to become over preoccupied with ideas of precision for even quite viscous glazes do, by definition, melt and some softening of quality from the scratched to the fired result is inevitable and is an aspect of the process better acknowledged than ignored. Even with very thin fluid wax mixtures it is difficult to scratch lines much closer than those shown without the danger of flakes of wax between the lines lifting off and this danger is compounded in closely spaced lines which cross.

*341 and 342* By using the two previous processes together, painting areas and lines with wax and scratching through resisted (and unresisted) glaze in lines and areas, the possibilities of the two can be combined allowing each glaze to show alone in lines and areas and allowing overlapped areas

While the preceding examples show opaque earthenware glazes the processes can equally be done with translucent glazes, allowing softer qualities to occur, and with stoneware glazes.

## PIGMENTED WAX: CUERDA SECA

*343 and 344* With normal wax resist, hot or cold, the thickness of the wax layer has no relevance to the colour or tonality of the finished work. In cuerda seca process the application of a wax resist is combined with the application of a pigment mixture so the thickness of the wax layer is relevant to the tonality of the pigment. As the proportion of pigment in a cuerda seca mix is limited if the resist quality is not to be impaired the danger is more that the pigment may be too light in tone rather than too dark so the aim should be to apply an even film of the mixture slightly thicker than with unpigmented wax. This is easily done by banding lines twice rather than once and painting other marks more slowly than usual. The pigment mixture can be one oxide or a blend of oxides. To be really smoothly paintable cuerda seca wax mixtures

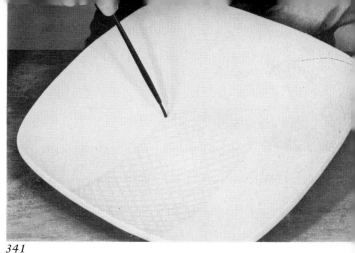

341

342

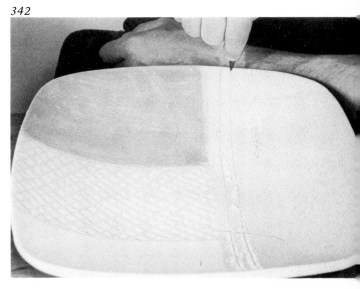

343

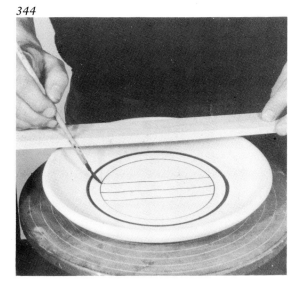

344

345

346

need to be kept somewhat hotter than ordinary wax resists. Once the resist and tonal qualities of a mix have been tested and are known application should present no other particular problems. As can be seen in 343 thickish glass as well as tin cans can be used to contain hot wax in a double boiler. With glass it is important that the glass is heated up in and allowed to cool in the water otherwise by putting cold glass into hot water or removing it from hot water to a cold surface the glass can break

*345* Traditional manifestations of cuerda seca usually use the pigmented wax as divisions between small areas of painted coloured earthenware glazes and it is surprising how effectively the wax works as a barrier when glaze is quickly dabbed on from well loaded brushes. In some contexts a slip trailer rather than a brush may be a more convenient way of applying the glaze

*346 and 347* In the Hispano-Moresque tiles which are the most common manifestation of the process the whole tile surface is treated but if only areas of cuerda seca are made on a larger surface, as here, these can be resisted with a normal wax mixture so the remainder of the surface can be glazed by dipping or pouring

347

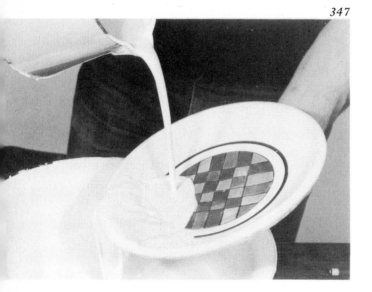

*348*

*348* Both the finish and the decoration of this small cup and saucer made of white stoneware clay involve the use of wax resist. The saucer is slightly under 4½ in. (11.5 cm) wide. Within the well of the saucer and the foot of the cup is the same unpigmented glaze as on the inside of the cup. All of these were wax resisted in whole or in part to allow the application of the green celadon on the remainder of the saucer and the outside of the cup. The simple bands on the saucer and the bands and brushwork on the cup were wax resisted and then banded all over with an iron bearing mixture leaving the green of the resisted celadon contrasting with the darker colours of the brushed pigment. This contrast and the contrast between the decorated and pale undecorated parts is typical of the remarkable balance between gestural freedom and precise controlled finish in the work of Harry and May Davis, 1960. *Crowan Pottery, Cornwall, England*

*349* This large dish, just under 18 in. (46 cm) in diameter, shows painted wax used as a resist between the application of a first and second layer of two glazes. Variety is added to the surface by the very controlled application of the second glaze in that the round, darker-toned area in the centre part is due solely to that part having a slightly different thickness to the remainder. Control of thickness of first and second layer in double glazing is a vital part of wax resist whether the aim is overall evenness or controlled unevenness. The wax resist itself shows an effective balance between broad and narrow marks. *David Winkley, 1980. Somerset, England*

*349*

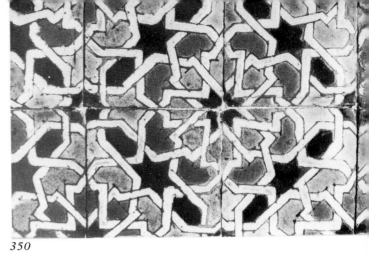

*350* These tiles are just under 5 in. (13 cm) square and are a typical example of the cuerda seca process. Two qualities deserve mention: firstly the contrast between the matt colour of the pigmented lines and the shine of the glaze areas and secondly the slight rounded relief which occurs on either side of every line caused by the glaze thickness and clearly evident in the right hand top tile of this illustration where the light reflects from the edges of the glaze areas. While the involved complexity of the work is obviously not inevitable with the process it is intriguing. Precision is one aspect of the work but it is not a mechanical precision and complex geometric thought combines with execution which in many places shows obvious errors, and yet the imprecision of detail does not detract from the precision of idea. The cuerda seca process was used by the Moors in Spain to replace the techniques of tile mosaics in which coloured glazed tiles were chipped to shape and assembled into astonishingly fine geometric mosaics. Fifteenth century AD. South-eastern Spain. *Victoria and Albert Museum, London*

*350*

*351* A less common use of cuerda seca is found on dishes and occasionally on pots contemporary with the tiles. The work rarely has anything of the intricate richness of the tiles and the cuerda seca line is used simply as a freely drawn coloured outline for larger areas of glaze. The quality is more related to the traditions of European peasant work than to those of Islamic ornament. This particular example, as can be seen from the running of the fluid glaze towards the edge not the middle, was fired upside down probably in a stack of similar dishes separated by stilts, the marks of which can be seen in the centre. Together with the better known tiles, cuerda seca work such as this underlines the possibilities of a process which, surprisingly, has been little used since sixteenth century Spain. About 1530 from Spain, probably Seville. *Victoria and Albert Museum, London*

*351*

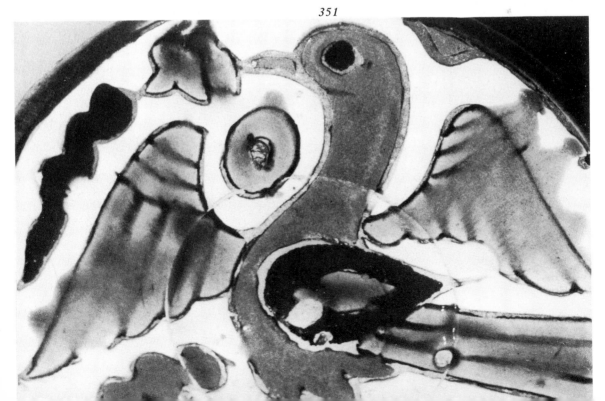

# Peelable latex resist

Emulsified latex cannot be thought of as a substitute for wax as a resist material. As a paintable material latex has a quite different quality to wax, hot or cold, though it is closer to cold wax, and it functions differently as a resist. Because at the end of each resisting action latex is peeled off subsequent resisting on any part of the whole surface is possible. Wax on the other hand because it is not removed, presents an ever decreasing part of the whole surface of an object for second and subsequent resisting actions.

It is never possible to scratch through a layer of latex resist in the way that wax resist painted onto an unfired glaze or leatherhard clay can be removed in lines or areas.

Emulsified latex is most commonly available as an adhesive, *Copydex* latex adhesive, but can also be bought specifically prepared as a resist.

The emulsified latex usually needs thinning with a little water to make it a more fluid consistency for painting. Care should however be taken not to overthin the mixture or the film of latex may be too thin and inclined to break as it is peeled off the surface. The latex can be thinned on a glazed tile or a saucer by taking three or four brushfulls of latex and adding one brushfull, or a fraction more, of water. No more than can be used in about ten minutes should be mixed or the mixture will tend to harden into rubbery lumps at its edges. For the same reason the small amount of the mixture should be spread out on the saucer as little as possible.

Although it is water based latex will, unless precautions are taken, tend to ruin brushes. Before any brush is dipped into latex or a thinned latex mixture it should first be well wetted in water. If the latex on the brush ferrule begins to become rubbery or if painting continues for longer than 20 minutes the brush should be well washed in running water before work proceeds. As soon as work is finished the brush should be washed with soap and well rinsed. If work is necessarily intermittent then the brush should rest in a saucer of water when not in use. If the latex is allowed to dry in the hairs of a brush then the brush is irretrievably spoiled but if the simple precautions described are taken then the latex has no detrimental effect whatsoever.

Latex can be used on leatherhard clay as a resist for poured or dipped slip but its adhesion on the damp clay is not strong and the film can tend to peel before or during slip application.

The most useful and most usual context for painted latex resist is with glazes both directly on biscuit and on unfired glaze surfaces. Here its peelability gives it unique possibilities both for the application of different glazes used singly in areas and in the sequential application of overlaps.

The degree of control which latex offers calls for the exercise of some caution. Care should be taken to see that the control offered by the process does not lead to inappropriately over elaborate results and tests should be made to ensure that the precise arrangement of layers and areas of glaze which is possible is visually evident and effective in the fired result.

The process has no tradition and has an inherent potential which is unexploited.

The illustrations which follow are of two parallel series, one of work directly on biscuit and the other on a touch-dry, unfired glaze surface.

*352 and 353* There is little difference between painting latex resist onto biscuit (even nos) or touch dry glaze (odd nos) surfaces. As soon as the painted latex has lost all signs of milkiness, and the surface has developed a dull sheen with a slight translucency, the glaze can be applied normally. One important point to watch is to try not to handle the latex at all as this can lead to the latex becoming detached from the surface. In particular any little rubbery lumps which occasionally may be picked up from the saucer of latex should be left on the surface. Likewise no attempt to scratch through the painted latex should be made. If part of the latex film does become detached it cannot be restuck nor, without removing all latex painting which joins up with it, can it be neatly removed

*354 and 355* When glazed, as here, the glaze is not dispelled from the latex but settles on it in a thin layer which dries more slowly than the glaze on unresisted parts. The latex should not be removed while the glaze on it is wet

352

353

355

354

356

357

*356 and 357* If all the edges of painted latex are within an object one edge must be loosened and lifted with a needle which can be used firmly on biscuit but has to be used with enough care not to damage the underlying glaze when latex is on glaze. If the latex extends beyond a working edge then it can be rubbed with a finger to loosen it. In either case it is a good idea, when applying latex resist, to decide where will be the most convenient place to begin to remove it and to paint an extra thickness there so the latex has a little extra body to grip initially

*358 and 359* As soon as an edge or end of latex is loose and has been securely gripped the resist can be simply peeled away. Though it adheres strongly to both biscuit and glaze surfaces it comes away from a glazed surface without so much as marking it. As the latex is pulled off it is stretched considerably and the thin resisted glaze layer on its upper surface is propelled in tiny pieces all over the place for a radius of about a foot (30 cm). There is no need to wear a mask as the pieces do not constitute airborne dust but they should be sponged off working surfaces before they dry and do create dust. The glaze on the latex must be touch dry before peeling begins or the tiny pieces of glaze will tend to adhere to the piece of work if they land on it. Where possible the work should be held vertically so the pieces do not come to rest on it

358

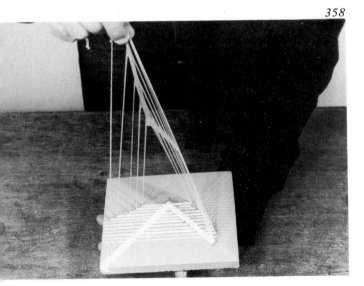

359

# Paper resist and stencilling

The distinction which can be made between paper resist and stencilling is that with paper resist the paper which produces the resist is not reused whereas a stencil may be used repeatedly. It might seem that both processes are limited to flat or cylindrical shapes and there is some truth in this. However the paper used in paper resist has a degree of stretch which allows it to accommodate some curve in two directions and, more obviously, a small stencil can be repeatedly applied to a large curved surface. In both instances what is possible depends on the content and size of the resist or stencil.

## PAPER RESIST

The commonly known form of paper resist is the use of paper to resist slip on leatherhard clay. Knowledge of the possibility of using the same process on glaze is less common but the process, either using glaze or oxide over the resist, is just as possible.

Technically the two factors of greatest importance for paper resist are the quality of the paper used and the wetting of the paper. The best papers to use are either newspaper or a strong tissue paper. Newspaper is a little thick but is readily available. If it can be found a strong tissue paper is better as it is more flexible when wet and of comparable strength. Whichever paper is used it should be thoroughly dampened before use which will make it expand. Complete expansion must occur before the paper is placed on the clay or glaze surface. Only if this has occurred is the risk of the paper edges buckling up while they are resisting removed. Apart from the control of the thickness of application of slip, glaze or oxide paper resist is otherwise free of technical problems.

Though it has distinct possibilities as a means of creating well defined areas of slip, glaze or oxide there is not a strong tradition of paper resist probably because it has not been thought of as a speedy production process. Occasional examples do however occur in Chinese ceramics.

By cutting through several layers of thin paper identical paper resists can be made. Stencils, by definition, are reusable so this is a means of repetition of paper resist rather than the production of disposable stencils.

360

## PAPER RESIST WITH SLIP

*360* The success of paper resist is mainly dependent on the care with which the paper is applied to the clay. However damp the paper is it should be well sponged down onto the surface with a damp sponge taking particular care that edges are well attached. When all the paper is in place the paper surface should again be sponged to remove any excess water from the surface

*361 and 362* The slip should be applied immediately the paper is finally in place. Pouring with great force where the stream of slip could lift edges should obviously be avoided but otherwise the slip can be applied by pouring or dipping in the normal way

*363* As soon as the slip approaches the touch dry state, usually about half an hour after application to leatherhard clay, the paper can be peeled off. The side of a metal kidney or a sharp pointed modelling tool are usually necessary to lift the edges of the paper and for this reason work which involves lifting off many small pieces of paper individually is usually avoided — though of course the quality of shape would be different, painted wax, because it does not have to be removed, would be a better resist material for such work

361

362

363

**364** Provided great care is taken that the junctions are well pressed onto the clay surface, paper can be overlapped

**365** This detail is from one of the series of plates by Bernard Leach entitled *The Pilgrim and the Mountain*. In some of the series both mountain and pilgrim are cut paper resist but in this example only the pilgrim is, the mountain being scratched through the slip. The black slip here is painted, rather than poured or dipped, giving the background a slightly uneven tonality. Despite this unevenness it is worth noting that the outline of paper resist is clear because the thickness of the paper, standing up in very slight relief, encourages a slight extra thickness to occur. This is clearly evident around the head, the feet and the bottom of the cloak. *Crafts Study Centre, Bath, England*

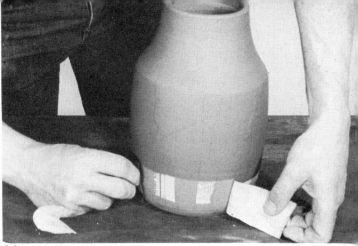

364

365

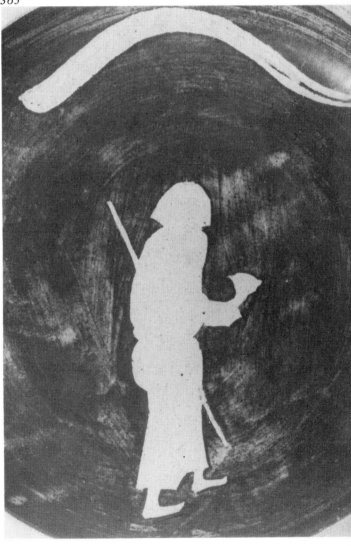

366 Here paper resist is combined with incising
into the resisted areas and through the slip. The
slip layer is an unusually thick one and the con-
sequent relief has become a strong element of
the work. Chinese. Sung Dynasty. *Victoria and
Albert Museum, London*

366

## PAPER RESIST WITH GLAZE ON GLAZE

*367* When the paper has been thoroughly dampened all surface water is sponged off it as excess moisture makes the paper stick to the porous glaze surface too readily making positioning difficult

*368* When it has been positioned the paper is pressed firmly against the surface in one or two places which is usually enough to hold it in place temporarily

*369* The paper is then firmly pressed onto the glaze with a small damp sponge so that all parts are fixed. Special care should be taken at the edges of the paper as loose edges can lift up during the application of the second glaze. The sponge will need to be repeatedly dampened but excess water as far as possible must be kept off the unresisted glaze surface so that a severely reduced porosity in some places does not lead to an uneven coat of the second glaze

*367*

*368*

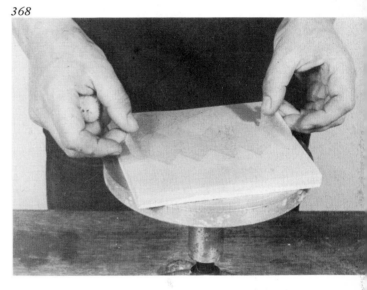

*369*

*continued on page 170*

**Plate 3**

a    **Relief modelling on Late Geometric Period large Greek pot.** *National Museum, Athens, Greece*
Though the light firing clay of this large vessel is necessarily somewhat coarse the surface of the vessel and the modelling are closely worked without being oversmoothed. The clay surface is treated with a thin separated slip which is given lightness by the paler clay beneath it. The separated slip has a waxy sheen rather than the hard gloss of some Roman separated slips. In this colour plate the way that the qualities of material combine to enhance the modelling is more evident

b    **Detail of a large ceramic bath.** Chinese. *Victoria and Albert Museum, London*
Though the means exployed are more complex than those at 3(a) the content of the work is comparably clear. It could be argued however that this clarity is due to evident graphic qualities rather than those of relief. That modelled relief, combined with other means, should lead to a quality which is primarily graphic merely extends rather than ignores the possibilities of the process

c    **Painted detail from Geometric Period Krater.** *National Museum, Athens, Greece*
This detail shows the coffin bearing chariot painted on a huge krater form. Geometric Greek pottery displays an ordered approach to painted decoration which is, almost without exception, organised in bands on forms of every size and shape. The sole materials used are separated slips of differing iron content on fairly light firing bodies. A pale slip covers the entire form and a darker slip is used for painting. The work is sometimes dismissed as cold and hard. Certainly the repetition of motifs is even and there is little evidence of inaccurate spacing or placing. But, examined in detail, there is ample evidence of a spontaneity of touch within the accurate repetition and, in the space filling motifs which surround most of the stylised representation, there is an almost gestural freedom. Because the work is Greek, order of course predominates but it is not overpowering

d    **Detail of Italian tin glazed and painted dish.** Caffaggiolo, dated 1514. *Victoria and Albert Museum, London*
Though wider ranges of colour than in this example exist quite commonly the control of colour and tonality in the painting of the triumphal procession is impressive. The slightly incongruous quality of the vigorously brushed blue background is typical of dishes painted in Caffaggiolo

e    **Detail of fluted porcelain jar.** Sung dynasty, China. *Topkapi Sarayi Museum, Istanbul, Turkey*
Spacing and tapering flutes evenly around a full bodied form requires careful measuring and repetition. Here the flutes taper slightly and spaces between the flutes taper more markedly to accommodate the changing circumference. The work shows accuracy without being mechanical and is a good example of the translucent green developed by some celadon glazes on a white porcelain body

f    **Detail of a large incised dish.** Sung Dynasty, China. *Topkapi Sarayi Museum, Istanbul, Turkey*
Though the incising is shallow the celadon glaze is given clear emphasis to the relief. The glaze is less shiny than the example at 3(e) and the colour difference is partly due to the slightly darker body

**Plate 3**

a
b
c
d
e
f

a

c

**Plate 4**

d e

**Plate 4**

**a** **Thrown stoneware pot.** *Bernard Leach. Crafts Study Centre, Bath, England*
Like the preceding plates 3(e) and 3(f) this example is of a form, with relief, which has been finished by being coated with a single glaze. Unlike those two examples the glaze here has developed some texturing on the areas without relief, partly because of the inherent nature of the clay. This texturing makes the emphasis which the glaze gives to the combed incising and the applied clay pellets much softer than would otherwise be the case

**b** **Tamba pot.** Japanese, eighteenth century. *Crafts Study Centre, Bath, England*
The robustly direct qualities of some peasant European pottery are sometimes somewhat akin to those of this pot but the intention is different as any runs of glaze and asymmetry of form are the result of a speedy production of objects which do not intend this — such occurances are allowed because of the 'lowly' status of the objects. The irregularity of the poured areas of this example are intentional and the asymmetry conscious. While aspects of the qualities of Tamba pottery can be very refreshing and invite, and have invited, emulation it is less than sensible not to acknowledge that to European traditions they are very foreign

**c** **Coiled and burnished pot.** *Judy Trim, 1980*
This very thinly coiled form is burnished. The yellow burnished colour derives from use of a body stain. The traditional association of burnishing and earth colours is a natural one, for red clays have the finest particle size, but it is not one which is technically inevitable. The stripes inside the edge contrast effectively with the simple, almost austere, burnished exterior

**d** **A detail of one of four large tiles flanking the entrance to the Sunnet Odasi in Topkapi Palace.** *Topkapi Sarayi Museum, Istanbul, Turkey*
For sheer brilliance of underglaze colour there is little that can match the work of Turkish potters of the sixteenth century. Production was centred in but not confined to the town of Iznik. The work was widely exported, some with contemporary English Elizabethan gilded mounts is known, but the finest work was reserved for mosque lamps and for tiles. Tiles were mass produced but fine ones were produced for particular use in mosques and palaces. The colour range was not wide, though it was wider than the blues of this example, including aubergine, brown, yellow and a range of greens but the colour quality was enhanced by the remarkably white background of the best work. The painting demonstrates extraordinary technical and graphic control. See also colour plate 1(c) and illustration 427.

**e** **Underglaze painted porcelain plate.** Ming dynasty, China. *Topkapi Sarayi Museum, Istanbul, Turkey*
The glaze of this example has a silky sheen rather than a high gloss. The grey blue, quite different from the colour of bought cobalt oxide, results from the use of an impure form of cobalt. Earlier examples of blue painting on a white ground do exist, notably on white earthenware bodies and on tin glazes at different times in Persian pottery but the mass production of blue and white porcelain in the Ching dynasty has its roots in the work of the Ming dynasty. Possibly more glazed pottery in various forms of blue and white — Oriental porcelains, European tin-glazed painted wares, the printed work of Staffordshire and other European centres — has been produced than any other form of glazed pottery. But the term 'blue and white' covers a range of quality and the single term and sheer quantity of the work tend to obscure the quality of particular types and particular examples. This work has a relaxed fluency and yet is highly organised. It shows a comparable graphic and technical control of painting to the tile of 4(d)

169

370

When the paper has been well secured the second glaze is applied in the normal way by dipping or pouring.

*370 and 371* As soon as the second glaze is touch dry the paper can be lifted at one end and peeled off. When the paper does not extend to a convenient edge a needle or fine pointed knife is needed to lift the edge of the paper

## PAPER RESIST ON GLAZE WITH SPLATTERED OXIDE MIXTURES

The application of the paper to the touch dry glazed surface is no different than for resist with glaze. The paper is first thoroughly dampened.

371

*372* Applying a dampened piece of thin paper to a vertical from is less easy than to the tile shown in figure 368. If it proves too difficult thicker paper may be used. If there is a knack it is to have the higher end of the paper rather damper than the rest with a little surface water on it and to press that end on, once the paper is positioned, so it grips the glaze at two or three points long enough to lift up the form into a horizontal position so the paper is resting against it

*373* If necessary the points of initial adhesion can be released and the paper repositioned. The paper is then stuck to the glaze as in figure 369 with a dampened sponge

372

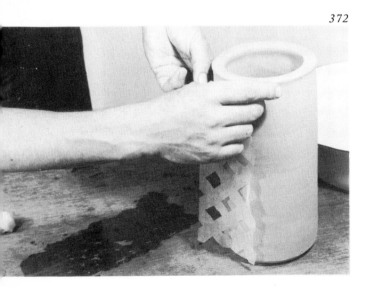

373

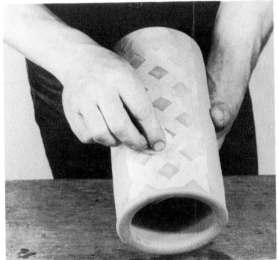

374 The splattered oxide is then applied. The process of splatter may seem at best anachronistic but this accords it less than its due. The quality is quite distinct from that achievable with an airbrush or spray gun: while directional control is as good as that with a fine airgun the granular texture of the colour is coarser than can be sprayed. The directional control gives a fine control over grading colour across a surface. To apply the oxide a stiff short bristled brush is dipped into an oxide mix and the ends of the bristles are stroked away from the glaze surface. As each bristle springs back into place it catapults a single drop of the oxide mixture forwards onto the glaze. The smaller the brush the greater the directional control. Toothbrushes and nail brushes both work effectively but should not be old with bristles bent at odd angles. The most even texture and the greatest directional control will be achieved with new brushes. In any experiments with splatter the factors to vary are the distance of brush from surface, the wateryness of the mixture, the strength of the stroking, the type of brush used and, because these have a fundamental influence on diminishing or retaining the granular texture of application, the oxide mixtures and glazes used

375 With thin paper the porosity of the glaze ensures that wet globules of oxide do not gather on the paper and run down onto the glaze and as both paper and glaze surface dry immediately the paper may be peeled off as soon as oxide application is complete

It would be wrong to consider that the sole application of splattered oxide is with paper resist. As with spraying, though the texture is always different, very subtle gradations can be achieved by directional splatter onto relief surfaces and simple forms and by merging areas of different oxides into one another.

374

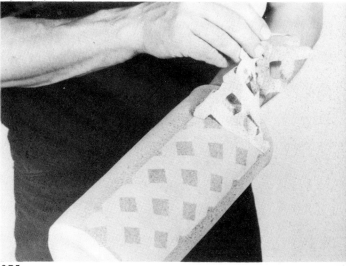

375

*376*

*377*

*376* The resist in this example is solely of the central painted roundel. The application of the splattered oxide onto the relief of the lobed form is fairly even, giving slight rather than exaggerated emphasis. The dish is tin glazed. Dutch mid-eighteenth century. *Victoria and Albert Museum, London*

*377* It is often not possible to be positively certain about what materials were used in processes in the past. Certainly the central octagon here is stencil resist and certainly the colour application is splattered. What material was used for the stencil is in doubt. Considering the cut shapes of the stencil, paper is quite impossible so thin sheet metal seems likely. The advantage of applying colour through a stencil by splatter rather than directly by brush or sponge is that the stencil acts as a mask and does not need to be in intimate contact with the surface. The white lines lightly scratched through the splattered oxide to the tin glaze on the edge begin to make a negative to positive contrast with the dark silhouette shapes of the stencil work in the centre but lack both the area and the quality of intricacy which could make a more effective contrast. English. Second half of the eighteenth century. *Victoria and Albert Museum, London*

## STENCILLING

In relation to rich traditions of stencilling in some fields there is little stencilled work of fame in ceramics. Certainly the process is less obvious and more limited for the more complex surfaces of ceramics. Stencilling has nevertheless been used fairly extensively. Tin glaze painted work from various sources contains stencilled elements, see for example 377, and it was still sufficiently common for ceramic suppliers catalogues of the 1930s to illustrate stencils which could be bought and to offer a stencil making service.

The basic requirement for problem free stencilling on any surface is a good stencil. It is most likely that stencils used in the past were metal, certainly the ones made in the 1930s were metal and were available in four different thicknesses. It is however the form as well, not just the material which makes stencils easy, or not so, to use. Commercially produced stencils have a lip at the edge formed as they are punched out and a true stencil knife is so bevelled as to make a slight lip as it cuts through thin shim.

Experiments with various ceramic materials using lipped, commercially available children's stencils have underlined the immense advantage of stencils with lips. In use the slight lip is placed downwards giving a good seal with the surface. If the back of the stencil is lightly smeared with grease or vaseline little or no colour creeps under the edge.

In the absense of stencil makers or the facilities to cut thin metal stencils, tolerable stencils can be made from cartridge paper but these, obviously, are unlipped. When the stencil has been cut the paper should be saturated in polyurethane varnish or a shellac solution to make it completely impervious. To get better penetration the polyurethane should be thinned with about a third part of white spirit. Shellac is either mixed by dissolving shellac flakes in methylated spirits or can usually be bought ready mixed as shellac patent knotting. If made thoroughly impervious such paper stencils will stand a reasonable amount of use.

From the process itself and its use in other fields the possibilities of stencilling are clear but it must be acknowledged that making or having well lipped stencils made presents a problem. If this can be overcome stencilling could be a very sensible process for some smaller scale of repetition production than would be reasonable by screen printing the process which, with others, has caused the complete disappearance of stencilling from the industry in the period since the 1930s.

When considered, stencilling should be used for its own qualities not, as happened too often in the past, as an inferior cheaper substitute for work which was initially painted.

378 The simplest form of stencil is one which has a single opening. Whether work is simple as here or complex, involving the use of several interrelated stencils each in use with a different colour, the placing of stencils is important.

378

379
380

379 Simple stencilling, whether with lipped or un-lipped stencils, can be done with almost any brush. Here the action is done in two strokes one from one edge to the middle and the other from the opposite edge to the middle. This avoids the risk of brushing colour under the stencil edges. More complex stencils should be painted with a more upright conventional stencilling action — stippling rather than stroking. Stencilling brushes now available are rather stiff for ceramic colours. When stencilling was more common stipplers and stencil brushes made specifically for stencilling with ceramic materials were available and were much softer

380 Stencils should be lifted off work carefully to avoid smudging the wet colour

381 The most conventional contexts for stencilling are with underglaze colours onto clay and with enamels onto fired glazed ware. It is, however, possible, as here, to stencil onto unfired glaze with a suitable pigment mixture. As always the stencil is carefully placed and firmly held in place

381

*382* The pigment here is applied with a sponge. The movement has no sideways effect at all in this being like the conventional stippling action, and even with complex stencils there is minimal tendency for colour to flow under stencil edges unless too much colour is picked up by the sponge or the mix is too fluid

*383* As the dry unfired glaze has a fairly immediate drying effect on the colour care in removing the stencil is necessitated more to prevent damage to the unfired glaze than for any risk of wet smudging

*384* This example shows use of stencilled decoration combined with painting. Just as has become the case with various printing processes, stencilling in the 1920s and 30s offered a cheaper alternative for mass production than painting. Here the stencilling is so combined with painting that the impression of the whole work is close to the varied complexity that can be a quality of painting. It is dangerous to be over dogmatic about what are the 'right' qualities of a given process especially one which clearly offers considerable diversity but rarely in ceramics has stencilling been used for the clear flat pattern which is naturally one of its qualities. 1920s or 1930s. English

*382*

*383*

*384*

# Some further resist possibilities

Though these few additional alternatives cannot be thought of as standard processes they do offer some interesting possibilities, mainly with on-glaze materials.

## THE USE OF ADHESIVE TAPES

The adhesion of various types of tape varies on different surfaces but is usually good on fired glaze surfaces but ranges only from poor to adequate on biscuit clay.

The use of clear adhesive tape allows precise, straight-edged areas to be resisted with enamels and commercial lustres.

*385* This tile shows painted lines of platinum which were resisted with clear tape. The tape can be removed as soon as the lustre has begun to dry

*386* These squares of yellow commercial lustre were resisted with clear tape and this illustration shows a problem which occurs when tape is overlapped. The resisted diagonal lines of tape which run from bottom left to top right were placed first and over these were placed the tape lines running from bottom right to top left. However carefully the overlapping tape is pressed into the edge of the slight relief formed by the first layer of tape, lustre does tend to creep along this edge. This is clearly a problem when clean hard-edged work is intended but it is a problem which creates a quality which is usable

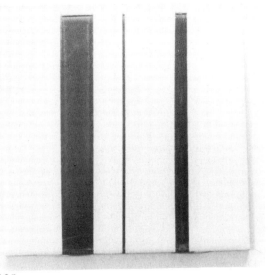

*385*

*386*

Clear adhesive tape works equally well with painted enamels. The greater viscosity of enamel colours eliminates the tendency for colour to creep along the joins of overlapped tape.

With masking tape the media of lustres and enamels react with the adhesive of the tape and material creeps under the tape edges so, for precise work with these materials, masking tape can be discounted.

*387* This illustration shows the frond-like growths which form as material creeps under the edges of masking tape. Again this is a problem which, in the right context and with appropriate material, for example pale commercial lustre, has some possibilities

With biscuit clay, however, masking tape is more clearly useful for some resist work. For areas of resist the tape can be backed up with paper.

*388* This biscuit dish has been prepared with tape and paper for resist with poured glaze. For shaped areas masking tape is easy to cut to precise shapes. If the biscuit is soft or rough it is not sensible to cut the tape on the biscuit so the tape is overlapped and assembled on the surface in the intended areas and is then peeled off and placed on a sheet of clean glass where it is cut with a sharp knife or razor blade. The overlapped and shaped tape is then returned to the biscuit surface — the tape loses none of its adhesion on the glass. When tape is overlapped it is easier to handle if it is consistently over-lapped in one direction. When the tape is to be backed up with paper the tape is first loosely pressed onto the biscuit and is only pressed down when the shaped paper has been slid under the loose edge of the paper. On some forms, with some areas of resist it is useful to fix any loose edges of paper well out of the way. This may involve cutting and taping the paper at the edges of the form, as is clear on the right-hand edge of this dish. After the glaze has been poured and the tape removed crisply defined areas of glaze are left. Work like this may be left as a clay to glaze contrast or, alternatively, the entire form  may be glazed again all over, with the same or a second glaze, for a single to double layer glaze contrast

387

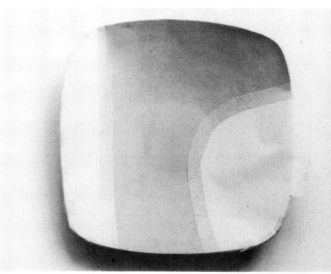

388

389

390

## REFRACTORY RESISTS WITH LUSTRE

This possibility concerns commercial lustres and works on the principle that a layer of refractory material is applied to the areas which are to be resisted and prevents contact and therefore adhesion between the lustre and the glaze surface. Being refractory the material is left in place and is cleaned off after the work has been fired.

Permanent white gouache colour is refractory at commercial lustre temperature and is eminently paintable. Some other colours of gouache work equally well but, whether white or another colour is used, tests should always be made as paint manufacturers do change the composition of paints from time to time. The two factors to check in tests are that the material is adequately refractory so that it can be removed easily and that it has no pigmenting effect on the glaze.

*389* The gouache colour is painted onto the glaze and allowed to dry thoroughly

*390* The lustre is then painted on

*391 and 392* After firing the entire paint surface is washed with soapy water. Fine abrasive powder can be used to speed the removal of any thick or stubborn paint but the abrasive powder must be fine as coarse powder will mark the surface of some lustres. Any shadowy stains left when the paint has been cleaned off are the result of lustre penetrating very thin gouache paint so care must be taken when applying the gouache that an even opaque layer is made

## COMMERCIAL AND OTHER RESIST PREPARATIONS

In addition to wax and latex emulsions some suppliers do market various other resist prepara-

391

392

tions, including screen printable resists. These are mostly intended for on-glaze use.

A variety of other resists can be mixed for use in particular contexts. In compounding any mixture consideration has to be given to the oil or water-borne nature of the material which is to be resisted and to how, whether and at what stage the resist material is to be removed.

## REACTIONS WITH COMMERCIAL LUSTRES

This topic is not strictly one of resist in that true resist is applied before the material which is to be resisted. The topic here is the reactions which occur if various liquids are applied to freshly applied commercial lustre. Mocha work, which is also not strictly a resist process, is somewhat similar to these reactions for, although it is dissimilar in that pigmenting material is added, it is related in that an added liquid disturbs and displaces a previously applied, and still potentially mobile, coating. With commercial lustre the process is effective because lustre is very sensitive to different thicknesses of application and because added liquids which are effective displace the wet lustre into uneven thicknesses. Liquids which can be used include white spirit, spirit of turpentine, benzene, linseed oil, prepared media and indeed

the reaction of any oil or spirit based liquid is worth testing. The effects of different liquids differ considerably and most liquids can be blended with each other to achieve a compromise of qualities. Soft soap can be effective if mixed to a fluid consistency with water. Water alone is too fluid and on all but flat surfaces tends to run off the liquid lustre and if applied to flat, horizontal surfaces merely floats the lustre off the surface leaving unlustred areas.

Marks are limited to lines and dots applied by brush, the latter being more controllable, and, like Mocha work, the process is one which can be controlled broadly rather than in detail.

When tests of different liquids are made it is important to ascertain the extent to which if any of the added liquids have adversely affected the adhesion of the lustre as this can, rarely only, be a side effect.

*393 and 394* These illustrations show examples of the sort of effect which can be achieved, though black and white photographs cannot do justice to the iridescent, reflective variety present in the lustres. 393 was done with spirits of turpentine with a small fraction of benzene added. 394 was done with linseed oil.

*393*

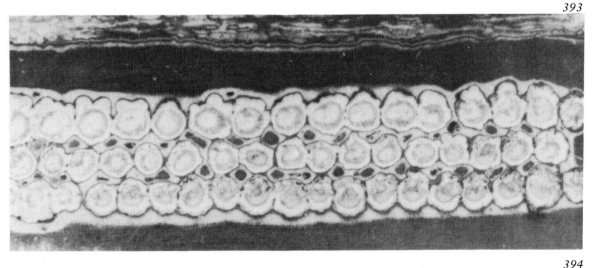

*394*

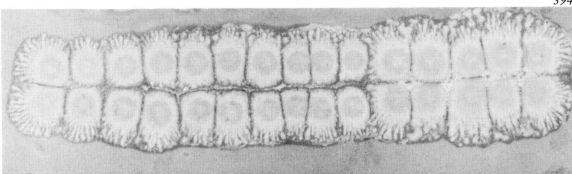

# Painting

Painting is the application by some type of brush, of some type of ceramic material, at some stage in the ceramic process.

These three factors and the touch and intentions of the painter form a complex equation which governs the quality of painting.

Painting, more perhaps than many processes, is strongly affected by stylistic conventions and people coming to it for the first time rarely do so without fairly strongly preconceived expectations. The intention of this section is not to investigate conventions, or styles but to describe aspects of the process which seem basic so that individuals may make what they will of the possibilities. The inclusion of a range of historical examples should not be allowed to obscure this intention and these should be seen as examples of the use of different brushes and materials in different contexts and not as examples of imitable style.

The process of application itself is so simple and yet so diverse that it defies concise description. Once brushes and the materials have been experienced so much is to do with touch and timing in response to these that sequential description with photographs would be repetitious and would reveal far less of actual process than with other processes. The form taken by this section is therefore rather different to the others in that the writing is accompanied by fewer photographs of demonstration, the concentration being on aspects of the three variables —brushes, the stage of application and the painting material — and factors relevant to these.

## BRUSHES

The principle of a brush is that the hairs, bristles or fibres which make up its working end will hold a volume of fluid material and will, as they touch and move across surfaces, readily and steadily give out this material. The hairs, bristles or fibres themselves are not absorbant and the fluid both clings to their surface and fills the spaces between them when the brush is charged. When charged a brush is full and rounded and as it works on a surface the body empties and shrinks as the material flows out.

The resilience of the hairs of a brush should be related to the viscosity of the intended painting material. The more fluid materials require brushes with soft fine hairs and the more viscous materials require brushes with stiffer coarser hairs — for example, Oriental brushes intended for ink painting have soft fine hairs while brushes intended for oil painting have coarse stiff bristles. In use the resilience of a brush is a factor of as much importance as its shape and for the brush to be effective must relate to the material context of use.

Within pottery there is a range of paintable materials which require application in different consistencies in layers of different thicknesses and brushes suitable in one context may be less so in another. Waterbourne pigment for example has a different fluidity to enamel mixed with an oil-based medium and slip needs a different thickness of application to underglaze colours. It is not easy therefore to generalise about the desirable quality of brushes for use in pottery especially when a diversity of individual intention is added to the range of possible materials and contexts. It can be said only generally therefore that brushes most useful in pottery tend to combine a material-containing volume of body with both a shape-retaining resilience of hair and a softness of working end. Animal hair, either of single type or a combination of types, is the almost universal material in brushes commonly used in pottery. Occasionally bristle brushes may be useful. A recent development is the manufacture of brushes with nylon 'hairs' and these are useful in some contexts.

Brushes exist in a great variety of sizes, shapes, hair types and qualities. Sable, squirrel, ox, goat and pony are the hair types most commonly found in European brushes and may be used alone or blended. The particular quality of hair depends not only on the animal but on the part of the animal from which the hair comes, ox ear hair, for example, is particularly resilient. The uncut ends of hairs taper and form a softer working end less prone to steaking so it is common to form brushes from uncut hair though some types such as cut liners are cut to shape. Oriental brushes exist in a bewildering variety of hairs — wolf, weasel, badger, goat, cat, dog and many others — as well as in diverse shapes and sizes.

Without acquired experience much of the quality and potential of a brush cannot be clear until the brush is handled and used. A small, well chosen selection including different qualities as well as sizes and shapes is a sensible beginning and will develop the experience needed to form a fuller selection of brushes. Whatever the manufacturers intention it is good to remember that the use to which a brush can be put is the first consideration in its purchase. One pitfall in buying brushes is that many are fine objects in themselves and they may be bought more for their intrinsic appeal than their potential use.

The illustrations which follow show a very small selection of common varieties of European and Oriental brushes. Most exist in a variety of qualities and all exist in a variety of sizes. All the brushes are shown wet and dry, dry brush above, wet brush below, to show the more defined shapes brushes assume in use.

**European brushes**

*395* Potters suppliers call this type of brush a majolica pencil while artists' suppliers refer to it simply as an artist's sable or a water colour brush. From small to medium, a finely graded range of sizes is available. Being sable the type is smooth working and resilient

*395*

*396* This type of sable brush is referred to as a 'one-stroke' by potters' suppliers and is sometimes called a 'lettering brush' by other suppliers

*397* This type of ox hair liner is usually called a square liner

*398* This brush is specifically intended for the banding of fine lines, a greater or lesser pressure producing a thicker or thinner band. Unlike the previous brush this type is manufactured not by power crimping the hairs into a metal ferrule but by gluing and tying the hairs and tying them into a quill. The handle is a tper fit in the open end of the quill. The type is called a cut liner

*399* A square bander. Banders of this and other
types clearly have a potential much wider than
their particular intended use

*399*

*400* Being made of fine soft hair and yet having
considerable bulk mop brushes, whether small
or large, are very versatile. The hair, usually
goat or squirrel, is glued and tied and the quill
is bound to both hairs and handle with wire

*400*

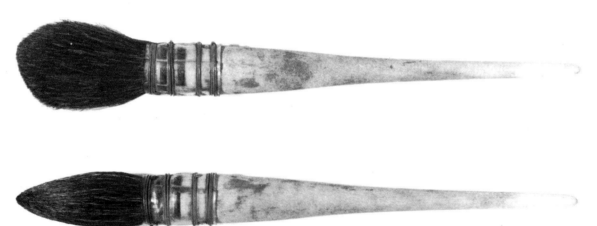

### Oriental brushes

*401* When bought European brushes are dry and their resilience can be felt by gently stroking them across the hand. Oriental brushes however are frequently sold stiffened into a crisp, rigid somewhat compressed shape. The stiffened hairs are often additionally protected by a removable bamboo cover. While this practice is effective in preventing damage it does prevent prospective purchasers from feeling the quality of the hair until after purchase when the water soluble stiffening can be washed out. Many Oriental brushes are intended for use with ink and these are fine and soft lacking the resilience often desirable in pottery brushes. The practice of stiffening hairs for their protection prior to purchase is not always done but is quite widespread especially with softer brushes and adds confusion to the confusingly wide variety which is available. Anyone buying Oriental brushes should always enquire what hair has been used so that experience relevant to future purchases is built up

*401*

*402* The same brush shown previously in stiffened form is here shown in wet and dry states

*402*

184

*403, 404 and 405* Few if any oriental brushes are cut to shape. The uncut hairs of most are glued and tied with silk and glued into round bamboo with or without an interconnecting sleeve of bone or plastic. Apart from the quality of the hair the variable factors are the diameter of the brush and the length of the hair. Those illustrated represent the medium size available. Very fine small and very large brushes also exist

*403*

*404*

*405*

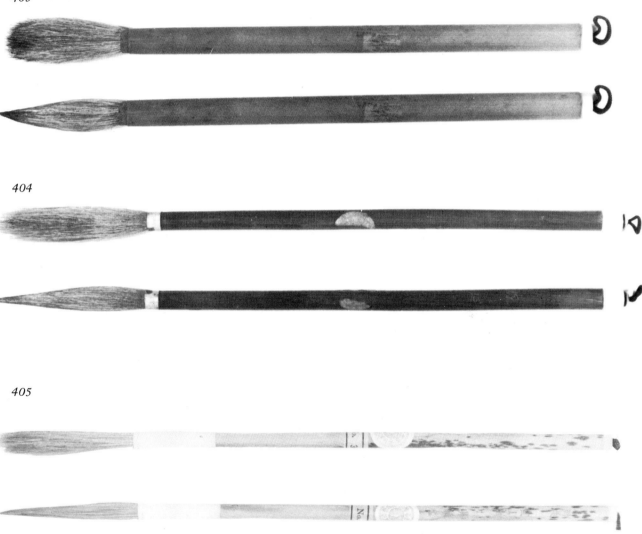

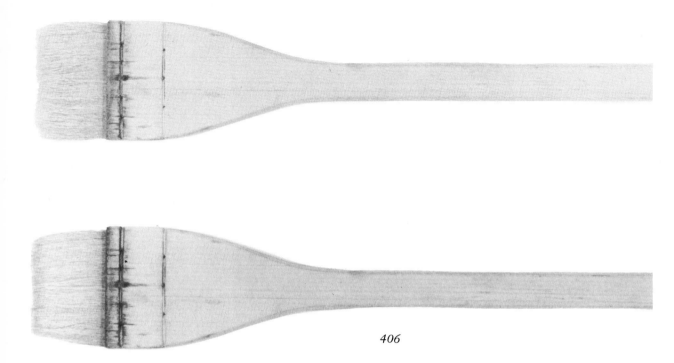

*406*

*406* There are some exceptions to the round
mounting of oriental brushes the most common
imported type being known as a 'hake' brush.
This is a full-bodied, soft, broad brush which
has diverse potential

The preceding illustrations are by no means
exhaustive of available types. Processes, materials
or particular mark-making intentions may well
demand different types, as for example the coarse
stiff brushes used for hakeme.

Such adaptations of brushes as occur are usually
purely an adaptation of function involving nothing
more than the decision to use a brush — house-
painting brushes or shaving brushes, for example —
for an application of say slip or oxide for which it
was not originally intended. At least one interesting
and useful adaptation can however be made by
careful cutting. The type of brush generally available as water colour or gouache brushes and sold
by pottery suppliers as majolica pencils can be
adapted in this way. A fairly full brush is the
starting point. The outer hairs are all shortened so
that the body of the brush tapers towards the
central core of hairs which are left uncut.

*407 and 408* Two cut brushes of slightly different form and volume are illustrated here, each in wet and dry states. In use the volume of the outer part of the brush acts as a reservoir replenishing the thin central part of the brush by which the painted material is applied. If the hairs are fairly resilient, which is common with this type of brush, the other part of the brush gives support to the thin centre part. Such brushes facilitate the controlled painting of long, fine lines, more or less as could be done with small brushes but with the advantage that the need for frequent replenishment is minimised. Being slightly less responsive to changes of pressure and less inclined to run dry such brushes can be used to paint long lines of even width. They are especially useful with the convention of painting which uses a number of washes of differing colour and tonality held together and detailed with linear painting and are to be found in use in the many small potteries producing tin glazed painting of this type particularly in Spain but also in Italy.

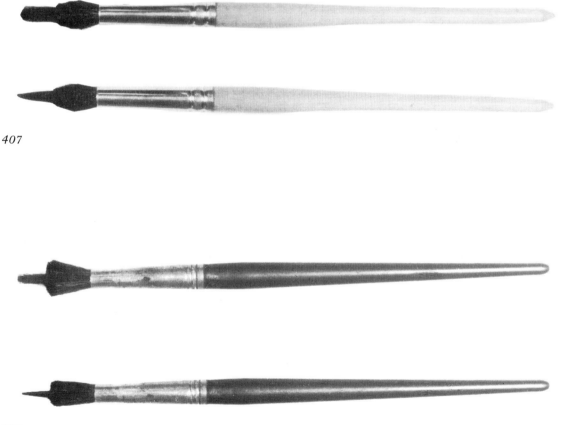

*407*

*408*

All brushes repay care. After use with water-borne materials they should be washed in water. After use with non-waterborne materials they should be cleaned in some suitable solvent, usually pure turpentine, and then be washed with soap in warm water. Strong detergents should be avoided as should excessively hot water. When washed the brush should be shaped to a point gently squeezing out excess moisture between the fingers. They should then be dried horizontally with their ends fully exposed to air. Some oriental brushes have a small silk loop at the top so they can be hang up to dry. Once dry brushes can be stored vertically in jars with their hairs uppermost. Brushes should never be allowed to rest vertically on their hairs as these can be irreversibly bent. In prolonged storage brushes should be protected from moths.

## THE POSSIBLE STAGES AT WHICH PAINTING MAY OCCUR

There are five main stages at which painting may occur: (1) leatherhard clay; (2) dry, unfired clay; (3) biscuit fired clay; (4) unfired glaze; and (5) fired glaze. Very exceptionally painting may be done onto plastic clay. Each of the five stages presents a surface which has different qualities as a ground for painting. The major factor which differs is the porosity of the surface. This porosity or lack of it is fundamental in conditioning the way the various possible materials may be handled as they are painted.

Leatherhard clay is a fairly broad stage but leatherhard clay and fired glaze both offer surfaces which in effect are nonporous as painting grounds. Dry, unfired clay has a fairly ready porosity. Biscuit fired clay, depending on the clay body and the temperature of biscuit firing, may range from having a strong porosity to being completely non-porous. Unfired glaze, depending on various factors, may have either strong or weak porosity — if the underlying biscuit is non-porous then the porosity of the glaze surface will be slight; if the porosity of underlying biscuit is strong then the porosity of the glaze will be strong; glazes with a high plastic clay content have a less strong porosity than glazes low in plastic clays.

Partly because of this variety of painting grounds and partly because of the needs and qualities of the painting materials themselves various media have been developed for use in different contexts.

## THE MATERIALS WHICH MAY BE PAINTED

There are seven groups of materials which may be painted: (1) slips; (2) engobes; (3) colouring oxides; (4) bought prepared colours; (5) glazes; (6) enamels; and (7) lustres.

*Slip* is normally painted onto leatherhard clay. Occasionally slips low in plastic clay, such as porcelain slips may be painted onto dry or even biscuit fired clay but engobes are more usual for this. Slip is painted in its waterbourne state and no medium is normally used.

*Engobes* may be intended for and painted onto leatherhard, dry or biscuit fired clay. On dry or biscuit fired clay the use of a water based medium may assist application.

*Colouring oxides* and *bought prepared colours* may be painted onto leatherhard, dry and biscuit fired clays and unfired glaze surfaces. The material adaptations and variations possible and appropriate to both these groups of materials when painted in different contexts are a complex subject not within the scope of this book. The painting of both these groups of materials on leatherhard clay is possible in simple waterbourne state but on dry and biscuit fired clay and unfired glaze the use of a water based medium is normal. Media are used when water alone inhibits control of the quality of painting intended. In particular, in contexts of porous grounds media reduce the drying suction of the surface and thereby increase the flow of material and the fluency of the action of painting. A variety of water based media can be purchased. Alternatively a medium can be mixed up. Two common alternatives are to add a drop or two of gum, either gum arabic the most common, or gum tragacanth, or several drops of glycerine to the painting mixture. Media have the secondary effect of strengthening and binding the painted material to the surface prior to firing. When the use of a medium is considered in this or other contexts it is worthwhile experimenting with different brands and mixtures as some will have a more appropriate feel than others.

Brief mention should be made here of the industrial practice of painting underglaze colours onto biscuit. The practice is long-standing and arose from the context of a production based on a high biscuit firing and a lower glaze firing. The underglaze painting was fired on in a low temperature 'hardening-on' firing between the biscuit and glaze firings. When it originated the practice allowed a greater colour range, as early colours were not very refractory, and it saved the colours from the adverse effects of the sulphates and carbonates generated in the biscuit firing. The cost and inconvenience of the additional 'hardening-on' firing is now questioned and much research has been directed towards evolving more refractory colours and evolving media which can be directly glazed over so that in some way the additional firing is avoided. In view of the cost, the traditional three firing sequence for underglaze painting should be seriously questioned in non-industrial contexts.

*Glazes* Of the groups of materials listed, glaze is the one least commonly used for painting. When painted, glazes are used in their normal water-bourne state.

*Enamels* are normally painted onto a fired glaze surface. Exceptionally they are painted onto vitrified clay. The enamels most commonly used are bought ready prepared in powder form but, using low temperature frits, enamels can be made from raw materials. Bought enamels are intended for industrial use and are pigmented for fairly thin application. It is normal to mix these with an oil based medium. In this form they constitute the most viscous of painting materials. Mixed up enamels, as opposed to bought ones, are often used more thickly and these can be prepared for use by mixing to a thickish glaze-like consistency with water but, equally, they can be mixed with media for thinner application.

Bought *lustres* and precious metals come ready for use in liquid form and thinners are supplied for any slight dilution which may be necessary to improve their flow. Such additions are easy to overdo and should be made with extreme care to less than the whole quantity available.

With all painting materials the concern with media is to give the painting materials the right degree of flow for the material to be applied in the intended context, at the intended thickness, with the greatest convenience. Personal preference based on experience of different media is more important than what is, or may be thought to be, general practice.

Underglaze colours and enamels may now be bought ready mixed in tubes as well as in their normal powder form.

Various materials which may be painted are also available in other forms and these extend their possibilities. Among these forms are underglaze crayons underglaze felt-tips and gold and platinum fibre-tips.

## INITIAL WORK IN PAINTING

There are many factors relevant to the quality of painted decoration — an understanding of the effect of the relative thickness of painted materials and of the grounds on which they are painted, of content, of placing, of colour and so on — but a fundamental factor is the painter's understanding of the qualities of brush he is using. Brushes do not make marks, they respond to direction. Inhibited painting is as stiff and dead as in any context and painting in ceramics is necessarily more direct than painting in many other contexts — reworked painting in ceramics becomes tonally confused and messy. Speed, however, brings with it the possible pitfalls of slickness but providing these are avoided most painting of quality in ceramics demonstrates the confidence of fluent unhurried directness — this is no less true whether the painting involves the use of a soft, floppy brush to paint broad, uneven areas of colour or a fine, springy brush to paint light, delicate marks in intricate configurations. The factors that can lead to this fluency are clarity of intention and experience with brushes and the materials and contexts of decoration.

Both clarity of intention and experience with brushes can be developed on paper. Work on paper may, of course, clarify intentions with any decoration process but there is a direct link which makes such work important with painted decoration. Experience of touch and timing in the use of brushes can be developed invaluably in work on paper but, valuable as it can be, the importance of such work must be kept in perspective for it is no substitute for the different feel of pottery materials or surfaces nor does it develop ceramic experience. An ink-filled brush, for example, will continue to make marks on paper long after it would have ceased to make marks in many porous ceramic contexts and, as further example, the colour and tonal effects of overlapped marks on a porous ceramic ground, which dries marks quickly, has no parallel on paper where painted marks stay wet for minutes. It is important therefore for beginners to balance the experience of work on paper with the experience of completing work in ceramic contexts.

409

410

*409* Working on curved surfaces is a very different experience from flat paper or tiles and rather than failing to achieve over elaborate intentions simply drawn shapes and lines can be a more useful start.

From the very beginning, the results of differing actions, brushes, materials and grounds should be observed so that the maximum information is assimilated as quickly as possible. It is vital that the experiments are fired so that the effects of different thicknesses of oxides and other pigments and materials begin to be appreciated.

Both the feel and the inherent visual quality of different grounds should be explored and compared.

*410* Here leatherhard clay is being painted with underglaze colours. Having no porosity the ground has a quite different feel to painting onto unfired glaze and the surface is quite different to biscuit, porous or non-porous. The unevenness within each mark which to some extent is inevitable can be used as a quality of directness providing the overall tonality of the painting is controlled

*411* Diluted colour can be spread into areas with broad soft brushes

*412* Thicker colour can be superimposed on pale areas to give darker tones of the same colour or, of course, contrasting colour may be applied

411

412

*413 and 414* Here an unfired tin glaze is being painted with oxide blends. The whiteness of a fired tin glaze ground is an important quality in itself but it can also serve to give brightness to thinly washed colour applied in large areas. With appropriately blended mixtures and with broad soft brushes this can be done with a good control of tonality but, as with all brushed areas, the colour should be applied so that the marks of application form part of the whole content

*415* With all materials and all brushes the repetition of marks, simple or complex, is a useful discipline. But it is a discipline which should not be too rigorous in its concern for initial accuracy. Too much emphasis on accuracy will only lead to dead, mechanical repetition. The emphasis should be on repetition of movement. When a movement can be repeated with fluency then the repetition of the mark will inevitably follow. Painting is not printing and an aspect of the quality of painting in which there is repetition whether that is from object to object or of units within an object, is the variation of detail within the repetition

413
414

415

*416 and 417* To make the marks for which they were intended some brushes have to be used quite particularly. Here a long haired liner is being used by drawing it along its own path with much of its length touching the surface

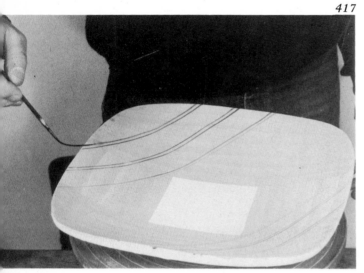

417

*418 and 419* An aspect which certainly deserves initial experiment is that of composite marks and different ways of painting areas. Different materials, grounds and procedures will determine whether or not the individual marks which form composite marks and areas show and the fact that in some contexts they do show means only that this is an additional aspect to be considered and used in the overall quality and content of painted work. 418 is a composite mark comprising four strokes painted with an oxide blend on tin glaze. 419 shows a small area built up of cross hatched marks painted with an underglaze colour onto biscuit fired clay and glazed, without a hardening on firing, with an earthenware clear glaze

418

419

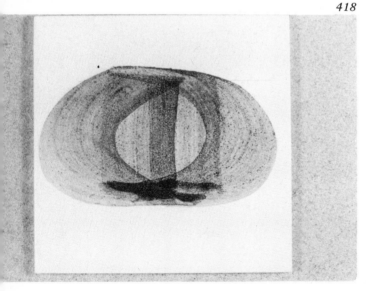

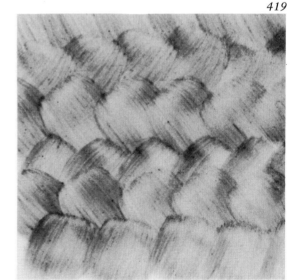

Whether intentions are precise or carefree, figurative or geometric it is very easy, when beginning to experiment with painted decoration, to become overconcerned with individual marks or groups of marks. It is important to remember that the spaces between and around marks are at least as important as the marks themselves. This of course is true of all decoration not just painted work, but it is particularly relevant to mention it in this context because painting is so direct a mark-making process that the necessary concentration on parts of the work can too easily obscure consideration of the relationship of the parts to the whole. It can be particularly instructive with painted work to consider the role of the reserved areas — the unpainted areas — to the overall work.

## UNGLAZED PAINTING

*420* Some types of Peruvian pottery, most notably Nazca pottery, show an extraordinarily wide colour range of slip usually painted in controlled areas of flat colour, often in more complex shapes than in this example. The use of flat colour and strong pattern on three dimensional form makes Nazca pottery distinctive and worthy of more attention than it has received. Nazca, Peru. 5 in. (12.5 cm) diameter *Horniman Museum, London*

*420*

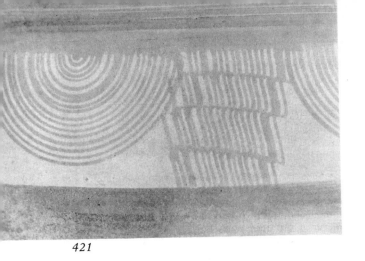

421

421 and 422 These two examples show the use of
a type of multiple brush developed by the
Greeks and much used on Geometric period
pots for the painting of concentric circles and
semi-circles. 421 shows a relatively rare freehand use of such a brush in a vertical wavy
movement and 422 shows the conventional
concentric use. The whole detail in 421 is
slightly under 4 in. (10 cm) wide and is from
the shoulder of a pot. Greek. Eight century BC.
*Archaeological Museum, Granada, Spain.* The
small bottle, 422, is eighth century BC. Greek
from Cyprus. 3½ in. (9 cm) high

422

*423*

423 The Greek 'red-figure' style is a good example
of reserved painting — the dark background not
the pale figure is the painted shape. The painting
of the linear details within the reserved figure
shape is fluent and confident and the line quality
is fine and controlled. The work indicates the
development of a very particular brush, fine
and resilient and with sufficient body to hold
enough material for long lines. The upper outline of the hair is scratched through the dark
slip. The separated slip used in Classical Greece
for painted decoration represents the highest
technical development of such slips, the use of
which was continued, though not for painting,
by the Romans. The roundel is 3½ in. (9 cm) in
diameter and is from the centre of a shallow
drinking cup. Greek 500-480 BC. *Agora
Museum, Athens, Greece*

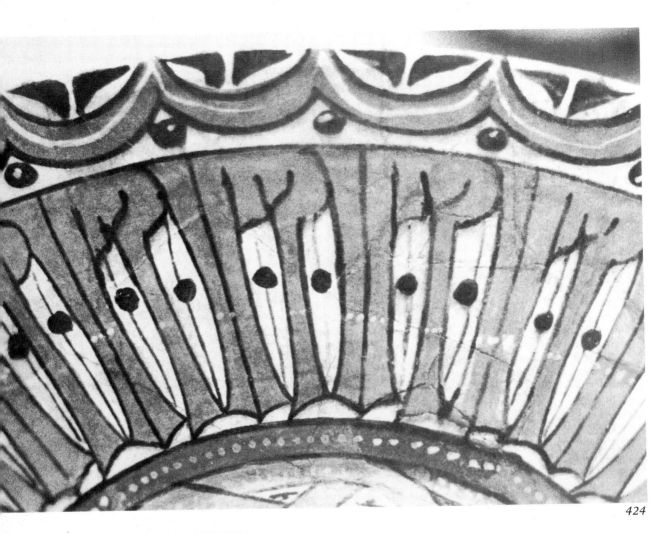

## UNDERGLAZE PAINTING

*424* Unless it is to be patchily uneven or unless each area is to be overpainted with a number of layers the application of slip as underglaze painting has to be very even and the slip itself needs a degree of opacity. The opacity of slip can be helped both by the addition of a staining material in quite high proportions — up to and even above 25% depending on the actual oxides — and by so balancing the consistency of the slip with the state of the clay ground that an evenly brushed application is facilitated. Whatever may have been their actual procedure the potters of Southern Russia and Afghanistan, in the eastern regions of the spread of Islam between the ninth and eleventh centuries AD developed slip painting which, as these details shows, demonstrates considerable material control. At least one of the slips, Armenian bole, which gives a colour range varying between reddy brown and tomato red, is a naturally occurring earth. This is always applied in a visibly thicker layer than the other slips. The range of colours in the other slips suggests a well developed understanding of the colour effect of different oxides and the easy, sometimes almost gestural, application could only be possible with carefully compounded mixtures. The body clay of this type of work ranges from buff to brown and is slipped with a white slip. The translucent glaze which covers the painting is very thinly applied. This detail is from a shallow bowl from Samarkand, now in Southern Russia. About tenth century AD. *Victoria and Albert Museum, London*

425 This detail of a Byzantine bowl demonstrates both the soft translucency and the harsh opacity which oxides and oxide mixtures used under a glaze can give. The painting was done on a white slip covering a dark brown clay. The glaze, though not very thin, has not encouraged the pigments to flow. This simple bold use of two colours of differing quality is typical of much peasant pottery which made direct and effective use of a small range of available materials. Diameter 10 in. (26 cm) approximately. Byzantine. Eleventh century AD. *Agora Museum, Athens, Greece*

425

426 The work of the potters of Isnik in Turkey is in complete contrast to the previous example. Here a range of very stable underglaze colours was developed and used on vessels and on the tiles with which most fine buildings were clad. Isnik potters made some use of Armenian bole but much of the rest of their delicate colour range could, on the basis of modern knowledge and practice, only have been derived not simply from blends but from calcined blends. They covered the sandy buff clays they used for tiles and the smooth lighter buff clays they mainly used for vessels with a slip of brilliant whiteness and their thin glaze is invariably craze free. This detail is from one of four immense tiles each measuring about 45 in. (114 cm) by 15 in. (38 cm) flanking the entrance to the Sunnet Odasi in Topkapi Palace in Istanbul. The painting is in shades of blue and turquoise and is as remarkable for its control of tonality as for its embroidery-like intricacy. *Topkapi Sarayi Museum, Istanbul, Turkey*

426

**427** This detail is from a panel of tiles which is adjacent to the previous example. Here the same degree of control is used to quite different effect. The brilliant whiteness of the flowers reserved as unpainted slip is the strongest element of the work but that same whiteness gives a brightness to the painted colours of the leaves and background. Colour technology and skill in painting combine to give tonal control. Even the inevitably evident marks of the painted background area are used to complement the crisp but fluent painting of the plants. *Topkapi Sarayi Museum, Istanbul, Turkey*

**428** The translucency of thinly painted underglaze colours on a light firing body is used to very distinct effect in this example. With the exception of the figurative details which are mostly defined with fine linear painting the work is composed of parallel painted strokes of differing and controlled tonality and colour. Rather than hiding the strokes of application these are used as a strong visual element in the work and help to unify the figure and its geometrically treated context. Painted by Susie Cooper for A E Gray & Co, Hanley, Staffordshire. English, 1925 to 1930. *Victoria and Albert Museum, London*

427

428

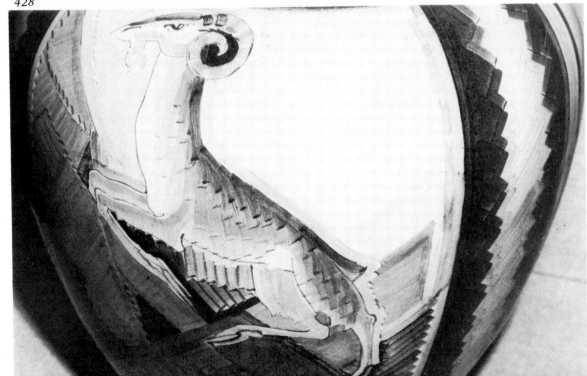

*429*

*429* One of the classic types of underglaze is painting on a porcelain body with cobalt based pigment. Over several centuries this type was produced in countless millions in China both for domestic use and for export. The painting is variable, depending partly on the date and the intended market, but whether the painting is fairly direct, as in this example, or shows a more careful use of graded tones the control of material is consistently admirable. This particular example shows the use of two tones of pigment the first being applied in broad washes and the second as a darker toned linear painting which details and outlines the wash. In this as in other contexts, the dilution of pigment to produce pale washes is more easily done by adding non-pigmenting material to the mixture than by water alone. The softness of Chinese blue is due to the use of impure cobalt ores as a basis for pigment. Modern pure cobalt oxide can be modified to soften its rather harsh blue by adding small proportions of iron and manganese oxides. China. Late Ming Dynasty. *Topkapi Sarayi Museum, Istanbul*

430

**430 and 431** In these two views of the same pot also the directness of the painting is as strong an element in the work as the figurative content. More than in the previous example the quality of painting is strongly related to the calligraphic traditions of its country of origin, China. While the quality of mark in the painting of the leaves is exuberant and accomplished the figurative intentions are not submerged in calligraphic purism for the leaves are detailed with sgrafitto through the painted marks and the painting of the peony flowers and the butterfly is handled quite differently though just as gesturally. The pot is fairly thickly slipped with a whitish slip and the underglaze painting has a consistent opacity. The painted material is probably either an ochreous earth with added pigment or a pigment with added clay. The glaze is very thinly applied. Tzu chou type. China. Sung Dynasty. *Victoria and Albert Museum, London*

431

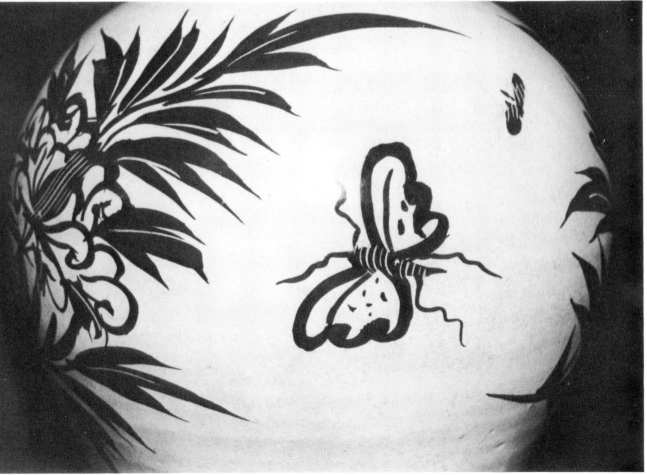

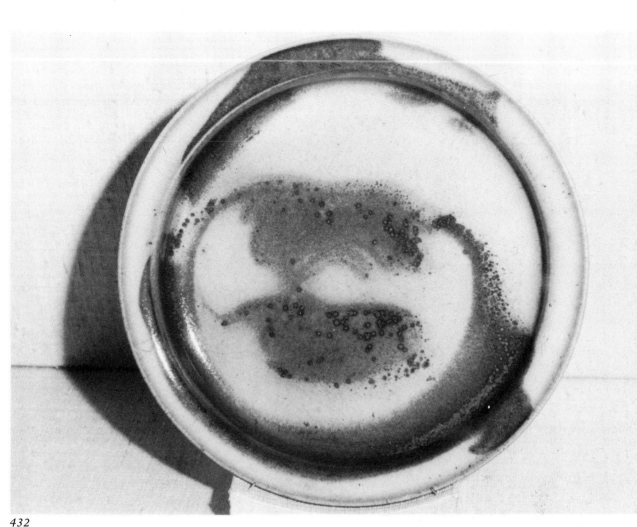

432

432 The paler areas of this plate are a pale opalescent blue glaze, known as a chün glaze, ranging almost to white and the darker painted marks are a pinky red colour derived from reduced copper. It is most likely that the copper pigment was applied directly onto the clay which is how this example can be justified for inclusion in a section on underglaze painting. Other examples do exist where a copper pigment or pigment and glaze mix has been freely painted over a chun glaze and such examples coupled with the peculiar depths of chun glazes and the vicissitudes of stoneware firings cast a little doubt on the definite classification of this example as underglaze. But certainly similar qualities can be achieved by the underglaze application which is suggested. As a contrast the example is an interesting one to include in underglaze painting as the difference of its quality serves both to extend the possible range of underglaze work and to define the conventions. With the aim that the colour shows clearly and is undisturbed by the glaze the common convention of underglaze work is to use stable colour under a clear thin glaze. To do the opposite, to use reactive colours under a semi-opaque glaze, clearly extends the range of possible qualities which, appropriately used, have different and interesting possibilities. Sung Dynasty, China. *Victoria and Albert Museum, London*

## OVERGLAZE PAINTING

*433* In general in overglaze painting stable colours are painted onto a stable light firing or white glaze while still in the unfired state. This example, of a classic much revered type, which is one of the exceptions to this general rule, shows an iron bearing pigment painted over a dark tenmoku glaze. The definition of the painting is slightly blurred by the reactive combination of the painted pigment and the glaze. The glaze ranges from a dark olive green where it is thin on the lower parts to a dark browny black where it is thicker on the upper parts and has a deep sheen rather than a bright shine. The pigment of broken, variable, rusty and golden colours has the tonal difference to be clear but does not form a strong contrast with the glaze. The control and definition of the form is softened by the casual unevenness of the glazing and the easy fluency of the relaxed though structured painting. The handling of the pot and its materials give the work a quiet sombreness which distinguishes it from the hard, reflective glossiness of much which emulates the type. China. 7¾ in. (20 cm) high. Sung Dynasty. *Private collection, England*

*434* This peasant work makes up what it may lack of classic control in its uninhibited execution. The iron based pigment is both stable and opaque on the thin glaze over which it is painted. The uneven tonality between the darker upper part and the light lower part is due to uneven atmosphere in the firing, the upper part being reduced and the lower oxidised. 15 in. (38 cm) high. South east Asia. *Private collection, England*

**435** Painting over tin glaze is probably the commonest historical example of an easily identifiable type of overglaze painting. Tin glaze is a term which sounds more specific than it is and, in fact, any glaze may be made opaque by the addition of tin oxide. Tin oxide acts as an opacifier because it is a fine, refractory oxide which remains suspended in the molten glaze taking little or no part in the glaze solution. Historically tin glazes have been made with glazes fluxed by lead alone, fluxed by lead and other fluxes and by leadless fluxes, and with glazes fluxing across a wide range of temperature, though usually within the earthenware temperature range. Though it is always true that the colour resulting from any oxide blend is governed partly by its context of use this is especially important to stress with pigments used on tin glaze, because of the specific sounding term. The only thing a group of different tin glazes may have in common is the opacifying effect of tin oxide and this difference will be clearly shown in the colour response of different oxide blends applied to each. Historically the handling of painting on tin glazes ranges from crudely direct, to fluently repetitive, to painstakingly controlled. This example of a 'blue dash' charger painted with tulips shows fairly direct handling being mainly composed of broadly brushed marks of paler colour detailed with a dark linear outline. The term 'blue dash' refers to the blue dabs regularly painted round the edge of plates and bowls. Last quarter of the seventeenth century. English. *Victoria and Albert Museum, London*

435

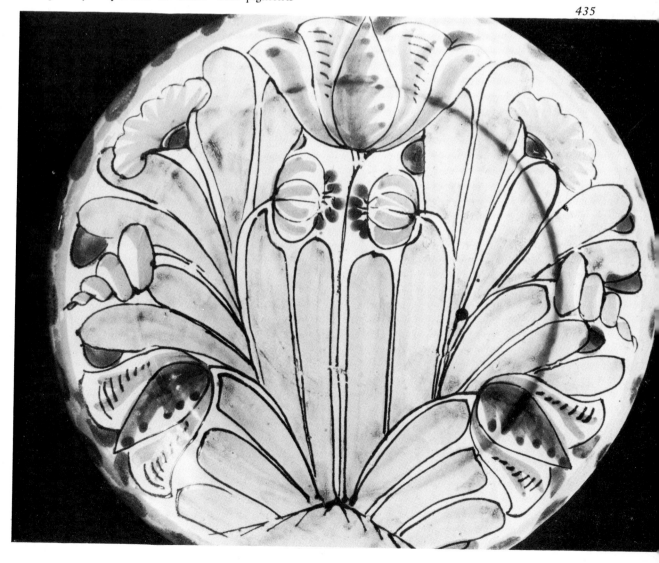

**436** This interesting detail shows an Italian Majolica painter at work on a dish. How accurate the scene is as an historical document is open to question: the way the painter's fingers are supporting the edge of the dish seems rather unlikely in view of the fragile nature of unfired glaze and it seems odd that the patrons for whose portraits the unpainted roundel waits should be watching the painting of the edge rather than sitting for the painting of their portraits. The six saucers of colour each supplied with two brushes and the way the painter is holding his brush are however interesting and more convincing details. Painted by Master Jacopo. First quarter of sixteenth century. Diameter of plate just over 9 in. (23 cm). Cafaggiolo, Italy. *Victoria and Albert Museum, London*

**437** This earlier Italian painted plate shows one possibility which was not developed in later work. The process is one of scratching rather than painting. If pigment painted overglaze is lightly scratched the pigment may be removed without removing the glaze. When this process is used on tin glaze painting it is possible to scratch to make white lines of re-exposed glaze within painted marks and areas. Such scratches are evident in the large leaves in front of and behind the painted hare. Florence, Italy. Mid fifteenth century. *Victoria and Albert Museum, London*

*436*

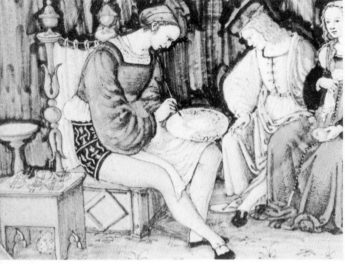

*437*

## ON GLAZE PAINTING WITH ENAMELS

Two rather different possibilities exist with this type of painting and are based in different qualities of enamel. One is of closely painted, detailed work and is evident both in European and Oriental work. The other is of more freely applied enamels of less detail and greater depth and is evident almost solely in Oriental work.

*438* This detail from a small dish of a painted quail well illustrates the degree of fine detail which is possible with enamel painting. The control is not solely of line quality and fineness but also of the graded tonality of small areas of colour. Though immensely controlled the painting retains a freshness in its evident speed of execution. Chinese. Ching Dynasty. About 1730-1740. *Victoria and Albert Museum, London*

*439* This roundel from the centre of a large dish shows a much broader painting of enamel. Though the work is held together with thin lines of thinly painted, densely pigmented enamel the glaze-like depth of the areas of coloured enamel is the dominant quality. Chinese. Ching Dynasty, reign of emperor Kang Hsi 1662-1722. *Victoria and Albert Museum, London*

438

439

*440* This example is of enamel painting applied directly onto the surface of unglazed, vitrified porcelain. The contrast between this and the material qualities evident in figure 438 serves to underline the very diverse possibilities of enamels. The rich fluid enamels have flowed into the incising to emphasise it but the colour and tonal contrasts of the freely painted areas of enamel are far stronger and these, not the incising, form the primary impact of the work. Kang Hsi period, China. *Victoria and Albert Museum, London*

*440*

## ON GLAZE PAINTING WITH LUSTRES

The quality of lustres, their sheen and reflectiveness, makes it difficult to do complete justice to lustre painting in black and white photography — the choice has to be made between allowing the lustre to be reflective, which tends to produce confusing results, or photographing it so that the lustrousness is not evident but that the form of the painting is clear. In the two examples which follow the second choice was made.

441

*441* The close texture and even distribution of the fine linear painting of the lustre give this dish a shimmering quality when the light plays on the lustre. The lustre on the small coils of applied relief adds reflectiveness. The simpler handling of the armorial centre is emphasised by the tracery which surrounds it. The brushwork of this tracery is typically Hispano-Moresque in its freedom, lightness and complexity. Spain. Mid-Fifteenth century. *Victoria and Albert Museum, London*

*442* The lustre on this tile delineates the hare and foliage by reserving it on the white glaze so the figure of the decoration stays constant being seen against a background which alternately is coloured, iridescent and reflective as the viewpoint changes. But the work has two levels for while the hare and foliage are clear the background is broken lustre, not solid, and the hare is dotted with lustre, not plain. This secondary level gives the work a more vibrant, light sensitive surface using the inherent quality of lustre to good effect. Persian. Fourteenth or Fifteenth Century. *Victoria and Albert Museum, London*

*442*

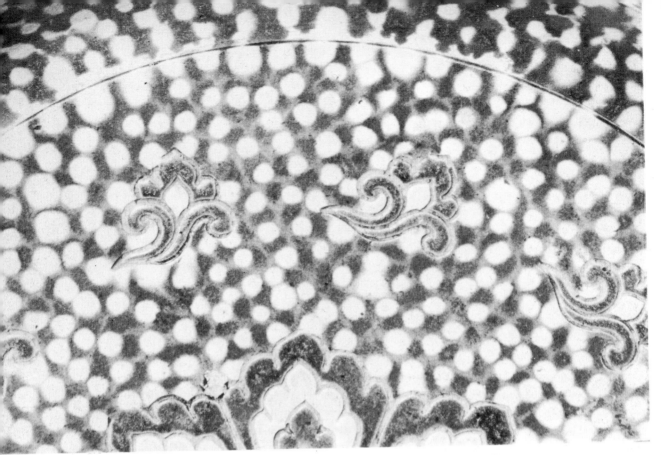

443

## GLAZE PAINTING

Glaze is neither a very convenient nor a frequently used material for painting. Glaze painting does nevertheless offer particular qualities especially when done with rich, fairly fluid glazes. Historically it is often difficult to say with certainty if particular examples have been painted or if the glaze was applied in some other way. In the two examples which follow painting certainly seems to have been the most likely process but whether this was the case or not is not vital, as painting is certainly the obvious way by which to achieve similar qualities.

*443* The obvious alternative here to painting is glaze trailing but regular dotting can also be done with a brush with both speed and control and the infill of glaze between the white and coloured dots has an evenness and thinness which suggests painting rather than trailing. The background of dots has a sparkle which is the result of an appropriate combination of material and means of application. Chinese. Tang Dynasty. *Victoria and Albert Museum, London*

*444* The fluid glazes of this example, especially the dark glaze, have run quite considerably but despite this movement the original areas of glaze application are clear. Sponging can be used to apply similar sized areas of pigment but it does not leave a thick enough layer to be a useful means of glaze application. The areas are too big to have been trailed and too intricate and controlled to have been poured. Application by brush seems therefore to be the only possible alternative but whether the areas were built up by dabbing or applied in a single action from some large soft brush cannot be determined. The large-scale mottling of this example, related to, but different in scale from, the previous one, shows a similarly appropriate combination of process and material. Chinese. Tang Dynasty. *Victoria and Albert Museum, London*

# Some further aspects of painting

## BANDING

Banding is an aspect of painting which can be applied to any round form. In conventional practice for the past three millenia it has been frequently used inside plates and dishes and on the outside of pots to define and contain areas of painted work.

Banding is done by centering a form on a banding wheel or other suitable turntable and applying colour to the revolving pot. Two distinct processes of banding exist: line banding in which the brush is held quite static and the width of band produced is therefore directly related to the size of brush; and wash banding in which the brush is moved, as the pot revolves, producing a wider line than the brush itself or an area.

A good banding wheel should have a strong momentum so that even at a slow speed it will continue to revolve steadily once it is set in motion. This momentum, while slightly dependent on the bearing and on good lubrication of this, is achieved mainly by the weight of the revolving head. Unfortunately many of the cheaper banding wheels now sold have lightweight aluminium alloy heads and, though they are adequate as turntables for handbuilt work, are useless for banding. Older patterns of floor standing banding wheels had heads with a long narrow shank which allowed the momentum of the head to be maintained by the free hand.

Banding may be done underglaze, on leather-hard or dry clay (industrially it may be done on biscuit), overglaze, on unfired glaze, and on-glaze, on fired glaze. The most even effects can be achieved by working on the least porous surfaces (leatherhard clay and fired glaze) as these offer the greatest opportunity for spreading the colour evenly and, to some extent, allow bands to be worked over until the intended evenness is achieved. Evenness of colour may not, however, be an aim and banding which shows some gradation of tonality and a directness of application may well be thought to have a preferable quality.

It is wrong to think of banding as being a mechanical process of painting. Touch is as important as in any type of painting and a confident, direct approach is demanded when working on dry clay for underglaze banding or on dry glaze. A line touched in a single revolution or an area banded in a steady spiral can have a freshness of quality which any painted mark can possess, and an over-worked band is like any other overworked mark in its deadness of quality.

As well as its use to contain other painted work banding can, of course, be used alone.

When working on leatherhard clay or on fired glaze brushes can be removed from the surface and replenished and the marks made by this can be eliminated in reworking the band. On a porous surface any band will show the history of its making so it is usual to use a brush which will hold sufficient colour to complete the banding without the need to replenish it.

445 Here a broad band is being washbanded onto a bone dry dish with an oxide mixture. Well-filled mop brushes are ideal for this type of work and, providing the painting mixture has the right fluidity, are not sucked dry by the porous surface even when considerable areas are banded. For the initial gentle touch and the first revolution the brush is held static and at a low angle

446 As soon as the first revolution is complete the brush begins a steady movement towards the centre. The steadier this movement is and the steadier the rotation of the banding wheel the more even will be the spacings of the spiral

447 Where a large area of banding is done on a porous surface, as here, the need for directness is stressed by the fact that the initial parts of the banding are dry before the area is complete. When the banding is complete the brush is held steady for one revolution to complete a circle and then gently raised from the surface. If the entire surface of a plate or bowl is to be banded a less obvious mark is left at the centre if the banding starts at the centre and finishes at the outer edge

448 Lines of stronger tone can be banded within broader lines or areas of wash banding. Liners used to produce narrow bands cannot have a body to contain colour so these are usually

445

446

448

447

made of quite long straight hairs their length, rather than any bulk, forming the reservoir. Clean, narrow, even bands are most easily produced if banding is completed in one revolution with a minimum of overlap. This is best achieved if the initial touch and the lift-off are gentle but also quick and sure and, obviously, if the touching pressure is even and the hand rock steady. A good lining brush is also essential if evenness of width is an aim

*449*

*450*

## HAKEME

The term *hakeme* is used both to describe an early Korean type of pottery and the process whereby slip was applied to this pottery. In hakeme a coating of slip is brushed over the surface of a pot and no attempt is made to eliminate the uneven thicknesses left by the brush. A light slip is generally used over a darker body and the slip is applied with a brush with fairly coarse, stiff bristles. The brush simultaneously applies the slip and combs it, very finely. When finished the thin parts of the slip virtually vanish and reveal the body clay and only the thicker slip shows a strong tonality. Finished pieces clearly reveal the paths taken by the brush.

While stoneware is the original and conventional context for the process the dissolving of thin slip into a glaze, on which the process largely relies, occurs just as readily in earthenware. And while a light slip over a darker body is usual the reverse can work just as well technically. Hakeme work is usually glazed but at stoneware temperatures when clay and slip are vitrified the process can, with a controlled application of tested materials, work effectively without glaze.

The term 'hakeme' is not generally used to describe single brushstrokes or groups of brushstrokes painted with slip and strictly is limited to brushpainted coatings of slip over the whole or large parts of the surfaces of a pot in which the brushstrokes of application are evident.

In many contexts the difficulties of applying an even coating of slip by brush are seen as a problem. Hakeme has the appeal that it accepts and exploits this. The process is a simple and direct one and it has qualities and possibilities which could be thoughtfully and more widely exploited.

*449* To apply sufficient slip fairly large brushes are used for hakeme. The brush is well filled with thickish slip. Hakeme can be done on newly-made pots but some degree of hardness can facilitate the application of a sufficiently thick layer of slip. The pot here is at an early leatherhard stage

*450* Replenishing the brush with slip as often as necessary the whole surface is covered. If work proceeds from top to bottom any runs of excess slip are removed as they occur — though in this context the odd splash or run may well be thought appropriate

451 The slight leatherhardness of the clay has taken the wet shine off the slip on the shoulder but it is far from touch dry. The initial layer of slip is still instantly affected by further use of the brush. At this stage the pot readily retains additional slip and some care should be taken not to build up too thick a coating which would be opaque. This danger is greatest with softer brushes. At this stage a stiff brush as well as applying slip behaves like a fine comb as the trailing bristles leave a finely ridged layer of thick and thin slip. The relative hardness of the clay when worked on with stiff bristles gives the process its clearest definition

452 The clay in this example is softer than that of the previous one — within the range of plastic rather than at the soft end of leatherhard. At this stage the body clay has virtually no drying effect on the slip so the brush should be frequently and fully reloaded with slip to ensure that a sufficiently thick layer is built up for the thicker slip to remain opaque

453 The major difference with softer clay is that because the clay has no immediate stiffening effect on the slip the entire surface stays wet and workable for much longer than with leather-hard clay and a stiffish brush seems to comb through the slip more positively. It does in fact do this but only by actually brushing into the soft clay — which could not occur with the stiffer clay of the previous example. If work at this stage is prolonged what may seem to be a positive configuration of brushmarks can be disappointingly ill-defined after firing because the brush has worked up sufficient slip from the body to diminish the tonal contrast of the slip. The temptation to overwork the slip layer should always be avoided but more carefully so with soft clay

451

452

453

454

*454* As the body clay and the slip vitrify the darker body colour burns through the thinnest slip clearly revealing the movement of the brush

*455* This detail is of the neck of a bottle by Bernard Leach. In this example the use of hakeme subtly but positively contributes to the softening of both the normally even tonality of a clay body and to the regularity associated with well defined thrown forms. The marks and splashes of the brushed slip are all evident. The softness of this example is in contrast to the harder qualities shown in figure 454. The possibilities of hakeme range both between and beyond the qualities evident in that contrast. *Craft Study Centre, Bath, England*

*455*

214

## PAINTING WITH CASTING SLIP

Casting slips, as they have a far lower water content than ordinary slips, may be applied by brushing, with no fear of flaking or peeling, to much drier clay than can ordinary slips. With some bodies they can be applied when the clay is dry.

For a smooth, even layer brushed engobe is arguably a better alternative but if water and casting slip are alternately brushed onto the dry clay surface an adequately even layer can be built up. Alternate brushings with water are necessary to minimise the tendency of the viscous slip to gather texturally on the clay surface.

A more interesting possibility utilises the viscous nature of casting slips and is in the creation and emphasis of textured surfaces with brushed slip. The clay state on which this work is possible is from mid leatherhard through to dry. If the clay surface is not smooth the slip will pick up on the high points of the surface in a single application and further applications are only necessary to deepen and emphasise the texture of the first layer. If however the clay surface is smooth several applications may be necessary for the characteristic type of surface to develop.

456 On smooth surfaces the first application should be made with a brush which is not too fully loaded with casting slip

457 An interval of a few minutes to let the previous application harden should be allowed between each application of slip. Deep, distinct texture can be built up very quickly with as few as two or three brushings. The process should not however be thought of as only permitting the creation of a single particular texture. The way the barely perceptible marks of throwing have been emphasised by gentle vertical brushing in the lower right hand corner of the painted area should be noted. By working on a surface before slip is applied, by scraping areas between applications, by controlled directional brushing and by gradually building up the surface, diversity and subtle gradation of relief are entirely possible.

456

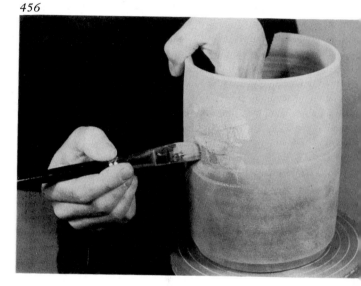

457

## PAINTING WITH GLAZE

Some sort of stroke making is the normal action by which materials are applied by brush but if this is done with glaze it tends both to apply the glaze very unevenly, from thick to too thin, and, if thin areas are brushed over, to remove the glaze already applied. The action used is therefore one of dabbing.

Painting with glaze has some possibilities if treated fairly broadly but is relatively unusual as a process of decoration by itself, but see figures 443, 444.

*458* As the brush is dabbed up and down it is moved across the biscuit clay surface building up intended areas to a controlled thickness. Full-formed, soft brushes perform this action best. The glaze should be of a consistency which will flow readily from the brush as it is dabbed but will not drip

*459* It is not easy with glaze painting to make areas of different glazes meet without any overlap but for the qualities of glaze painting small overlaps probably do not matter. Here a large mop brush is being used to fill in spaces between areas of contrasting coloured glazes with a clear glaze. Such brushes are best when painted glaze has to be applied to large areas. The apparent unevenness which dabbing creates can be somewhat alarming but providing the actual layer of glaze applied is even the uneven surface has little effect even on the tonality of coloured translucent glazes

*458*

*459*

## THE APPLICATION OF COLOUR BY SPONGING

Although the action of this process is closer to stamp printing than to painting the absence in this book of any description of the various mechanised printing processes and the frequent combination in historical examples of sponged and painted marks makes this a convenient context for a mention of sponging.

There are two rather separate aspects of sponging: on the one hand open textured natural sponges may be used for the application of colour in textured areas; alternatively cut sponge of close texture may be used to print repeated units of flatter areas of colour. In both these instances it is usual to add gum to the waterborne pigment and, in both, colour may be applied either as underglaze or on top of unfired glaze.

The rather more open textured use of sponge applied colour is found fairly commonly in the representation of trees and foliage in seventeenth and eighteenth century work on tin glaze.

The use of cut sponge printing, neither shown extensively in demonstration nor in examples, deserves some mention as an aspect of nonmechanised printing. In the nineteenth and early twentieth centuries it was in wide industrial use as a more variable printing possibility than the engraved printing of underglaze. Suppliers, as late as the 1930s, offered both an immense range of cut sponge motifs and a sponge cutting service. The material used was a finely textured quality of root sponge which allowed fine, intricate sponge stamps to be cut and gave flat colour. Such cut sponges were used exclusively with underglaze colours for application to biscuit. The possibilities of cut sponge stamping were extended by the even more intricate and fine possibilities of india rubber and various rubber composition stamps. These permitted the use of overglaze colours such as gold as well as underglaze colours. Colours used with rubber stamps were mixed with a viscous stamping medium. The present extensive use in industry of offset printing onto curved forms with flexible pads may be seen as a sophisticated development from these hand applied rubber stamps.

460 If an evenness of texture and tonality is intended in using pieces of natural sponge to print textured areas of colour then care must be taken to duplicate the degree of light pressure required and neither to overload the sponge nor to have too fluid a colour mix

461 Slightly greater pressure or more watery, pigment will result in denser, less broken areas of colour

462 Cut synthetic foam rubber, in use here, has obvious possibilities for fairly bold simple work but lacks the dense resilience which would permit the cutting of more intricate shapes. Anyone interested in working more intricately with stamps should, in the absence of a fine quality of natural root sponge, experiment with different qualities of synthetic sponge rubber to find a type which combines the right degree of porosity with a very close and resilient texture. Alternatively, or additionally, experiment with stamps cut from more rigid rubber offers related possibilities

460
461

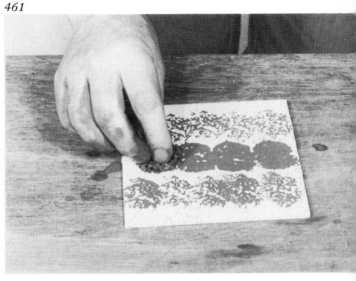

462

463 Sponging here is used more subtly than in the following example to build up different areas of various shapes. The diminished tonality of the headgerows and trees in the background is very controlled. English. Eighteenth century. *Victoria and Albert Museum, London*

464 In this early eighteenth century tin glazed painted commemorative portrait of Queen Anne overlapped sponged marks of very even tonality are used to represent foliage. English. *Victoria and Albert Museum, London*

463

464

# Ground laying

It is extremely difficult in the painting of areas of colour to eliminate brushmarks. The process of groundlaying was devised to overcome this problem. Its particular possibility in its traditional industrial context is the production of areas of even colour on flat and curved surfaces. With the advances that have been made in printing processes groundlaying has been largely superceded and, as it is a labour intensive process, it is now rare though it does remain a relevant process for the application of flat areas of colour to surfaces which are too curved to be easily printed.

Groundlaying oil, mainly consisting of fat oil, linseed oil and spirit of turpentine, can be bought from most suppliers. It is a very viscous mixture and in use is thinned with an equal part or more of spirits of turpentine.

Before any glazed surface is groundlaid it must be thoroughly cleaned of dust and fingermarks. This must be done with a non-fluffy rag to eliminate the creation of further dust and with a cleaner such as methylated spirits which will remove the grease of finger marks.

465 The thinned groundlaying oil is then dabbed evenly over a manageable part of the intended area using a clean, flat, soft brush

465

466

467

468

*466, 467 and 468* The oil is then brushed out evenly over the surface. As in these three illustrations the brushing is done in short gentle strokes — the brush glides onto the surface, moves along it and glides off. The action must be a gentle one spreading and evening out the dabs and is repeated over every part of the area several times, criss-cross fashion.

Adjacent areas are then dabbed with oil and this is brushed out until the entire area is covered. As the thinned oil has a tendency to become tacky quickly, only small areas at a time should be dabbed with oil. When brushing out is complete the surface should be held to the light so that any 'holidays' — small areas devoid of oil — can be seen and touched in. The brushed oil is so pale in colour that bare patches are difficult to see except against the light.

The next action is the bossing of the brushed oil. For this a boss of silk is needed and this should be made in advance.

*469* Groundlaying bosses consist of a round disc of stiffish card which acts as backing for a pad of cotton wool about ¾ in. (2 cm) thick. Finely woven silk is stretched round this pad and tied at the back with silk or, alternatively, it may be taped

An interval of time between the application and the bossing of the oil is always necessary for the

469

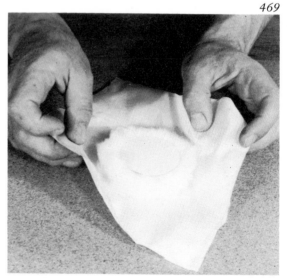

oil must dry to the right degree of tackiness before it can be effectively bossed. Some experience is needed to judge the right moment for bossing and the inexperienced should have trial pieces to accompany initial work. The test is to hold the trial piece near to the ear and to lightly touch the oiled surface with a finger tip. If the oil is noticeably soft and sticky it is not ready; if the finger feels a slight tackiness and releases with a pinging sound the oil is ready; if no tackiness can be felt the oil is too dry.

It is important that the whole process of groundlaying is done in as dust-free an atmosphere as possible but it is especially important that between applying and bossing the oil no dust settles on the surface as dust, hair and fluff clearly mark the finished fired colour. For the same reason clean terylene overalls should be worn and woollen clothes, which harbour dust and generate fluff, should be avoided.

How long the interval is between applying and bossing the oil depends on various factors. The interval may be less than an hour or may be several hours and as the oil has to be bossed at the right moment it is obviously important that the ability to assess the likely interval of time is developed. The initial dilution of the oil is a prime factor in determining how quickly the oil dries — the less viscous the painted dilution the more quickly the oil will dry. Warm rooms with low humidity also accelerate the drying time of the oil. Strong air circulation and draughts should be avoided because they increase the risk of dust.

470 Bossing is at the same time a simple and highly skilled operation. The intention of bossing is to even out any unevennesses in the brushing of the oil and to eliminate brush-strokes. The action is a fairly fast up and down movement steadily working across the whole surface

471 The application of powdered enamel colour is done over a shallow plate or tray. Initially a quantity of colour is spooned onto the centre of the groundlaid area

472 This colour is then spread out with a pad of cotton wool. The lower surface of the cotton wool should be loaded with powdered colour from the plate and is then used to spread out the heap of colour on the oiled surface.

470

471

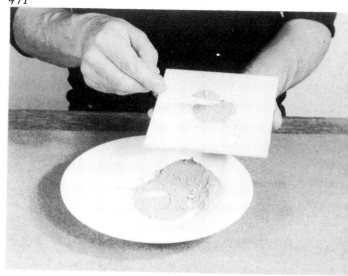

472

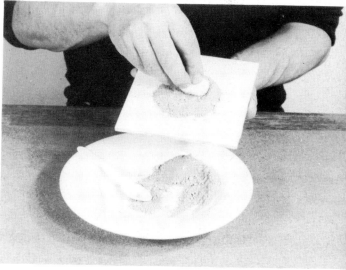

Obviously cotton wool which is not loaded with colour should at no time be allowed to contact the bossed oil surface or the evenness of the colour application will be irretrievably spoiled, due to specks of cotton being stuck to the oil

473 The action is light and done with a circular motion, spreading the colour out form the centre continuously

474 Excess colour is pushed off the edges of the surface so that it returns to the plate

**473**
**474**

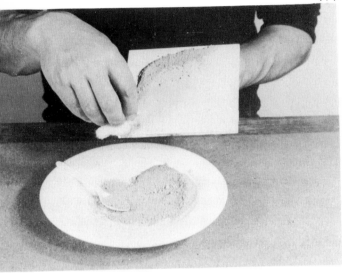

475 When the entire surface has been covered it is gone over again with the cotton wool pad which is repeatedly loaded with powder from the plate. This is done using the pad with a light circular motion and ensures as even as possible a layer of colour. Finally, without reloading the cotton wool pad, the surface is dusted to remove specks of colour which are not adhering to the oil

While it is possible to groundlay up to the edges of forms which have sharply defined edges, such as the tile illustrated, the difficulty of brushing and bossing oil evenly over an edge means that it is not possible to groundlay over the edges of hollow forms and that there is usually some unevenness of the extent of groundlaid colour at such edges. The bossing operation spreads the oil slightly and it is not possible to brush or boss the oil to precisely defined shapes. With perhaps the one exception of groundlaying the entire surface of a tile it is therefore usually necessary to clean up the outer edges of groundlaid areas.

**475**

*476*

476 Whenever groundlaid colour has to be cleaned off parts of a surface the extent of the area of colour is first usually defined with a line scratched through the dried oil and colour. Excess colour is then removed by scratching up to this line. Groundlaying oil dries very hard and a sharp knife or other appropriate metal tool offers a precision and speed not possible with wooden tools. Care should be taken that scrapings of the removed colour are not left on either the groundlaid or the cleaned surface. It is a sensible precaution against unwanted specks of colour to give cleaned areas a wipe with a cloth dampened with white spirit which has a softening effect on the dried oil. While it was possible to groundlay the entire tile surface, to leave a precise ungroundlaid margin is only possible if the dried colour is cleaned back to a line

Prior to firing, groundlaid colour areas should be handled as little as possible and always with care, the main danger being scratching. Before the work is fired the oil must be allowed time to become thoroughly dry.

Even though many of the enamel colours now marketed are lead free the actual application of enamel colour should be done in an extraction booth because of the hazards of silica and metal oxide dust.

The evenness of tonality of groundlaying is dependent on the evenness with which the brushing and bossing of the oil are done. The actual tonality of the fired colour depends both on the inherent tonality of the particular colour used and on the thickness and dryness of the layer of bossed oil. Most colours are capable of developing adequate strength with a single groundlaying but a few paler colours only work satisfactorily if a second layer is applied after the first has been fired on. The application of more than one layer, though it adds to the firing cost and to labour, allows the creation of very rich colour and offers the advantage of improving the evenness of the tonality as any dust specks in the first coat are minimised by the second.

Groundlaying has been little used outside the industry perhaps because its usage in the industry has inhibited thought about its actual potential. The possibilities of mixed colours and overlaid colours are diverse and the possibility of sgrafitto through groundlaid enamel is almost totally unexploited. The principle of groundlaying is attractive in its simplicity and it is practice not principle which limits its use to enamel colours. It is, for example, possible, by refiring to glaze temperature or near to it, to fire underglaze colours and blended pigments of metal oxides, applied by groundlaying, in-glaze and this aspect offers particular qualities which are also unexploited.

# Scratched decoration: incising and sgraffito

Within the field of scratching there are three distinct but related areas. Firstly there is pure incising — scratching directly into the clay — finished with a translucent glaze or left unglazed. Secondly there are various other treatments of marks scratched into clay. Thirdly there is sgraffito — scratching through one material back to another. The two terms *incising* and *sgraffito* tend to be used rather loosely, often interchangeably, but the distinction is an important one: with pure incising the relief of the scratched clay surface, whether glazed or unglazed, remains as the primary element of the work; with sgraffito the contrast between the scratched and the underlying material is the primary element. With the second of the three areas — other treatments of marks scratched into clay — a colour or tone contrast rather than the relief of the mark itself is the primary element which, unlike pure incising or sgraffito, is not the simultaneous result of the scratching.

There is little cause with any of the three areas of scratching to show or describe the process in serial detail as scratching is far less complicated than many ceramic processes. The concentration in the three sections which follow is therefore on such brief description of the process as seems necessary and on examples which point to the range of possibilities in different contexts.

## INCISING

The quality range of incising places it much closer as a process to carving than to sgraffito. Indeed if there is a clear dividing line at all between carving and incising it can really only be argued to be one of scale, in that the depth of relief is lesser with incising. Incising can unobtrusively occur on the insides of plates and bowls while carving belongs on the outside of pots and bowls. This distinction is not just one of function and incising can of course equally occur on the outside of forms but the greater depth of carving needs the space and the lightness of the outside of forms to be rightly revealed.

Both pointed and chisel-ended tools are useful for incising. Almost any pointed tool can be used to make a simple incised line but for broader marks the exact nature of the tool does play an important part in governing the sort of marks which are possible. Two other important factors are the nature and the condition of the clay. Linear incising with a sharp point can be done in any clay at any dryness but the quality of line is directly related to the dryness of the clay and to its inherent texture — the drier and the coarser the clay the more jagged will be the line. The use of chisel-ended tools drawn across the clay reveals the textural nature of the clay more obviously and the fluent, more gestural marks which can be an aspect of incising with such tools can really only be done with smooth plastic clays, with no tendency to tear, at an early leatherhard stage. The precise time for such work depends mainly on the clay body and partly on the tools. Only experiment can determine the precise conditions which enable particular work to be done.

The possibility of fluent mark-making, related as it is to a lesser relief than carving, is a further factor which distinguishes incising from carving.

Where the intended finish of incising is with a pale translucent glaze it is obvious that a light firing clay should be used.

477 Pure linear work drawn with a sharp pointed wooden tool can be done at a fairly late leather-hard stage when all tendency of incised marks to burr up has ceased. Greater control of fine linear work is more possible at this stage than earlier providing the clay is not too dry

478 A pale translucent glaze reveals the slight relief

479 The incising in this detail was done with a chisel-ended tool used to cut away a sloping relief to outline the foliate shapes. Persian. Twelfth century AD. *Victoria and Albert Museum, London*

477
478

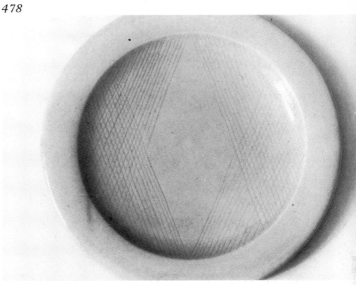

479

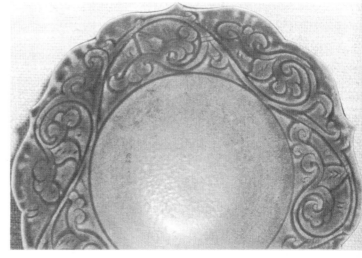

480

481

*480* Likewise in this bowl the incising was scraped with a chisel ended tool slanted at a slight angle. The soft and consistent tonal grading of the glaze across each of the incised marks is a simple and effective emphasis of the slight relief. The smooth clay was clearly cut at exactly the right stage to permit a gestural fluency but even so the consistency of repetition is remarkable. Chinese. Sung Dynasty. *Victoria and Albert Museum, London*

*481* This detail is from a large dish slightly over 20 in. (50 cm) in diameter. The work here combines the use of chisel-ended tools to outline the main shapes with pointed tools to draw in linear detail. The slightly fractured edges of the chisel-cut marks suggest that the stage of work was relatively late but clearly, from the fluency of the curvilinear drawing, the clay was no more than leatherhard. The fractured edges are probably therefore the result of the subsequent removal at a dry stage of a burr formed when quite soft clay was incised. The tonal emphasis of the glaze belies the extreme shallowness of the relief. Chinese. Sung Dynasty. *Topkapi Sarayi Museum, Istanbul, Turkey*

The behaviour of glaze on a relief surface is fundamental to the quality of glazed incised work and deserves some mention. The range of possibility is broad and it is not enough simply to use any pale translucent glaze. Some glazes are so stable they do not move in response to the relief and simply cloak it. Others are too fluid and over-react giving rather hard emphasis. What is needed is a glaze which is fluid enough to respond to slight relief, viscous enough not to flow on a form and which develops the intended degree of tonal difference at slightly differing thicknesses. There is not an easy answer and stoneware is not necessarily better than earthernware. Whatever type of firing is possible, careful testing to establish the behaviour of different glazes on relief is necessary. It is an area of glaze technology that has not been subject to extensive research. What is certain is, firstly, that the materials used in the glaze suspension govern how the glaze takes on the relief surface when the glaze is applied by dipping or pouring and, secondly, that the chemistry of the glaze governs how it behaves on that surface during firing. Exactly what pattern there is in these physical and chemical factors remains to be fully documented.

482 The contrast between the combed incising on this plant pot, applied on a revolving wheel, and the work of the Persian and Chinese examples, 479 to 481, could hardly be greater but it does serve to emphasise that the possible range of the quality of incising is considerable. In that appropriate glazing can serve to emphasise a subtlety of relief, albeit intended for glazing, which would otherwise be indistinct, incising which is made to be unglazed is of necessity bolder in quality, revealed as it is by light and shadow alone. Diameter just under 22 in. (55 cm). Early twentieth century. *In the gardens of the Generalife, Granada, Spain*

483

*483* Though African pottery is widely appreciated in Europe relatively little is known about the great diversity of processes which were, and to some extent are, used. The diversity is in part the result of local conventions and in part a response to differing materials. Though the gloss of this polished pot, resulting from the use of graphite, is striking its combination with incising is more so. The shine extends over every angle of the crisp incising completely refuting the possibility that it is the result of any conventional burnishing. (See also colour plate 2A.) From Uganda. 5 in. (12.5 cm) high. About 1910. *Horniman Museum, London*

## OTHER TREATMENTS OF MARKS SCRATCHED INTO CLAY

In the simplest sense all the possibilities in this area are the same in that they use the existence of scratched marks in a surface as a convenient means of containing an applied material that emphasises those marks. Inlay is a particular example of one possibility that has become a separate process. It is a relevant example to quote because with inlay the depth and edge definition of marks must be such that inlay is possible without the risk of a loss of definition when clay or slip is scraped away. Likewise, though in a less extreme way, it is important with all the possibilities that the depth and definition of marks is appropriate for the application of the intended material.

The most obvious possibilities involve the use of oxide and glaze.

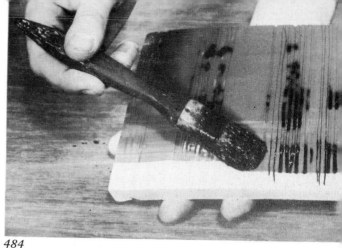

484 Oxide can be brushed onto clay at fairly early stages in the drying cycle. The earlier it is brushed on however the more tendency it has to combine with the clay surface as a slip-like mixture. This makes it difficult to rub down with control so it is usually brushed on at the dry or nearly dry stage when the oxide itself is dried by the porosity of the dry clay in a matter of seconds. For applying oxide in this way any broad brush may be used as the sole aim is to apply an all over covering. Even as the oxide is applied it tends to run into the scratched marks more thickly than it is left on the surface

484
485

485 As soon as the oxide is quite dry the surface can be rubbed down. This has three effects: firstly the streaky brush marks of application are rubbed away; secondly the thickness of oxide on the surface is reduced; thirdly the thickness of oxide in the lines, especially the fine ones, is increased by the oxide rubbed off the surface. Most oxides can be readily rubbed down just with the fingers but some tend to combine rather more strongly with the clay surface and for these a dry cloth can be used to rub them down. Pure oxides, oxide mixtures, body stains and underglaze colours may all be used in exactly this way. An important precaution to take when rubbing down work is not to blow the dust around. The dust should be tipped or tapped off the object and sponged off the work surface with a wet sponge or scraped into a container for re-use. Where possible rubbing down should be done in an extraction booth.

486

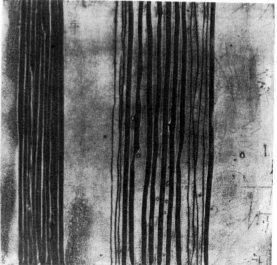

486 The fired tile shows the strong tonal contrast between the rubbed surface and the scratched lines. It is interesting to note the way the oxide has picked up the other marks and texture of the clay surface. Painted and rubbed oxide is in fact an extremely useful process for emphasising fine texture

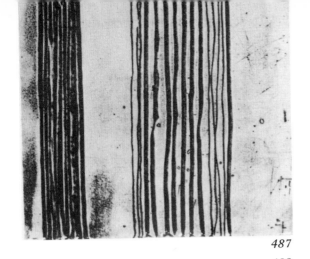

487 A clear glaze will dissolve the thinnest of the rubbed oxide and thereby increase the contrast

488 Instead of rubbing the painted oxide it can be scraped off the surface with a metal kidney. The scraped dust should not be blown around

489 Especially with unglazed work, though obviously with glazed as well, this painting and scraping process gives a much starker contrast than painting and rubbing. Though the surface is not flush this is sometimes referred to as oxide inlay

490 Where incising is reasonably deep and is well defined it is possible to apply glaze to the whole surface and then to scrape it off leaving it only in the lines. The entire surface can then be glazed again with a different glaze. This possibility works rather better if dark toned glazes are used in the lines and are overglazed with paler glazes than if the opposite possibility is tried

487
488

489

490

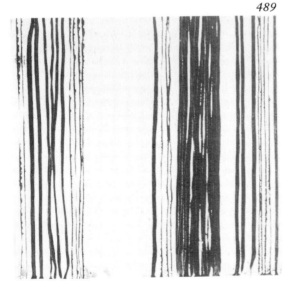

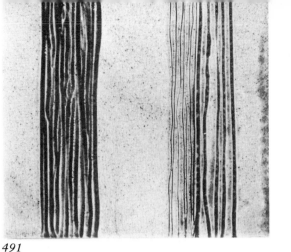

491 With an appropriate combination of glazes the process works very clearly. Though somewhat time consuming it has possibilities in particular contexts

492 Somewhat related to the previous possibility when incising has been glazed and still shows clearly defined relief it is possible to reglaze the surface and to leave the second glaze in the incised marks

493 Unlike the previous possibility 490 and 491 the process does involve an additional glaze firing but similarly it has possibilities in particular contexts. Dark glazes may be used over light or as here a pale opaque glaze may be used over a darker glaze. This latter possibility focuses attention on the tonalities of the work and diminishes awareness of the relief. As can be seen with some of the finer lines if there is insufficient depth, the glaze may tend to be lifted out of the lines when the surface is scraped

491

492

493

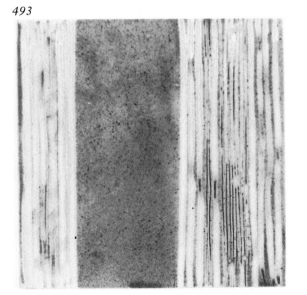

231

494

If occasion demands it, it is entirely possible to extend the idea of scraped lines containing colour on into other materials such as enamel.

494 The scratched decoration here is simply emphasised with a rubbed oxide mixture, the faint texture of the surface being the result of salt glazing. In this example as in the descriptions for figures 484 to 493 the relief of the lines is subordinate to their tonality which distinguishes all other treatments of scratched marks from the simple glazing of pure incising and gives such treatments a stronger visual link with sgraffito. Hannah Barlow. Doulton's, about 1910. *Victoria and Albert Museum, London*

## SGRAFFITO

Historically the commonest application of sgraffito is through slip. In very many cultures where dark firing iron-bearing clays were abundant, and light or white-firing clay deposits were rare or unexploited, the only way of making lighter toned or brighter coloured pottery was to coat the red clay body with a slip of the rarer, lighter clay. For pots made like this to scratch through the pale slip to the contrasting dark body was a direct and obvious means of decoration. Sgraffito can however be done through a whole range of materials and while scratching needs little description there are a number of factors relevant to different contexts which should be described.

The primary quality in sgraffito is the contrast between the scratched lines and areas of the revealed ground and the applied covering. Necessarily a relief equal at least to the thickness of the applied covering is involved but, with only rare exceptions, the lines and shapes revealing the contrast, not the relief, are the important aspects.

For sgraffito through slip any of the tools relevant for incising may be useful and for the removal of large areas of slip the addition of broader ended tools may be necessary if the texture of the revealed clay is to remain unobtrusive. Sgraffito through unfired glaze requires only such tools as the intended marks may dictate but scratching through enamel or lustre does demand sharply pointed metal tools.

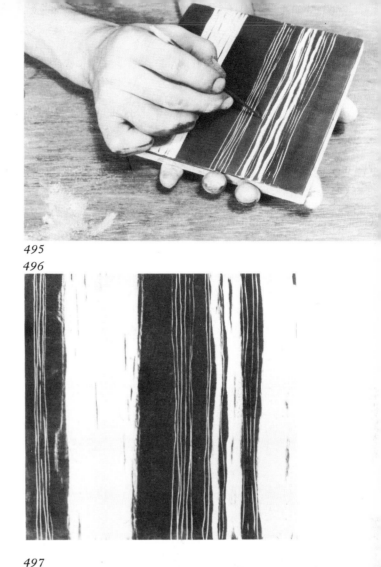

495
496

495 Oxide, oxide mixtures and underglaze colours are alternatives to slip, though applied at a later stage, for sgraffitto on unfired clay. The oxide is applied in the same way as shown in figures 484-485, except that it is rubbed very gently with the finger ends enough only to even out any streaks from the brush, not enough to thin the layer. The clay should be dry or nearly so when it is scratched and at this stage the gentlest of pressure will scratch crisp, fine lines

496 The definition of the sgraffito will remain unaltered by firing providing the original oxide application achieved the right degree of thickness but a glaze application, unless the oxide mixture approaches an engobe in composition, will almost certainly blur the sgraffito marks and show up unevennesses in the oxide ground. This underlines that it is the stability of slip which makes it such a good context for sgraffito

497 Really fine lines can be cut through slip with any sharp point such as the far end of this tool. Broader lines, as here, can be conveniently cut with the rounded corner of a chisel-ended tool. The cut is always a scraping cut with the working part of the tool at an acute angle to the clay.

497

498
499

498 Keeping the surface of scratched areas reasonably smooth is a frequent concern which is best met by the use of broad tools. Wire ended modelling tools are useful for this and canted over at an angle as here can be used to work to a reasonable edge. The main use of such tools is for the speedy removal of areas of slip

499 To finish clearly defined edges a short length of strip metal makes a really smooth cutting tool. Wider versions of the same sort of tool can be used for cleaning up and smoothing scratched areas but the wire tools are better for the initial removal of slip

500 If edges of areas are scraped to a precise shape in a number of actions a burr of clay can form if the slip and clay are a bit soft and, rather than letting this dry, it is very easy to remove the sharpness by lightly running a finger round the edges

500

**501** Linear work, especially fine linear work, is somewhat inclined to suffer from sharply burred edges if the slip is a bit soft. Prevention is better than cure and this can be avoided by allowing the clay to become progressively drier until scraping does not form a burr. Whether sharpness is present or not it is a useful practice with linear work to brush firmly over the surface with a broad dry brush at a late leatherhard stage. This clears all the slip and clay debris from the lines and, additionally, if there is sharpness, softens it. As the clay is still leatherhard there is no hazard of creating airborne dust

Raw glaze, especially when applied to leatherhard rather than bone dry forms, is an interesting context for sgraffito for as well as the normal colour and tone contrast there is the additional surface contrast of body and glaze. Physically raw glazes have a strength, in the raw state, somewhere between slip and glazes for biscuit and are easy to scratch, especially in a linear way. Work is easiest at the leatherhard stage as soon as the glaze is touch dry. One point to watch is that in the speedy ease of drawing which is possible clay is not burred up into the glaze

**502 and 503** Sgraffito through glazes applied to biscuit should be done as soon as the glaze becomes touch dry. If it is left much longer than this the glaze surface tends to become too fragile to handle safely. The feel of this sort of sgraffito with the tool working against the hard biscuit surface is quite different to working on unfired clay

501

502

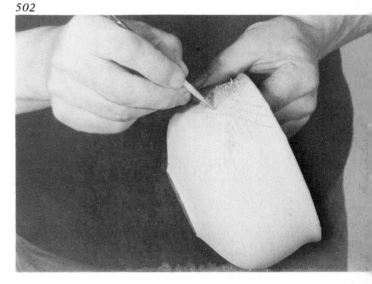

503

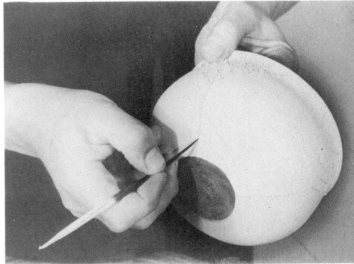

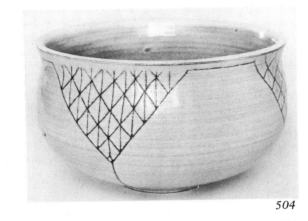

504

504 One of the incidental qualities of sgraffito through glaze back to clay is the rounded relief at the edge of the glaze areas. This is an earthenware tin-glaze on a red earthenware body

505 and 506 Sgraffito through unfired glaze applied over a fired glaze, as here, has a different feel again, the smooth fired surface of the glaze offering no resistance to the tool. Because the adhesion of glaze onto a fired glaze surface is much less than its adhesion onto biscuit the chance of quite large flakes of glaze loosening and lifting off at edges and where lines cross or are close is correspondingly greater. The chance is greatest where the unfired glaze is thickest. Except with very thin applications of glaze this fracturing is inevitable. If more precise qualities are intended slip sgraffito on clay is a more appropriate process. Firing always softens and alters this fracturing somewhat

505

506

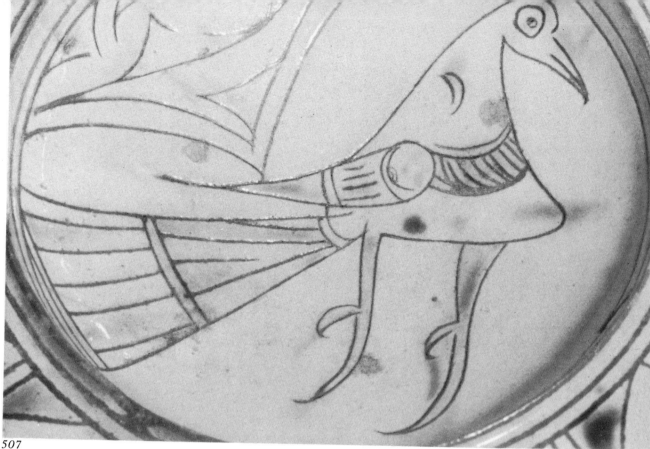

507

507 This example shows a simple linear use of sgraffito through a light slip to a darker clay. The fluency of line is most readily achieved at some point in the early to mid-leatherhard stage. The work is typical of the Mediterranean pottery which preceded the use and spread of tin glaze painting and which, as peasant ware, continued parallel with it. Byzantine. *Victoria and Albert Museum, London*

508

A development from linear sgraffito through slip is to remove the areas defined by lines.

508 A line through a pale slip to a darker body clay reveals little more than the general tonality of the underlying clay. When areas are removed the texture of the body clay, smooth or coarse, is revealed. The existence of a physical or colour texture in the underlying clay body has obviously to be acknowledged visually but presents no visual problem. At some stages however the removal of areas of slip from a coarsely textured clay can lead to a rather messy surface. If the sgraffito is limited to lines at the leatherhard stage leaving the areas till the nearly dry state then a granular texture will result. If the areas are removed at the leatherhard stage then the grog or sand in the clay will give a linear texture to the scratching which may not relate well to the reserved areas and may need smoothing. Here the rather granular background is an effective contrast to the boldly drawn figures. English, fourteenth century. One of a set of tiles from Tring in Hertfordshire. *British Museum, London*

*509*

*509* This detail is from a thrown jug just over 7 in. (18 cm) wide and 8 in. (20 cm) high and shows a solution to the problem of removing large areas of slip from a smoothly thrown convex form. Such work is necessarily painstaking, the danger is that it can become and look laborious. The solution used here was to scrape the slip away in short diagonal strokes, each stroke being about ¾ in. (2 cm) long. No attempt has been made to smooth or remove the marks of the strokes. The quality of the strokes is fast and crisp but they leave only a barely perceptible mark, evident to the eye and the touch as a slight undulation and visible here in the area beneath the cottage, and detracting neither from the quality of the form nor from the remaining reserved areas of slip. English, dated 1949 made by W. Fishley Holland at Clevedon in Somerset. *Craft Study Centre, Bath*

*510* Recessing the areas of removed slip to give reserved areas a slightly raised relief is a possible and interesting aspect of sgraffito and is evident in this fragment of a Byzantine bowl. *Museum of the Agora, Athens, Greece*

*510*

*511* The element of relief is even stronger in this example which is a combination of carving and sgraffito rather than one process or the other. The layer of glaze is exceptionally thin scarcely filling the relief at all. Chinese. Sung Dynasty. Tzu-Chou ware. *Victoria and Albert Museum, London*

*512* Sgraffito here is through a brushed mixture probably of a heavily oxided slip. The combination of sgraffito and painted marks is a diverse and common one. Japanese. Made by Ogata Kenzan VI about 1912. *Crafts Study Centre, Bath*

*512*

513 Raw glaze offers the easy freedom of linear sgrafitto in a similar way to slip. The crisp relief of the scratching is clearly evident in the unglazed areas. Whether or not there is as strong a tone contrast as here the surface contrast of clay to glaze is more varied and often subtler than the phrase 'matt to shiny' might suggest and is always an element of sgraffito through raw glaze, as is the light-reflective rounding at the edges of all glazed areas. Chinese. Sung Dynasty. *Victoria and Albert Museum, London*

514 Though the major impact of this bowl is created by the bold almost exuberant lustre painting, the thin sgraffito lines through the lustre are an important element. Slightly under 9 in. (22 cm) diameter. Egyptian. Twelfth century. *Victoria and Albert Museum, London*

513

514

# Piercing

Piercing is, as the name suggests, decoration cut through the walls of a form.

Historically the quality and nature of piercing has varied from free to precise, from figurative to geometrically formal and from fairly large scale to very small.

It is limiting, though the commonness of this work probably makes it inevitable, that when piercing is considered examples of English eighteen century pierced creamware and its later derivatives come to mind. While much of this work shows exemplary finish and the best shows extraordinary virtuosity it should be remembered that its content and quality represents a fairly narrow range of the actual possibilities of piercing. The commonness of this type of eighteenth century work and the content and quality it represents is more of a comment on the availability of a diligent and cheap labour force than on the real breadth of the possibilities of piercing. The eighteenth century examples are further limiting in that, piercing is often the only technique of decoration. The possibilities of piercing may be extended by combining it with carving, incising, painting and other processes of decoration.

Clearly the effect of the process of piercing the walls of a vessel limits its function.

Whether functional, semi-functional or purely decorative the visual possibilities created by piercing are governed by an awareness of the wall thickness of vessels and sight through that thickness.

Technically piercing may be divided into two distinct processes: knife cut piercing and tool cut piercing.

Through most of the eighteenth century, small scale, repetitive piercing was done with shaped punches it is wrong to imagine that all of it was done in this way. Some of the more elaborate centre pieces, especially and obviously those which include non repetitive units, were knife cut. While such work shows remarkable skill the natural possibilities of knife cut piercing are with larger and freer piercing.

## KNIFE CUT PIERCING

*515* Knife cut piercing of fairly large holes through a relatively thick walled pot can be done with the clay softer than with a thin walled pot. Most of the tools sold as potters' knives have rather thick blades and are therefore rather clumsy for such work. A piece of hacksaw blade ground to a point and sharpened makes an excellent tool for this as it is thin. The teeth should be ground down or ground away to give a more comfortable grip and the handle can, of course, be bound with string or masking tape

*515*

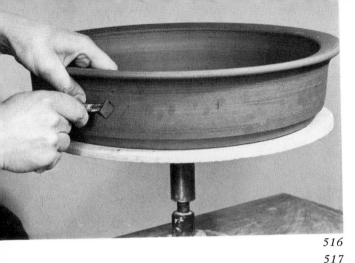

516 The initial cut is a push cut to the shape of the intended hole but smaller than it. If the piercing involves a repeat the work should be spaced and marked out

517 When four cuts have been made the clay piece can be levered out by twisting the knife

518 The hole can now be enlarged by slicing away more clay. A thin bladed, sharp pointed knife is essential to take fine cuts. The outside shape and the chamfer of the piercing should be finished at this stage. The inside shape of the hole will be a little ragged and can be finished later

519 For smaller holes the initial hole can be more conveniently cut with a hole cutter (see also figures 534 to 536)

516
517

518

519

520 The small initial holes can then be enlarged with a number of pushing and slicing cuts

521 Finally the inside edge of the hole is chamfered both to tidy up the edges and, by slightly more or less chamfering, to give the cut hole its final shape

522 For knife cut piercing in a thin walled pot and for cutting holes which are not straight edged in thicker pots an altogether finer tool is needed. For this also a piece of hacksaw blade appropriately ground makes an excellent tool. The cutting part is ground to reduce the ½ in. (1.25 cm) width of a hacksaw blade to about $^3/_{64}$ in. (1 mm), ground to reduce the thickness and sharpened on the inner edge. In essence the cutting end of the tool is like a rectangular sectioned, rather than a round, needle and is sharp on one edge. It is fine enough to cut through thin walls without deforming them and narrow enough to cut tight curves

523 Even with a very fine tool it is better when piercing a thin walled pot to cut an initial hole and enlarge this to the final size, even if the piercing is far smaller than in this example

520

521

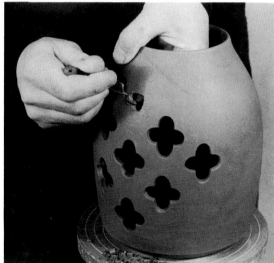

523

522

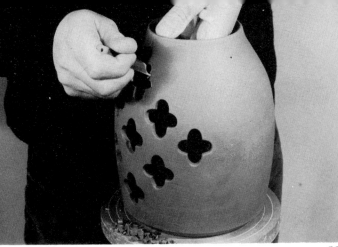

524
525

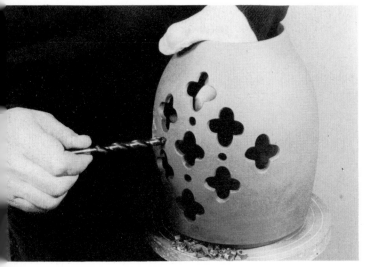

526

524 In any piercing, projecting points, such as in this example, can easily chip or break off and to avoid this cutting movements should always be inwards from projecting points

525 The sharpness of edges is commonly part of the quality of piercing and arises wholly naturally from the process. It is however often necessary to remove specks of clay from the cut surface and edges and if this is done by a very gentle sponging with a slightly damp sponge it has a barely perceptible softening effect on the sharpness of edges. If a slightly, or more fully, rounded quality of edge is wanted it should be done at this stage and the sponging should be preceded, if and as necessary, by cutting or scraping with the piercing knife

526 Conventional wood or metal working drills, available in a vast range of sizes, can effectively be used to make round holes in clay. They need a little pressure to start them cutting but then they should be pressed very lightly indeed and twisted backwards and forwards between the fingers. If they are pushed too hard they will burst through the clay leaving a very jagged back edge to the hole

*527* Single flute (527) and double flute (528) drills are the available types.

*528* The latter is the more expensive type and for wood and metal is the superior type by far. In clay both cut adequately but the double flute, simply because of the clearance which the second shallow flute gives to the narrow cutting edge, seems to work more cleanly

## TOOL CUT PIERCING

In the absence of readily available tools of various shapes and sizes, with the exception of round hole piercers (see 534 and 535) tools for piercing have to be improvised or made. Hollow section metal extrusions are one possible type of material to shape. A skilled metal worker could form cutters from shaped and soldered sheet metal.

*529* Tools designed to cut half a shape at a time and made from hollow section metal should be filed with a slight point which makes both the start of the cut and placing easier. All cutting edges should be sharpened with an inner bevel

*530* In use the tool is placed in position and pushed through the clay. Inside edges are much neater if a pad of leatherhard clay is held firmly against the clay wall

*531* With the pad removed it can be seen that the tool has just pierced through the wall

527

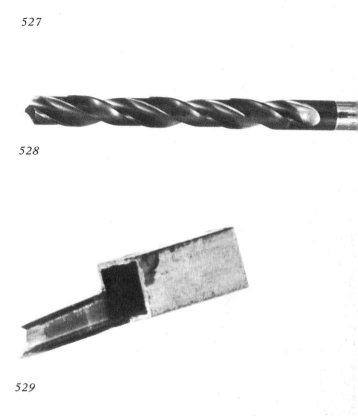

528

529

531

530

532

533

532 The tool is pushed through again to cut the two opposite sides of the square

533 It is usually far easier when cutting parallel sided holes like this to push the loose square of clay right through to the inside and flick it off the tool than to try to withdraw it through the hole

534 and 535 Round hole piercers are made in two types: tapered hole piercers (534) and parallel sided hole piercers, (535) both in a variety of sizes

534

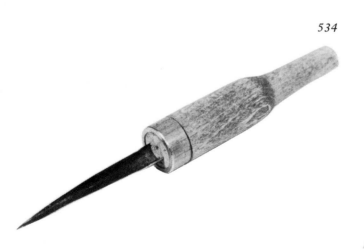

535

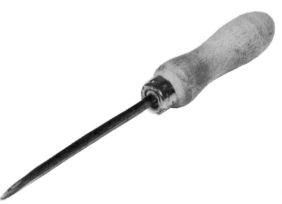

536 In use half round cutters are pushed into the clay and twisted between the fingers and thumb. Within reason the more they are twisted the cleaner is the cut, especially the back of the cut. Once parallel sided cutters have pierced through the wall they should be twisted once more and withdrawn and they will lift the plug of clay out of the hole. Tapered cutters, as here, are likewise pushed into the clay and simultaneously twisted. The further they are pushed through the wall the wider the hole they make. In enlarging holes they cut fine shavings not, obviously, a solid plug and these too will emerge with the tool after a final twist

536

537 and 538 Tools which work as punches are straightforward to form from tube. Three aspects of the design of this type of tool are important: firstly the part which connects the cutting end to the handle should be less than half the section of the cut shape so that the cut pieces, as they are pushed along the tube by new pieces being cut, are not trapped; secondly the cutting end should not be too long so that the friction of the cut pieces passing along the tube exists for as short a distance as possible; thirdly, and most importantly, the inner section of the tool should at least be parallel and should not get narrower. This last aspect is very important. With thin material which needs no sharpening to cut through the clay there is no problem in producing a tool with a parallel inside the tool. With thick material however the need to combine a sharp end to the tool with a parallel inside shape necessarily involves bevelling the outside of the tool towards the cutting edge. In use such a tool makes a slightly tapered hole in the clay combining some degree of impressing with its primary cutting role

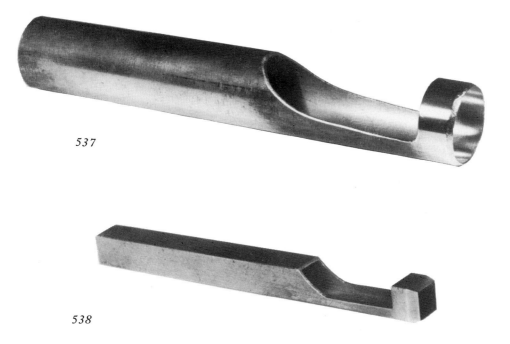

537

538

539

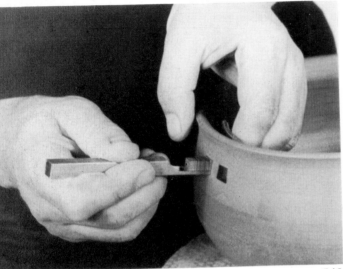

540

539 Tools of this type are extremely easy and quick to use, so quick in fact that, in repetition use, it is easy to imagine that the major problem is a loss of concentration on careful placing (see 546). Leather, held on the inside of the form, helps to support the tool as it cuts through the wall

540 All shapes except round must only be pushed and clearly cannot be twisted. With good punches the action is clean and fast

541 The inner shape of this mug is a simple cylinder. The lower part is double walled. The knife-cut flower and leaf shapes which terminate the incising are pierced into the cavity between the two walls. English. Dated 1703. *Victoria and Albert Museum, London*

541

542

542 This fine beaker, less than 4 in. (10 cm) wide, has a number of bands of incised decoration. In the top band fine incising is combined with delicate piercing. All the piercing is filled with a milky glaze. There is no technical problem in filling small pierced holes with glaze. If the biscuit has a ready porosity and the glaze is any thicker than watery thin small holes and narrow slots need no inducement to fill up and holes filled with glaze before firing will only clear if a glaze is very fluid. Holes can never be filled flush with the surface so as well as its obvious translucency work of this type has an additional quality of relief. Persian. Thirteenth century AD. *Victoria and Albert Museum, London*

543 This extraordinarily fine piercing, less than 2 in. (5 cm) across, is functional as well as decorative in intention, being the strainer in the neck of an unglazed jug. Egyptian. *Victoria and Albert Museum, London*

543

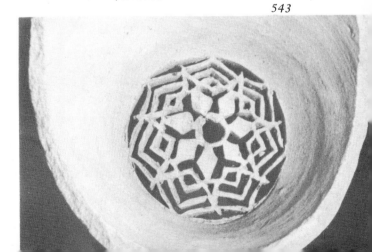

**544**

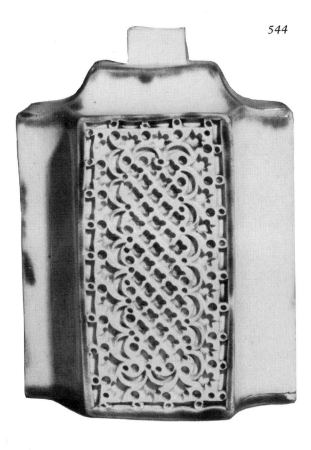

544 Punch-cut piercing of clay supported flat on a work surface can be taken to extremes. It is difficult to imagine that this perforated slab could have survived drying, firing and glazing except in this context attached, after piercing, to the flat side of a pressed bottle. The work is cracked in many places but the idea of the use of piercing as relief is an interesting one. English. Second half of the eighteenth century. *Victoria and Albert Museum, London*

545 This dish is a little less than 7 in. (17.5 cm) wide and its edge is slightly more than ¾ in. (2 cm) wide. Within the edge the piercing falls within a band fractionally under ⅝ in. (1.7 cm) wide. It is certainly not an example of good quality pierced creamware, technically or otherwise, but it has a typical intricacy and as an example of punch-cut piercing it is interesting. As can be clearly seen in the left hand side all three of the different shapes of hole taper considerably through the thickness of the dish. The star shape shows an outline which is crisply impressed. The many cracks show the pressure exerted on the clay by the close spacing of the piercing actions. The need for a firm support on the back of the work is obvious. The evidence all points indisputably to the use of a punch with a tapered outside section. English. Late eighteenth century

545

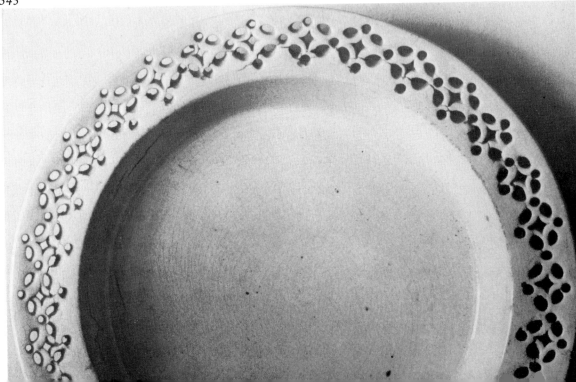

546

546 The piercing here is punch-cut through a mould-formed salt glazed dish. The placing of the piercing is somewhat inaccurate showing the need for sustained concentration on this when using fast cutting punches. English. Third quarter of the eighteenth century. *Victoria and Albert Museum, London*

# Carving

Carving, facetting and fluting all involve cutting or scraping clay in some way. Facetting and fluting are, by definition, limited in scope, being formal aspects of carving.

There is no clear dividing line between carving and incising but carving is generally used to describe broader and deeper relief than the finer marks associated with incising.

With a material as easily cut as clay carving is not a complex process.

The quality of mark and surface made is as much dependent on the dampness or dryness of the clay being carved as by the tools used. A hollow clay form can be carved at any stage, from as soon as it is rigid enough to withstand the pressure of carving right through to when it is bone dry. A solid clay tile or block may, as it has no walls to collapse, be carved as soon as it is formed. Modelled work can be subsequently modified by carving. Very soft clay however is rarely carved as it tends to stick to tools and clog them. Most carving occurs at some point in the leatherhard stage when the clay can be cut quickly and crisply neither clogging tools with a sticky softness nor resisting them with a hard dryness. Once clay passes a certain state of dryness and this state varies from clay to clay, depending largely on the plastic clay content of the particular clay body, each cut into the surface will produce a mark with fractured or torn edges and may produce a fractured or granular surface. Whenever bone dry clay is carved every cut will reveal the texture of the body, so with sanded and grogged clays a marked granular texture will occur. Carving bone dry clay is rarely done, especially with thin forms as these are obviously fragile, and, if and when it is, precautions should be taken against the creation of airborne dust.

Tools for carving clay are by no means as specific as those for carving harder materials and all manner of objects may be useful. Tools relevant to carving may be thought of as working in three categories: wire tools which remove clay from the form in strips or sheets; metal or wooden tools which remove clay by making chisel or knife cuts; tools which remove clay by scraping. Wire tools are normally hoop tools made of rigid brass wire formed in various shapes but flexible wire either held taut in a harp or by hand can also be used in some contexts. Many tools can be used either to cut or scrape and would clearly fall into both of the second two categories.

There are no great technical problems associated with carving. Clearly the thing to avoid with hollow forms is carving right through the clay wall. If deep carving is wanted in some areas clay can be added to these parts before carving commences. This is much better than risking extreme thinness at the deepest points of carved marks for, in fact, not only should carving not pierce the wall but it should not nearly do so, certainly not with long marks for these may develop into cracks. Particular care should be taken when deep carving impinges on an edge of a hollow form. When a carved form has a considerable range of thicknesses unrushed drying and gentle handling when dry will minimise the chance of cracks developing.

The content of carving may range from fine relief, revealing gently graded translucencies in porcelain, to bold, craggy work of considerable depth. Because clay comes in so many types and can be worked in varying states of softness or hardness the range of quality possible is probably wider than with the harder materials conventionally associated with carving.

It should not be forgotten with the breadth of possibilities available that carved form and relief in clay, like that in any other material, is revealed by light and shadow. It is all too easy to diminish the effect of carving by some even slightly thoughtless subsequent treatment. This is not a condemnation of any oxiding or glazing or other subsequent colouring treatments of carved clay. But it is perhaps unusually important with carved relief to be clear at the beginning about what subsequent treatment, if any, the carving may have. Knowledge, for example, of the way a particular glaze behaves on relief will fundamentally affect the quality of carving which is appropriate.

547 When carving is to be repetitive it is helpful to use drawn marks to establish the proportions and placing of the work. Even when carving is to be freely asymmetric some rough guide-marks can be helpful as carving is often a slower, more meticulous process then many others and one danger is that careful concentration on work in one area may inhibit a constant awareness of the relationship of that area to the whole

548 Some state of leatherhardness, depending partly on the intended quality of carving and partly on the nature of the clay, is the usual state for most carving. A sharp pointed, chisel-ended tool is used here, knife-like, to cut the main shapes of the intended relief

549 Softish leatherhard clay can be cut away quite effectively by scraping with a chisel-ended tool. The clay should be firm enough to come away cleanly without sticking to the tool

550 Sharp, thin tools can be pushed into the clay, chisel-like, in a paring action

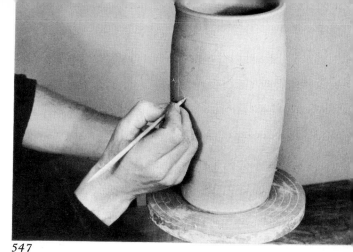

547

548

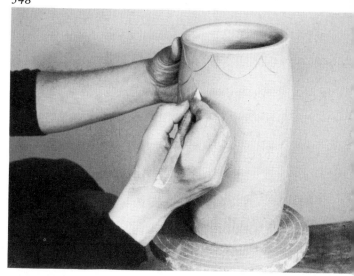

550

549

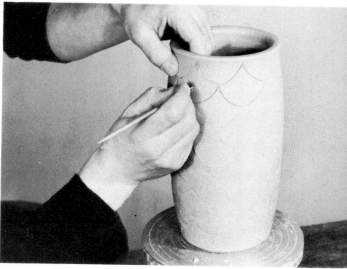

551

552

**551** Here a tool sharpened on its side as well as its end is being used in a scraping cut defining, and deepening the relief of the scale shape

**552** Even when the clay is firm enough to be cut quite crisply some actions, especially at the sharp edges of relief, may produce an unwanted burr which can be softened at this stage with gentle finger pressure

553

**553** While the main relief shapes produced are always the primary interest of carving, surface is an aspect which cannot be ignored. Here the slight but consistent marks of the carving complement the main shapes

554 Using metal, or sharp wooden, tools in leatherhard clay carving can be quite gestural in quality. Here the strong horizontal of an incomplete turned spiral, is being broken by vertical cuts. Work of this kind is on the border between carving and incising. Whether it is the one or the other does not matter, what is important is that it is realised that the faster, freer marks associated with incising on a small scale may be done deeper and larger

555 and 556 A free sort of carving can be done for work limited to slabs or relief tiles simply by slicing through a thickish slab of clay with a wire. Quite complex relief can be made by uneven upward and downward movements of the two hands as the wire is drawn through the clay. By using a wire tautly stretched in a strong harp slightly different effects can be achieved. Wire-cut facetting is a further context for work of this kind though the depth of such work is clearly restricted by the wall thickness

554

555

556

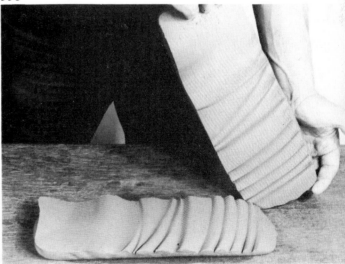

557

557 The detail of a carved Chinese brush pot shows work of an intricate, meticulous quality combined with incising and piercing. Most of the carved forms are fully rounded so little of the original thrown surface remains. All the marks of cutting and scraping have been smoothed away yet the work is not oversoftened or overworked in quality. The thin pale glaze is neither so matt that it obscures the fine incising nor so shiny that it confuses the relief with reflections. Chinese. Made in the early eighteenth century in the style of Sung Dynasty Ting ware. *Victoria and Albert Museum, London*

558 This detail from a large Persian tile shows an entirely different quality of relief. The difference is heightened by the use of bright colour and contrasting tone. Much as in wood or lino blocks for printing, though with fundamentally different intention, the relief here is created beneath the surface by carving away clay to leave the calligraphic and foliate shapes as the only remaining parts of the original surface. Wire ended tools to remove strips of clay are useful for this sort of work. From the soft, rounded quality of the recessions it is likely that the carving of this tile was done at a very early leatherhard stage. The strongly contrasting colour and tone might seem to query the need for relief but the carving is deep and well defined by its sharp edges and the relief gives the surface emphasis which otherwise would have been lacking. The particular treatment with colour gives emphasis to the calligraphy and in its architectural context would have combined clarity with a typically Islamic complexity. From the wall of the tomb mosque of Buyan Kuli Khan near Bokhara, now in Uzbekistan, USSR made about 1360. *Victoria and Albert Museum, London*

558

*559* Like the Persian tile of 558 the carving on
this Chinese jar leaves the drawn shapes on the
original surface. In this case these shapes are
detailed and emphasised by freely drawn incising. The relief of the carving is relatively deep
leaving the work sharply revealed by light and
shade. The textural strength of the irregular
linear background gives clarity to the simple
shapes of the men and their horses. China. Late
Ming Dynasty. *Victoria and Albert Museum,
London*

*559*

# Facetting

Facetting is the creation of a number of flat sides around a previously formed pot. In jewellery, precious gemstones are facetted into a variety of forms and here the term is a precise one. In pottery, where many sided forms can be readily constructed by slab building and can, less obviously but entirely possibly, be coiled and thrown and pots can be pushed or beaten into more angular shapes, the term is used more loosely. The distinction made here is the strict one and is between facets which are cut into previously formed pots and other means of making pots angular. By far the commonest context for cut facets is thrown pots.

Facetting can be done on thrown pots in one of two ways either by cutting with a wire or by cutting with some form of facetting tool. With the former process fecetting occurs either as soon as or shortly after the pot has been thrown while the clay is still soft enough to be readily cut with a wire. With the latter process the exact time for facetting is determined partly by the clay body in question and partly by the intended quality but is only rarely done later than a fairly early stage of leatherhardness.

Thrown pots which are to be facetted must be made with somewhat thicker walls than is normal otherwise it is not possible to cut into the walls to form facets. Exactly how much thicker the walls should be depends partly on the nature of the pot and partly on the intended nature of the facets. It is simple geometry, in the context of vertical facets on basically vertical pots, that it is straightforward to form many facets on the sides of a wide cylinder with not unusually thick walls and that as the number of facets and the diameter of the cylinder decreases so the wall thickness must increase to accommodate the facets.

Wire cut facets can be made while a pot is still attached to the wheel or they can be made on a bat or workboard when it has been removed from the wheel. Cuts can be made upwards or downwards. The most direct process is to use a single strand or twisted wire held taut and by this means a surface which is less truly flat than the term facet implies can be made. The alternative is to use wire stretched taut in a harp.

Cutting facets on leatherhard pots with a facetting tool involves either making, finding or adapting something to use as a tool. Facetting tools work on the same principle as planes for wood in that the cutting edge projects from the body and in passing over the surface removes a shaving as thick as the projection of the edge from the body. Quite apart from the objections of diverting them from their intended use, woodworking tools have the serious drawback that they are designed to be used two handed on material which is held in a vice and they are difficult to use one handed with control even though they cut clay so easily. In fact a potato peeler, designed as it is to be used one handed is a tool which is easier to use and, in that it will work on concave as well as convex or vertical profiles, is more versatile. One limitation however is that being designed for potatoes they do not exist with cutting edges much wider than 2 in. (50 mm). If the possibilities of facetting are to be seriously explored it is undoubtably necessary to make a number of specific tools. How these are made and whether pipe material, to develop the idea of a potato peeler, or sheet material, to construct a plane-like cutter, is more appropriate will depend on specific intentions but before any are made, available tools of the types mentioned should be used and studied to understand their principles and to see how they can be improved on as facetting tools.

It is of course also possible to make facets by scraping with a metal kidney, but this is slower than both wire or tool cutting.

The qualities of facetting depend on various, very variable aspects. Perhaps the most important aspect is the dimensions and proportions of the facets themselves, not just the simple height to width relationships but also the number that can be seen and whether these are regular or irregular. How and where the facets stop or start is also visually important — the round, thrown origin is evident somewhere and makes an inevitable focus, not just of edge, where round becomes angular. The nature of edges between facets is an obvious quality and in part is determined by the quality of surface. There is a distinct, direct quality to wire or tool cut facetted surfaces which is an important element in the overall quality of a facetted pot. Cut facets can show an immense range of quality from free and spontaneous through to hard, precise qualities. Facets formed or modified by scraping are not a part of this range and are distinctly different most noticeably in edge and surface. The scraping of facets may sometimes be an appropriate process to prepare for a further exploitation of the possibilities of a facetted form with some further processes like perhaps inlay or painting but in most instances where this is not the case scraping tends to deaden the particular liveliness of cut facets.

## WIRE CUT FACETTING

*560 and 561* For wire cut facetting all that is needed is a wire. Brass or stainless steel wire both have a reasonable life. The wire may be single strand or twisted. It is always better to mount the wire in wooden toggles at each end. This makes the wire much easier to stretch taut. Care should be taken that the wire does not develop kinks as these are very difficult to remove and will always leave their mark on the cut clay

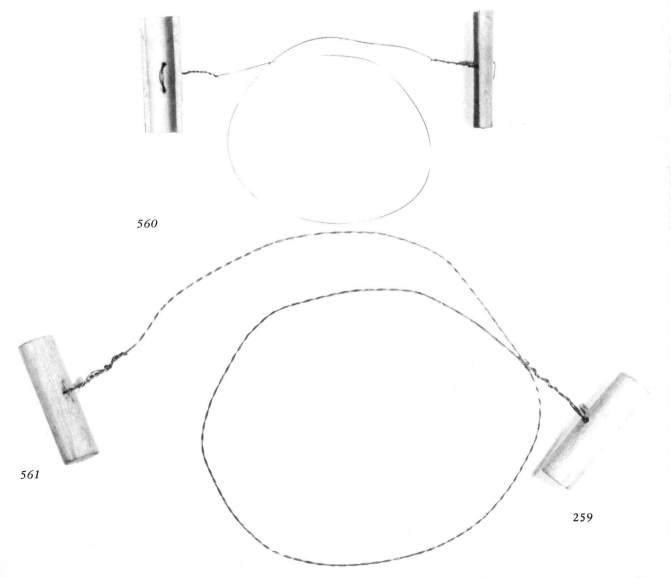

*560*

*561*

562
563

562 A twisted wire will always leave its particular furrowed texture on the facets. Twisted wires tend to leave a more jagged top edge than single strands, especially if the cut is made upwards

563 In use the wire is stretched taut. This dish is being cut less that 15 minutes after it was thrown — the clay is therefore still in a soft plastic state

564 The wire is simply drawn up from the bottom to the top of the thrown form within the thickness of the wall

564

*565*

*565 and 566* A somewhat cleaner edge is left if, rather than being drawn out of the top horizontally, the wire is angled to cut both along and up through and edge. When facets are cut through a thickish top edge which is not flat in cross section an angular change of form which is not horizontal is inevitably created. What is produced depends on the exact nature of the thrown edge form and it is a readily variable and visually important aspect. In this instance the broad inward sloping flat edge has led to a distinct scolloping

*566*

## TOOL CUT FACETTING

*567* Facetting tools can be based on the principle of the potato peeler which will remove shavings of clay up to the depth of the projection of the cutting edge from the tool. Thinner shavings can be removed by tilting the cutting edge so that less of it is projecting above the leading, and blunt, front edge of the tool. In clay it is far easier to use at its full depth as holding it steady at less than this is not easy

*567*

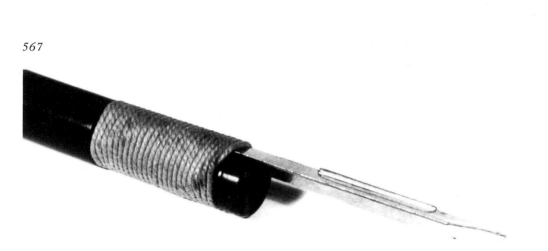

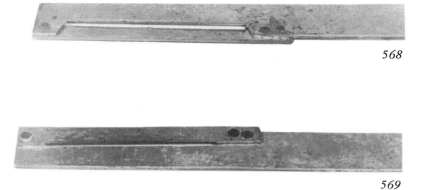

*568*

*569*

568 and 569   The two views of this home made
tool show the simple construction which
improves on the potato peeler in that it permits
a much broader cut and will produce really flat
surfaces. The small strip of metal is filed to a
cutting edge and is rivetted on. In use the front
portion rests flat on the uncut clay, the shaving
passes through the slot and the flat back of the
smaller piece of metal rests on the cut clay.
Each shaving is the thickness of the metal of
the cutting edge. The tool can be used on
convex but not on concave profiles

*570*

*571*

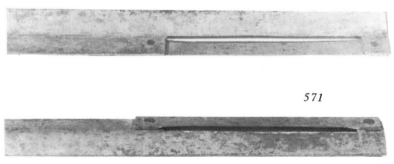

570 and 571   The two views of this tool show one
of similar construction to the previous one but
with a body bent in its length like the potato
peeler. To produce flat facets this tool is not as
good as the previous one but unlike the previous
one it can be used on concave profiles

572 In use facetting tools may become clogged if the clay is too soft so most tool-facetting is done to clay of medium leatherhardness, about the same consistency as for most turning. For really controlled cuts the clay should be of as even a consistency as possible from top to bottom. This is easily ensured by inverting the pot onto its top edge so this does not become too dry. If the facetting tool is held in both hands for steadiness then the facetting should be in a downward direction as the necessary pressure if applied upwards would simply tilt the pot and no cut would be possible. If the pot is supported by, or held in, one hand and the tool therefore used in one hand, then cutting can be done in any convenient direction

573 With a good tool it should be perfectly easy to remove shavings right down the full height of a pot in one movement. When this is done the pot should be placed on the edge of a banding wheel or some other support so the hands can pass beyond the base in an uninterrupted movement

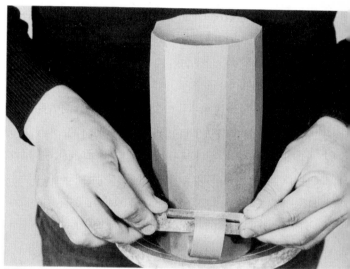

573

574

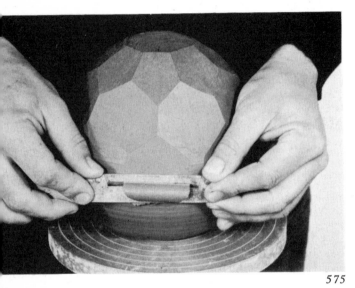

575

*574, 575 and 576* On forms where this is possible facetting tools can also be used to form facets more akin to those on gemstones. If precision is intended a flat rather than a convex tool should be used and cuts should be two handed and downwards with the pot inverted as necessary

*577* A surprisingly effective facetting tool can be made by cutting a slot with a sharp knife in a length of split bamboo and sharpening one edge of this slot into a cutting edge. The cutting edge is upper most in this illustration. As always with bamboo it is the outer casing which is left to form the cutting edge as this is the hard, durable part

576

577

264

*578* The tool requires quite firm pressure in use
and while it can be used one-handed, if the pot
is appropriately steadied, it is easier to use two-
handed. Like a potato peeler and the tool in
figure 570 and 571 it can be rotated to reveal
more or less of the cutting edge and thereby
remove a thicker or thinner shaving. In use it
feels more like a scraper than a plane and it is
complementary rather than an alternative to
metal tools producing a less precise, less
mechanical facetted surface

*579* With plates the extreme edge may be likened
to the sides of a more vertical pot and plate
edges can be facetted. The rough shape or even
the finished shape may be simply cut with a
knife, or at a softer stage with a wire, but a
piece of surform blade is a better tool despite
the fact that some potters frown on their use.
Certainly the full size surform plane, like the
carpenters plane which some advocate, is a bit
cumbersome to use one-handed but broken
pieces are more sympathetic and easy to use
with clay and work effectively. Being in fact
numerous miniature potato peelers arranged in
a flat plane, a surform tool has the distinct
advantage over a knife in that it can be made to
cut absolutely straight (though it will also
readily form a convex curve). In a few quick
movements it can remove more clay, with more
control, than a knife in a single slower cut. Surform tools or pieces of blade that have been
used with plaster should never be used with
clay as there is a strong danger if the clay parings
are reclaimed that they will be contaminated
with plaster

*580* A 2 in. (5 cm) length of surform is the ideal
size. A shorter length is difficult to keep straight
and longer is simply unnecessarily cumbersome.
Surform blades, new or used, are brittle and are
easily broken into pieces of useful length. New
blades are unnecessarily sharp for clay and
blades which would be blunt for woodwork will
give good service with clay

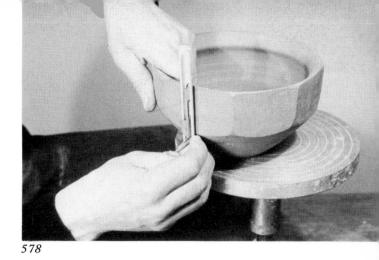

*578*

*579*

*580*

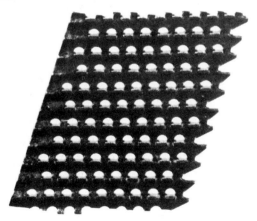

581

582

581 Because of the nature of its many cutting edges a surform tool does not however leave either a smooth surface or precise edges. Work on a plate edge should therefore leave the facets oversize so they can be finally pared to shape with a facetting tool

582 In the context of a plate it may be desirable to remove extreme sharpness from the top and bottom of the tool cut edge. A damp chamois held round the edge and worked gently along each facet will do this without oversoftening the angle

583 The finished plate demonstrates both the distinct shape made when cut facets and thrown roundness occur in an edge and the tonal break which occurs with many glazes on sharp edges

583

*584* The facetting in this teapot has a preciseness without being mechanical. The shoulder is nearly flat producing only a slight curve at the top of the facets but the lower part of the form joins the sides at less of a right angle resulting in a fuller curve at the base of the facets. The details of the lid, lugs and spout echo the crisp quality of the facetting. *Andrew Crouch, 1979. England*

*584*

*585*

*585* Crispness is not a quality of this bottle by Bernard Leach. There are many facets so the vertical junctions between them are gentle rather than pronounced. The facets follow the convexities and concavities of the form and therefore widen and narrow with it — slightly irregularly. The facets began above the substantial foot and finish under the full and flaring top edge so neither the base nor the top reveal the external polygonal edge which is common with facetting. Though there is a slight colour and tone change on the angles the thick dark glaze visually and actually softens the angularities of the facets. While it is fundamental that this pot is facetted it is also fundamental that none of the obvious emphases have been made. *Craft Study Centre, Bath, England*

267

# Fluting

Fluting is the making of evenly spaced, parallel grooves up part or the whole of a pot. Through its architectural associations and through its usage in ceramics the term implies a degree of formality and gestural, uneven marks are not referred to as fluting. In direction flutes can vary from a strongly slanting spiral to the truly vertical. In cross section the grooves of fluting can range from sharp angular ones to full rounded curves.

The application of fluting to a cylinder is a straightforward matter. As the circumference of a cylinder is identical at any height the whole surface can be fluted by spacing the flutes to meet evenly or to leave even spaces of original surface. On forms with concavities or convexities, or both, in their profiles the circumference of the form changes from height to height so, to cover the form evenly and for each flute to extend to the full height of the fluting either the flutes or the spaces between them, or both, must widen and taper with the form, or the more formal conventions of fluting must be ignored.

As with both carving and facetting, pots which are to be fluted may need to be made a little thicker than usual but this does depend on the context. It is possible, for example, especially with flutes of angular section to make very distinct though shallow flutes on thin walled pots. In this context with porcelain, fluting can be used to make a pot with subtly varying translucency.

With any particular clay whatever state of leatherhardness is ideal for turning, when the clay cuts really cleanly, is also right for most fluting though when flutes are scraped onto a thin walled pot this is better done a bit later.

Flutes can be formed in one of two main ways or in a combination of them. They can be scraped with wood or metal tools with shaped sharpened ends held more or less at right angles to the clay or they can be cut with specifically made fluting tools which remove shavings of clay leaving shaped

grooves. The former process can be thought of as a formal extension of incising or carving while the latter is a type of clay planing. Flutes can also be cut with wire loop tools but these are less controllable and produce a more variable groove than the two other types of tool.

Flutes which are scraped are generally made in a series of strokes. The first stroke establishes the length and direction of the flute and subsequent strokes deepen and define it. The form of the flute is largely determined by the tool itself. If they are painstakingly worked, scraped flutes can become rather dead but visual freshness can be retained if the number of strokes is kept to a minimum working as quickly and directly as is compatible with the intended quality. Old hacksaw blade pieces or similar strips of metal filed to shape at one end or both, make good tools and boxwood, bamboo or other hardwoods can also be used.

Flutes made with a specific fluting tool can be cut with considerable control in a single simple movement. Once an efficient fluting tool has begun to cut it is easy to make a long flute of even width and depth. With some tools especially those of angular or deeply arched, rather than hemispherical, cross section it can also be easy to make a gently tapering flute. Bamboo fluting tools can be bought but not in great variety. Fortunately they are relatively easy to make. Metal tube or bamboo are both easy to cut and to file to shape and a range of sizes of hemispherical sectioned tools can be made like this. Copper tube is much softer than brass and with this once the cutting part has been made it can be readily bent to deeper arched or angular sections. Brass tube is usually thicker-walled and is more durable.

The quality of fluting is determined partly by the quality of cut surface but importantly by the direction, width, depth and form of the flutes themselves and by the shapes of original surface, if any, left between the flutes. Forms moreover may be fluted for less than their full height, contrasting fluted against unfluted surface. Though superficially it may seem a narrow field fluting can in fact offer a range of interest and quality even within the limits imposed by its' definition.

586 This bamboo tool is readily available through most potters' suppliers. The cutting edge is deeply chamfered on the inside to facilitate the passage of a clay shaving without clogging and thereby to allow an even flute to be formed

586

587 The slight chamfering at the end beyond the cutting edge allows the body of the tool to be tilted clear of the pot leaving the cutting edge exposed with a sole beyond it long enough to keep the cut steady and short enough to allow controlled passage over convex and most concave profiles. The cutting edge is formed in the extreme outer skin of the bamboo which is the hardest and most durable part

587

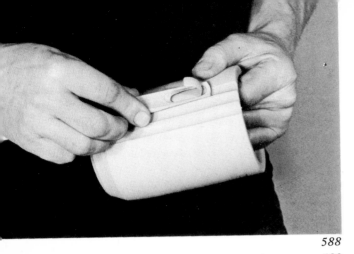

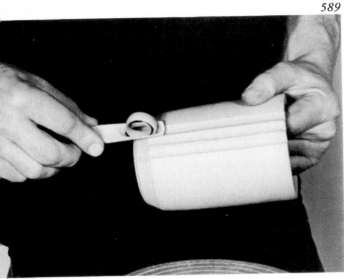

588
589

*588 and 589* In use the tool is pulled. Within the leatherhard state most clays will cut fairly smoothly as a long shaving is removed. This tool tends to work best at its full depth. It is not easy to use it to produce a tapering cut. Bought tools such as this are not made in a variety of widths or depths

*590, 591 and 592* With a sharp knife or a saw and some files it is both quick and easy to make fluting tools from short lengths of bamboo. A variety of diameters of bamboo allows tools of differing dimensions to be made. Like the bought tool the softer wood behind the cutting edge is removed. Unlike the bought tool, home-make tools can have two cutting edges so they can be pushed or pulled. Clearance for holding is given by the complete removal of the half of the bamboo in which the working edge is cut. This is possible because while the bought tool is cut from bamboo of some considerable diameter, certainly too large to be practical to use in the round, the home made tools are cut from round bamboo ¾ in. (20 mm) and less in

*591*

*590*

*592*

diameter. The lesser diameter of the bamboo enables a deeper flute of more rounded section to be cut. The length of the part which contains the cutting edges limits the concavity in which such tools can work. When they are being pulled to cut all these tools have effective depth-stops, formed by the bamboo which connects the working end to the body. A range of sizes can be made from bamboo of different widths.

*593 and 594* In a fairly tight concavity tools cut in the round may be used by being pushed or pulled as is convenient

*595* Such tools, a larger size is in use here, are not easier or more difficult to use than bought ones when long, continuous flutes are being made

*596* They are, however, because of their deeper, rounder cross section much easier tools to use when widening a flute to produce a tapered cut. Here one side of the tool is recutting and widening a flute on one side in a pushing action

593

594

595

596

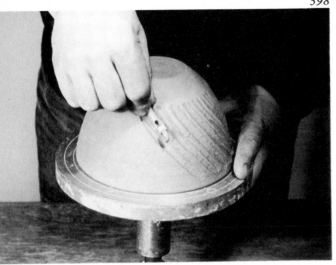

597
598

597 The depth and width of flutes appropriate for any form are finally a personal decision but depend at least in part on consideration of proportion. If only because of the breadth home made tools can bring to this consideration they must be considered a necessary part of any wide ranging exploitation of fluting. A narrow flute is here being cut in a small thin bowl. Not all fluted pots are robust and when softish leatherhard clay is being fluted care should be taken to avoid accidental distortion. Here the fingers inside give a firm support to the slight pressure of the tool

598 A different support here is an alternative guard against distortion

599 Some clays, in some states, especially some of the less plastic porcelains and semi-porcelains which are marketed can tend to tear when they are fluted. Often this has nothing to do with the sharpness, or lack of it, of a tool but is to do with the inherent qualities of the clay body. The tearing may be unacceptable to some, and in some contexts, but appropriately treated it can combine texture and relief in a way which can be exploited

599

*600, 601 and 602* Fluting tools filed from metal tube extend the possibilities of bamboo tools especially when the section of the cutting edge is reshaped. A tool with an eliptical section can be much more effectively used to cut thin shallow flutes and broader deeper ones than any tool with a cutter of circular cross section. As with bamboo the tools can be made to cut when pulled or pushed or both

*600*

*601*

*602*

273

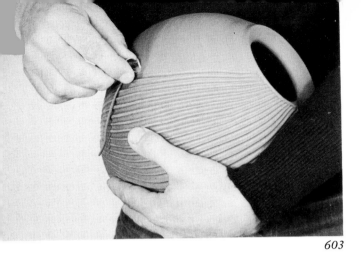

*603*

603 Here a tool of eliptical section is being used to cut flutes which taper from thin to thick and back to thin. This taper can be achieved in a single cut. Reworking one side of a flute to widen it as in figure 601 with a tool of circular section is completely unnecessary once the fairly simple control necessary to taper a cut has been achieved

604 and 605 A different and effective fluting tool can be made from a flat strip of metal. The illustrations show one made from brass $\frac{5}{8}$ in. (15 mm) wide and $\frac{1}{16}$ in. (1.5 mm) thick. The angle bent at the end allows the flat strip, used as a handle, to be held well clear of the pot. The projection of the shaped cutter slot is the maximum depth of cut and the curvature beaten into the cutting edge and the short piece of metal beyond the cutting edge forms the cross section of the flute

*604*

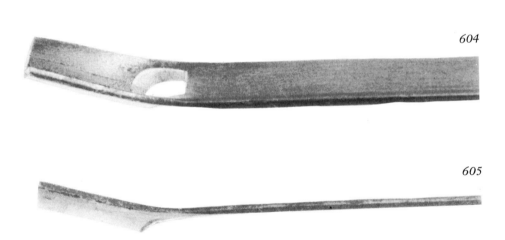

*605*

606 Fairly firm pressure is needed to engage the cutting edge

607 Like the bought bamboo tool shown in figures 586 to 587 this tool is pulled and like that tool, with the projection beyond the cutting edge resting in the cut clay, flutes of controlled, even size can be made very simply. This type of tool will not readily produce flutes of tapering width

608 Scraped fluting is really only a formal aspect of incising and the tools do not differ, being filed from any convenient rigid flat metal strip

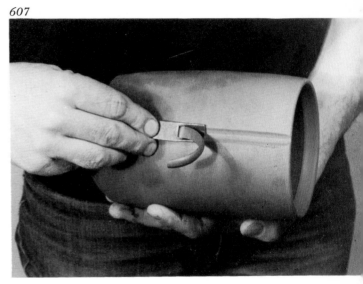

*606*

*607*

*608*

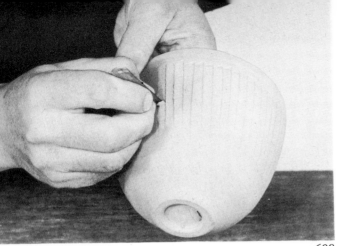

*609* In fluting of this type the first one or two strokes define the edge and depth of the flute. The third and fourth strokes remove more material and broaden the mark. Such flutes are scraped quite quickly. Control is better achieved through the repetition of action than by painstaking correction. Jagged edges between flutes can be rubbed away as the clay hardens. To slightly soften the quality the whole surface could be gently sponged

609

*610* This detail of a full-formed Sung dynasty Chinese porcelain jar shows the classic finish. The glaze is a pale translucent green and the clay is white. The raised parts of the flutes stand out paler where the glaze is thinnest and as the glaze inevitably thickens towards the deepest parts of the flutes so the colour grades darker. From the widest part of the jar the flutes taper considerably towards the narrow foot and slightly towards the neck. Interestingly the section of the flutes is eliptical not hemispherical. *Topkapi Sarayi Museum, Istanbul, Turkey*

610

*611* This fluted celadon bowl by Bernard Leach also uses the tonal emphasis of a pale translucent glaze but the quality of fluting is different. While the fluting of the Sung jar is soft it also has an almost mechanical precision and regularity. This fluting of Bernard Leach's has much more variety in detail. Both in going up each flute and in passing horizontally across the fluted surface the eye is held by irregularities. *Craft Study Centre, Bath, England*

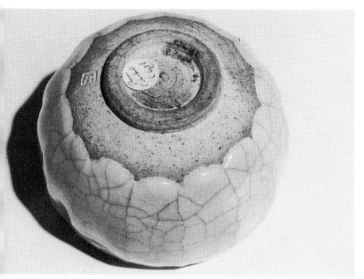

**612 and 613** This small bowl of Katherine Pleydell-Bouverie's might perhaps be called facetted not fluted for the relief on the walls is wider and shallower than the term 'fluting' suggests but the slight concavity can be argued to take it into the field of fluting rather than facetting. Beginnings and endings of flutes are areas of potential focus and are therefore visual problems demanding clear thought. Here both problems are very particularly solved — subtly at the top edge, which simply tapers slightly between the high points of the flutes, and distinctly at the bottom where the thick glaze is finished where the relief of the fluting ends. The thickish, crackled opaque glaze gives a totally different effect to that common with translucent glazes. The glaze does nothing to visually emphasise the fluting (except at the base) and yet the effect is intriguing for what can be felt to be there and seen to be there is not seen to be emphasised. *Crafts Study Centre, Bath, England*

612

613

# Sound practice in the use of materials: health and safety

Some of the materials used in ceramics are toxic; many are a serious health hazard if inhaled as airborne dust.

The brevity of this section should not be seen as any reflection on the seriousness of the subject.

Various laws apply to the practice of ceramics in factories, workshops and educational institutions. Though these laws do not apply to those working alone, the hazards exist and individuals should be as careful as those bound by law. Laws also apply to the metal release from various categories of functional pottery when this is offered for sale. Anyone who makes or sells ceramics should be aware of the various legislation which applies and where there is doubt they should consult the Health and Safety Department of their Local Authority for literature or advice.

In a book concentrating on decoration processes two factors deserve particular mention. Firstly, all steps should be taken against the creation of airborne dust. Processes involving the scraping of dry clay should be regarded as hazardous and avoided whenever possible. And whenever water borne mixtures are spilled they should be sponged up before they become dry. Secondly, protective clothing should be worn. Terylene overalls are best for dry work and waterproof overalls for all wet work. (For photographic convenience and continuity the demonstration sequences in this book ignored the normal requirements for the wearing of particular overalls.) Overalls, it should be stressed, only fulfil their function if they are removed on leaving work areas and if they, and towels, are regularly washed.

In addition to the legal literature on Health and Safety, material suppliers' catalogues give information on the hazards associated with ceramics and indicate the materials considered toxic.

# Glossary of terms

This glossary includes only terms contained in the text of this book

**Biscuit**   This term refers to clay that has been once-fired, without glaze. Biscuit fired clay may be highly porous or non-porous, depending on the intended glaze firing temperature and the clay body in use and to some extent on personal preference. The term 'bizque' is sometimes used interchangeably with biscuit but this can lead to confusion as 'bisque' is commonly used to refer to the finish of clay objects completed without glaze.

**Carbonising**   This, or 'smoking', is a term used for the subsequent treatment of biscuit fired clay. It is entirely distinct from the firing of clay, by whatever method, though it is true that carbon particles may also be trapped in clay during firing itself if the atmosphere of the firing is sufficiently reducing to allow this. Carbonising involves subjecting fired clay to an atmosphere of carbon laden combustion – because of the combustion heat is inevitably involved but the degree of heat is of a totally different order to that of firing. This exposure to combustion may be within a heap of smoldering sawdust or may be done by supporting the form and holding burning paper or sticks against it. Clay which is to be carbonised should be relatively low-fired or the carbon penetration of the clay will be only slight.

**Celadon**   The term celadon covers a range of high-fired, translucent glazes usually pale in colour and varying from pale blue grey to grey green through to pale and some darker bottle greens. The entire range is the result of the reduction of iron oxide. If celadon glazes are oxidised tan colours result. A definitive celadon is the result not just of a particular glaze with a small proportion of iron oxide usually less, often much less, than 2.5% but is the result of the use of that glaze on a light-firing or white clay. The colour resulting from the use of celadon glazes on some darker clays may still be recognisably celadon but at a certain point of darkness the term ceases to apply, whether the glaze itself is a celadon or not.

**Chun**   The term Chun covers a small range of unpigmented high-fired glazes which in common have a quality of opalescence which has a blue or green or milky white tinge. The science of this type of glaze is rather vague in that what produces the effect is recorded in numerous glaze recipes but why is the subject of some doubt.

**Classical Period, Greece**   This period, dating from about 575 to about 330 BC, covers the time within which the most renowned Greek sculpture, architecture and ceramics were produced.

**Crawling**   Crawling is a fault in glazes in which the continuity of the glaze layer is lost during the firing revealing areas of unglazed clay. The fault is sometimes the result of too thick an application of glaze. Some glazes are more prone to it than others. A sign that crawling may occur is when the dry, unfired glaze develops a lattice of fine cracks. Lightly rubbing such cracks to fill them with glaze dust can sometimes prevent crawling but persistent crawling of glazes is a problem needing a more radical solution usually involving an adaptation of the recipe to alter the physical characteristics of ingredients. One possible further cause of crawling is dusty biscuit.

**Crazing**   Crazing is a glaze fault in which the fired glaze layer develops a network of fine cracks. The condition is caused by the glaze having a greater shrinkage as it cools than the clay body. With earthenware when the glaze firing is at a lower temperature than the biscuit crazing may be stopped by increasing the temperature of the biscuit firing. Otherwise it is corrected by altering the glaze or the body composition. Less flux or more silica, or both, in the glaze will decrease its contraction and may effect a cure. Alternatively more silica in the body may work. There are limits to which the silica and flux ratios in a glaze can be altered after which its other characteristics will also be changed. Alterations to the silica content of bodies are more time consuming but in some instances are a better alternative. No way has been found of preventing crazing in the low-fired high-alkali glazes used with copper, for turquoise, and manganese, for aubergine.

**Engobe**    The term engobe suffers from somewhat vague usage. While some people use the term interchangeably with 'slip', to others it has the preciser meaning of mixtures of material in composition somewhere between those of conventional clay slips and of glazes. If this latter meaning is accepted engobes may be thought of as mixtures of materials containing substantially less plastic clay than conventional slips and containing silica together with some fluxing material. Whereas with conventional clay slips the adhesion of slip to body is achieved mainly by the plastic clay content of the slip which has inherent powers of adhesion and which allows the slip to shrink as the body dries from the plastic stage at which the slip is applied, with engobes the adhesion of engobe to clay body is achieved mainly by the action of the fluxes in the mixture. Constituted with appropriately small quantities of plastic clays engobes can be applied to both dry and to biscuit fired clays. Because engobes achieve adhesion and strength through the action of fluxes they tend to be constituted to work within a given temperature range.

**Geometric period, Greek**    This period of Greek art dates from about 950 to 630 BC. Work of this period was less highly regarded than Classical when the Western European collections were being formed in the nineteenth century and is much better represented in Greek museums.

**Grog**    Grog is clay which has been fired and subsequently ground up for incorporation into clay bodies. Grog is graded for size by the sieve mesh through which it will pass. The grogs most commonly available are fireclay grogs but grog may be made from any clay. Though grog of larger than about 80 mesh size imparts a tactile and visual texture to bodies, fine grog, smaller than say 120 mesh size, may be present in bodies without being evident to the touch or visually. All grog additions, whether fine or coarse, affect the quality of plasticity of any body.

**Hellenistic period**    This is the period during which the previously non-Greek areas conquered by Alexander the Great were Hellenised. The period is from about 330 BC until the emergence of the Roman Empire in the middle of the first century BC.

**Hispano-Moresque**    This is the name given to the pottery made under Moorish influence in Southern Spain from about the twelfth to the fifteenth centuries, mostly but not exclusively decorated with painted lustres on tine glaze. The Moors brought with them the knowledge of working with lustres during the Islamic conquest of Spain and, although the lands ruled by the Moors diminished from the thirteenth century onwards until their final expulsion from Granada in 1492, the use of these processes and stylistic influences, partly through craftsmen who remained, continued for some considerable time. The term Hispano-Moresque is applied to pottery produced in Spain from the twelfth century which demonstrates Moorish influence on style and process.

**Hollow and Hump Moulds**    These are the two types of one-piece press moulds used to make dishes. Hump moulds are sometimes called mushroom moulds. With hump moulds the clay is pressed over the convex mould, the inner surface of the dish being formed against the mould and the outer being pressed by hand. With hollow moulds the exact opposite is true, the clay being pressed into the concave mould and the outer surface of the dish therefore being mould formed and the inner pressed by hand.

**Kang Hsi period**    Kang Hsi was the second of the Ching dynasty emperors and reigned China from 1662 to 1722.

**Krater**    This name is given to the large stem bowl forms used by the Greeks for mixing wine and water.

**Majolica**    The term was first used in Italy to describe imported Hispano-Moresque wares which reached Italy via the island of Majorca. It then became used to describe Italian tin-glazed painting on tin glaze. An alternative spelling is maiolica.

**Ming**    The Ming dynasty of emperors ruled China from 1368 to 1644. During the Ming dynasty cobalt blue painting on porcelain was developed both for home markets and for export and enamels were used for the first time in China.

**Leather hard**   Leather hard is a state of firmness of clay when it can be easily impressed with a fingernail but not by the finger end. Clay at this stage has sufficient resistance to be readily cut.

**Molochite**   Molochite is fired china clay ground down to a graded fineness. It is available sieved very fine (200 mesh) in which state it may be used in glazes or in fine clay bodies. In its coarser grades it is used as a white and highly refractory grog.

**Mycenaen period, Greek**   This period coincides roughly with the second half of the second millenium BC when the Greek culture was based on Mycenae which had strong links with the Minoan culture of Crete. Strictly the period is briefer than this as Mycenae was destroyed in about 1200 BC.

**Plastic**   Clay in the plastic state is at its most formable, firmer than when soft but not approaching leather hardness. The term can however be confusing — a highly formable clay in an ideal state for use may be ambiguously referred to as highly plastic, refering both to its quality and its state. A clay which has poor forming qualities even in its most plastic state has poor plasticity or is 'short'.

**Plasticity**   Plasticity is a clay's quality of formability. There are many aspects of plasticity and strictly plasticity can only be assessed somewhat generally unless the precise context of use is defined — clay, for example, which rolls out well for forming in pressmoulds may not form readily or stand up well in throwing.

**Pressmoulding**   This term covers the making both of enclosed forms and small solid forms in piece moulds and open forms in one-piece moulds. With all press moulding plastic clay not slip is used which makes a clear distinction between this and slip casting. With open forms the clay is simply pressed into or over the mould. With enclosed forms the clay is pressed into the moulds and the keyed parts of the mould are pressed together.

**Refractory**   Refractoriness is the ability of a material to withstand heat. The greater the heat it will withstand without melting the more refractory the material is said to be.

**Short**   Shortness is the opposite quality to plasticity in a clay body — a short body has poor forming characteristics.

**Slip**   Outside the industry the term slip refers to clay in a liquid state. As well as referring to the liquid state of the material it also refers to its nature as a mixture which is predominantly clay and which if stiffened would form a clay body. Some slips intended as coatings have a proportion of flint added, red slips to make them more refractory and white slips to make them more opaque, but such additions rarely exceed 15%. When non-clay additions exceed this amount the nature of the material mixture approaches proportions where the slip would more properly be called an engobe. The term slip is sometimes used interchangeably with 'engobe' which does not assist clarity for the demarcation line between slips and engobes is a rather imprecise one, even though ultimately their natures are definably different. In industrial usage the term slip needs qualifying to have any precision of meaning, for reference may equally be made to a glaze slip as well as a clay slip and in this context the term merely refers to a liquid suspension of materials.

**Slurry**   Slurry is a very wet and uneven mixture of clay. It is like slip in consistency, though a little less wet, but unlike slip in that it is unmixed and therefore uneven.

**Sung**   The Sung Dynasty emperors ruled China from 960 to 1279. The Sung Dynasty is particularly known for its refinement of porcelain and the development of various high-fired glazes.

**Tang**   The Tang Dynasty emperors ruled China from 618 to 907. While the Tang dynasty is best known for its lively earthenware the development of simple form and the materials of porcelain and stoneware was advanced by the end of the Tang dynasty.

**Tenmoku**   The term tenmoku covers glazes of a variety of dark colours ranging from bluey blacks and dark olive greeny blacks to blacks with a textured surface of rusty brown to mirror blacks. The main factor common to the many variations of tenmoku is that the glaze is pigmented to the point of saturation with iron oxide, additions between 8% and 12% being most common. Temmoku is an alternative spelling.

**Terracotta**   Loosely this term is used to refer to any red earthenware clay. More correctly it refers to finished objects made in red earthenware clay, fired without the use of glaze. Unglazed finished objects made of other clays are referred to as 'bisque'.

# Further reading

There are few books solely concerned with decoration. This list of further reading concentrates on books which have some practical coverage of aspects of decoration but those concerned with the related topics of materials and firing are not included.

Billington, Dora *The Technique of Pottery, 1962,* revised by John Colbeck 1974, Batsford

Clark, Kenneth *Practical Pottery and Ceramics,* 1964, Studio Books

Cooper, Emmanuel, *Potter's Book of Glaze Recipes*, 1980, Batsford

Cooper, Emmanuel, and Royle, Derek, *Glazes for the Studio Potter*, 1979, Batsford

Fournier, Robert *Illustrated Dictionary of Practical Pottery*, 1973, Van Nostrand Reinhold

French, Neal *Industrial Ceramics: Tableware,* 1972, Oxford University Press

Leach, Bernard *A Potter's Book,* 1940, Faber

Noble, Joseph V. *Technique of Attic Painted Pottery*, 1966, Faber

Rhodes, Daniel *Clay and Glazes for the Potter,* 1957, Pitman

Rhodes, Daniel *Stoneware and Porcelian*, 1960, Pitman

Shafer, Thomas *Pottery Decoration*, 1976, Pitman

Shaw, Kenneth *Ceramic Colours and Pottery Decoration*, 1962, Maclaren

# Addresses of suppliers in the UK

**General suppliers**
*Deancraft Ceramic Suppliers*
Lovatt Street, Stoke on Trent, Staffs ST4 7RL

*Ferro (Great Britain) Ltd*
Wombourne, Wolverhampton, WV5 8DA

*Fulham Pottery Ltd*
210 New Kings Road, London SW6 4NY

*Harrison Mayer Ltd*
Meir, Stoke on Trent, Staffs ST3 7PX

*Podmore Ceramics Ltd*
105 Minet Road, London SW9 7UH

*Podmore & Sons Ltd*
New Caledonian Mills, Shelton, Stoke on Trent, Staffs ST3 7PX

*Potclays Ltd*
Brickkiln Lane, Etruria, Stoke on Trent, Staffs

*Wengers Ltd*
Etruria, Stoke on Trent, Staffs ST4 7BQ

A number of the general suppliers above have local agents, purchasing from whom may represent a considerable saving on carriage rates from Stoke on Trent. All the above suppliers produce full catalogues.

**Suppliers of brushes**
*Cowling & Wilcox Ltd*
26/28 Broadwick Street, London W1V 1FG

*Reeves*
Lincoln Road, Enfield, Middlesex EN1 1SX

*George Rowney & Co Ltd*
12 Percy Street, London W1

*Winsor & Newton Ltd*
51 Rathbone Place, London W1

**Suppliers of oriental brushes**
*Guanghwa Co*
7/9 Newport Place, London WC2

**Toxic metal release tests** are undertaken by some of the general suppliers listed and also by
*British Ceramic Research Association*
Queens Road, Penkhall, Stoke on Trent, Staffs

**Lustres and precious metal supplier**
*Hanovia Ltd*
Engelhard Industries, Valley Road, Cinderford, Gloucestershire

**Suppliers of bulk powdered clays**
*English China Clay Co Ltd*
John Keay House, St Austell, Cornwall PL25 4DJ

*Watts, Blake, Bearne & Co Ltd*
Park House, Courtenay Park, Newton Abbot, Devon TQ12 4PS

Small amounts of the clays of these two bulk suppliers can be bought from regional agencies, in the case of the former company, and from some of the general suppliers listed, in the case of the latter company.

**Supplier of brushes, media and some tools**
*E.W. Good & Co Ltd*
Barker Street, Longton, Stoke on Trent, Staffs

# Addresses of suppliers in the USA

## General Suppliers

Amherst Pottery Supply
44 McClellan Street
Amherst, MA 01002

American Art Clay Co (AMACO)
4717 West 16th Street
Indianapolis, IN 46222

A.R.T. Studio Clay Co.
921 Oakton Street
Elk Grove, IL 60007

Baldwin Pottery
534 La Guardia Place
New York, NY 10012

Byrne Ceramic Supply Co, Inc
95 Bartley Road
Flanders, NJ 07836

The Archie Bray Foundation
Country Club Avenue
Helena, MT 59601

Cedar Heights Clay Co
50 Portsmouth Road
Oak Hill, OH 45656

Capital Ceramics, Inc
2174 South Main Street
Salt Lake City, UT 84115

Del Val Potter's Supplies Co
Queen Street and Ivy Hill Road
Philadelphia, PA 19118

Eagle Ceramics
12266 Wilkins Avenue
Rockville, MD 20852

Earthworks Studio Supply, Ltd
420 Merchants Road
Rocherster, NY 14609

Ferro Corporation
4150 East 56th Street
Cleveland, OH 44144

Hammill and Gillespie, Inc
154 South Livingston Avenue
Livingston, NJ 07039

Harrison Bell (associate company of
   Harrison Mayer Ltd)
3605A Kennedy Road
South Plainfield, NJ 07080

House of Ceramics
1011 North Hollywood
Memphis, TN 38108

Leslie Ceramic Supply Co
1212 San Pablo Avenue
Berkeley, CA 94706

Minnesota Clay
8001 Grand Avenue South
Bloomington, MI 55420

H.C. Muddox Clay Co
5975 Bradshaw Road
Sacramento, CA 95826

Ohio Ceramic Supply Co
Box 630
Kent, OH 44249

Pemco Division, Glidden Co
5601 Eastern Avenue
Baltimore, MD 21224

Rovin Ceramics
6912 Schaefer Road
Dearborn, MI 48126

Seattle Pottery Supplies
400 East Pine Street
Seattle, WA 98122

Standard Ceramic Supply Co
Box 4435
Pittsburgh, PA 15205

Van Howe Ceramic Supply Co
11975 East 40 Avenue
Denver, CO 80239

or

4860 Pan American Freeway
N.E. Albuquerque, NM 87107

Western Ceramic Supply
1601 Howard Street
San Franciso, CA 94103

Jack D. Wolfe Co, Inc
724-734 Meeker Avenue
Brooklyn, NY 11222

### Oriental Brushes
Aiko's Art Materials Import, Inc
714 North Wabash Avenue
Chicago, IL 60611

### Brushes and Modeling Tools
Sculpture House
38 East 30th Street
New York, NY 10016

### Sponges and Chamois
Florida Sponge and Chamois Co
2495 Long Beach Road
Oceanside, NY 11572

### General Suppliers, Canada
Barrett Co. Ltd
1155 Dorchester Boulevard
West Montreal 2, PQ

Clay Crafts Supply
1004 Taylor Street
Saskatoon, SK

Ferro (Canada) Ltd
354 Davis
Oakville, ON

*continued ...*

## General Suppliers, Canada
*continued*

The Green Barn Potters Supply
P.O. Box 1235 Station A
Surrey, BC

HIRO Distributors
518 Beatty Street
Vancouver, BC

Plainsman Clays Ltd
Box 1266
Medicine Hat, AL TIA 7M9

Pottery Supply House
P.O. Box 192
Oakville, ON L6J 5AZ

## Laboratories which will test for metal release

Bio-Technics Laboratories, Inc.
1133 Crenshaw Boulevard
Los Angeles, CA 90019

Coors Spectro-Chemical Laboratory
Box 500
Golden, CT 80401

Pittsburgh Testing Laboratory
850 Popular Street
Pittsburgh, PA 15220

The Twining Laboratories, Inc
Box 1472
Fresno, CA 93716

# Index

# Index to examples illustrated

Illustration numbers only are given.

**DATE DUE**

| | | | |
|---|---|---|---|
| | | | |
| | | | |
| | | | |
| | | | |
| | | | |
| | | | |
| | | | |
| | | | |
| | | | |
| | | | |
| | | | |
| | | | |